THE SOUL OF YOSEMITE

Finding, Defending, and Saving
the Valley's Sacred Wild Nature

Barbara J. Moritsch

CJM BOOKS
ROCHESTER, NY

Copyright © 2012 by Barbara J. Moritsch

All rights reserved. Except as permitted under the U.S. Copyright Act of 1976, no part of this publication may be reproduced, distributed, or transmitted in any form or by any means, or stored in a database or retrieval system, without the prior written permission of the publisher.

For large quantity orders and promotional materials, contact publisher:
CJM Books
P.O. Box 565
East Rochester, NY 14445
www.CJMBooks.com

Cover art photography © 2002 Barbara J. Moritsch
Used with permission by CJM Books

Cover art adaptation and design by
Chris Murphy / CJM Books. All rights reserved.
Text set in Georgia

ISBN-10: 0983179727
ISBN-13: 978-0-9831797-2-6

Library of Congress Control Number: 2011944436

To:

Tom, Marc, Mom, & Dad

CONTENTS

ACKNOWLEDGMENTS   i
PROLOGUE   iii

PART ONE
GROWING UP WITH CLAM AND COOT

CHAPTER 1	How I Came to Care	2
CHAPTER 2	Coming of Age in Wildness	7
CHAPTER 3	Anchors	12
CHAPTER 4	Getting on with It	21
CHAPTER 5	Anything but a Passive Observer	24
CHAPTER 6	The Best Jobs in the World	31
CHAPTER 7	The Perfect Summer	34
CHAPTER 8	Finding My Niche	41
CHAPTER 9	On Fire and Getting Burned	49
CHAPTER 10	Steep Learning	59
CHAPTER 11	You Can Go Home Again	68

PART TWO
BEARING WITNESS

CHAPTER 12	The Lorax, the Flood, and the Top 15+2	78
CHAPTER 13	Radical Environmentalists	86
CHAPTER 14	Legal Actions and "The Yosemite Way"	96
CHAPTER 15	Waging War	104
CHAPTER 16	Convolution, Obfuscation, Desecration	114
CHAPTER 17	Honesty and Integrity Need Not Apply	126
CHAPTER 18	The Hidden Costs of Flushing	137
CHAPTER 19	Troubled Waters	148
CHAPTER 20	Burned, Trampled, Grazed, Plowed, and Bulldozed	158
CHAPTER 21	Killing Them Softly	169
CHAPTER 22	And the Damage Done	182

PART THREE
ROOTS OF PROBLEMS, SEEDS OF SOLUTIONS

CHAPTER 23	A Murder, a Curse, a Riot, Some Restoration, and a Few Revelations	196
CHAPTER 24	Essential Wildness	203
CHAPTER 25	Yosemite *Is* Different	213
CHAPTER 26	First, Do No More Harm	225
CHAPTER 27	Embrace Transparency and Humility	240
CHAPTER 28	Establish Limits	252
CHAPTER 29	Liberate Natural Processes	264
CHAPTER 30	Cultivate Reverence, Not Relevance	276
CHAPTER 31	Transcend Economics	288
CHAPTER 32	Imagine	295
CHAPTER 33	In Wildness	309
EPILOGUE		314
FOR FURTHER READING		319
ABOUT THE AUTHOR		

ACKNOWLEDGMENTS

My deep, heartfelt thanks go out to the many people who helped me write this story. Thank you to my first writing group, with whom the idea for this book was born: Margaret Eissler, Bridget McGinnis Kerr, and Carol Blaney. Thank you, Kate Riley and Marlene Gast, for unstinting support, thoughtful insight, and friendship as we worked through chapter after chapter. Thank you, Jan van Wagtendonk, Rod Nash, Alfred Runte, Jill Kuraitis, Mary Jo Cartledgehayes, Vicki Jo Lawson, Nan Perigo, Dawn Adams, and Ellen Eberhardt, for invaluable feedback. Thank you, George Whitmore and Greg Adair, for your support and your tireless efforts to help Yosemite Valley. Thank you, Chris Murphy, for all your help and patience with getting this book put together. Thank you, all of my cohorts in Yosemite who have asked to remain anonymous.

Thank you, Natalie Goldberg, for sharing your wisdom and showing me I already had everything I needed. Thank you, Terry Tempest Williams for urging me to tell my story. Thank you, David Abram, Dave Foreman, Gary Snyder, and Jack Turner for breaking trail through your writings, which provided me with inspiration and the courage to speak my truth. Thank you, Linda Eade, Librarian at the Yosemite NPS Research Library, for all of your support and help.

Thank you, John Muir, Frederick Law Olmsted, David Brower, John Lennon, Rachel Carson, Henry David Thoreau, Ansel Adams, Aldo Leopold, and Edward Abbey, for giving us all guidance as we try to find a better, unpaved path in this world.

Thank you, Cali and Leo Moritsch-Nichols, for never leaving my side through the writing process. Thank you, Mom, Dad, and Marc for everything, always.

And, thank you, Tom, for your endless patience and Zen Master wisdom, and for supporting me in all ways without reservation in this endeavor.

PROLOGUE

The screen door squeaked softly as I pushed it open and stepped out into a quiet moonlit night. Venus and a few faint stars hung low in the western sky. A distant dog barked as I walked around to the west side of the El Portal Community Center and across the parking lot to my pickup. The door squeaked again when my writer's group friends exited and headed off in the opposite direction. I wasn't alone, though; my moon shadow danced with me across the gravel to the springtime rhythm of the River of Mercy.

The small hamlet of El Portal perches on an almost level spot on an otherwise steep slope in the foothills of California's Sierra Nevada. North of the Community Center, narrow roads twist uphill into a maze of hobbit homes. To the west, offices and neighborhoods spring from the landscape. To the south, the Merced River flows to the Central Valley. And, to the east, Yosemite National Park stretches up to the Sierra Nevada crest.

Driving east out of El Portal, I passed the Yosemite View Lodge and park entrance station before climbing into the mountains. It was late on a Wednesday; I was alone on the road.

Upon entering the gates of Yosemite, I was transported into another world, a dynamic extravaganza of rock, light, and water. A big winter storm had passed through the canyon a few hours earlier, leaving the sheer rock walls dark and wet. Ephemeral white waterfalls cascaded down narrow, almost vertical, rock-strewn chutes. Sheets of silver water danced like shifting veils across dark gray, impassive granite faces. Whispers of cloud fragments parted like old, tattered curtains to reveal a brilliant full moon. Each and every drop of water in this landscape caught, magnified, and reflected the brilliant outpouring of moonlight, and the resulting kaleidoscope of sparkle shot right through my eyes to illuminate the center of my being.

I sank more deeply into the seat of the truck and grinned to myself in the pale glow of the dashboard lights as John Muir's words echoed through my head:

"Climb the mountains and get their good tidings. Nature's peace will flow into you as sunshine flows into trees. The winds will blow their own freshness into you and the storms their energy, while cares will drop off like autumn leaves."

The gift of clarity the mountains and the moon gave me that spring night via the ageless, timeless dance of light on water brought me back to myself and helped me regain my balance. Since I'd moved to Yosemite Valley two and a half years earlier, I'd changed from a confident professional woman to an anxious, under-employed woman. Somewhere along the way I'd lost my identity, my sense of purpose. Was it a mid-life crisis? Was it due to shifting hormones? Was I miserable because I'd left a great job at Point Reyes to pursue my Yosemite dream, only to wind up in a job so frustrating and painful I had to quit after only nine months?

I asked myself these questions a thousand times. The answers were always the same: yes and no. It was true the past few years had been a time of intense change and personal growth, but my state of inner turmoil ran much deeper. Gazing up at the shining, wet granite that brilliant March night, I recognized the root of my troubles was buried deep in the granite and sand of Yosemite Valley, intertwined with roots of oak, pine, deergrass, and sedge. The source of my grief, anger, and pain became crystal clear. I was watching Yosemite Valley die a slow death, both ecologically and spiritually, and it was breaking my heart.

PART ONE

GROWING UP WITH CLAM AND COOT

*"I only went out for a walk,
and finally concluded
to stay out till sundown,
for going out, I found,
was really going in."*

John Muir
Journal 1913

CHAPTER 1
How I Came to Care

Journal

Mom, Dad, and my adopted aunt, Beth, came to visit last week. We all sat out on the back patio one hot afternoon and sipped iced tea while Mom reminisced about a long ago camping trip in the coast redwood forests of California.

"Do you remember when we slept outside?" she asked me. "On cots? When we woke up we were surrounded by thick fog, and our sleeping bags were all wet."

I had a wisp of such a memory, but no details came to mind.

"You always wanted to sleep outside when we camped. So it was you and me outside, and Dad and Marc in the camper," she grinned slightly and her eyes took on the recessed glow of the past. "And then there was the time we woke up and there were chipmunks running around, back and forth, over our feet."

I dug deep to recall fragments of that big adventure. Thanks, Mom, for telling these stories; and thanks for your willingness to sleep outside, regardless of weather and wild animals. These experiences nourished my young soul like mountain streams feed cottonwood seedlings, affecting my life in ways neither of us could have predicted.

♦♦♦

The forest stretched forever in all directions. The giant trees were cloaked in fibrous red-brown bark, and their dark green crowns were almost invisible because they were so high in the sky and so densely packed. The towering redwoods pulled eyes and energy irresistibly upwards.

Beneath the trees the mood was damp and dimly lit. Scattered tufts of sword ferns, huckleberry bushes, and thick clumps of grass grew where filtered sunbeams penetrated the forest canopy. A small stream gurgled, out of sight, but close by.

My family—Mom, Dad, my older brother Marc, and eight-year-old me—had just piled out of a very small, rented, cab-over-camper after a several hour drive. We lived on the rural east edge of Sacramento, in a burg called Fair Oaks, and this trip to the coast redwood forest was a venture deep into the unknown.

"Okay," my Dad said. "Here we are. We're camping now." He pulled an aluminum chair strung with blue and white webbing into its full upright and locked position and sat down with a sigh.

"What are we gonna do now?" Marc asked as he dragged a stick through the dark humus-rich soil under our feet.

"Well, I don't know. What do you do when you're camping?" Dad cast a long look at Mom, a clear appeal for help. Many afternoon hours loomed ahead of us before we could default to the known routine of fixing a meal.

Mom, as usual, came to the rescue. "I think I hear a creek. Let's see if we can find it."

We spent the rest of the week learning how to camp, learning that camping mostly involved not "doing" much of anything. This concept must have been foreign to my engineer father; I suspect camping was Mom's idea. We took meandering walks through the forest, played with rocks in the creek, got our tennis shoes and pants wet and dirty, tried to fish, prepared gourmet meals featuring hamburgers or hotdogs, and played Yahtzee and Password. After the last light of day receded, we sat, silently arrayed around the campfire, watching flames flicker and dance.

Thus began our family tradition of camping. I can't remember a single vacation that didn't involve camping, except obligatory visits to relatives. Our initial forays were into California's coastal redwood forests, but before long we discovered the wonders of the Sierra Nevada—Yosemite and Sequoia national parks. Once bitten by the Sierra bug, we never went anywhere else.

Before I entered the hallowed temples of the Sierra, though, we left Sacramento. We migrated south to California's central coast, chasing employment.

Our new town was called Orcutt and was located just south of Santa Maria between the Pacific Ocean and the oak and chaparral clad slopes of California's Coast Range. The town was tiny, planted in the middle of flat agricultural lands that churned out lots of strawberries, sugar beets, and broccoli, among other things. Before long, we became very familiar with the earthy odor that emanated from sugar beet processing factories west of us, carried to our noses by prevailing coastal breezes. A half hour drive north, a long strand of public beaches—Oceano, Pismo, and Avila—beckoned. We answered the call of the sea before we even finished unpacking boxes.

The fog was pea-soup thick when we pulled into the almost empty parking lot. It was mid-morning on a winter Saturday and I was ten years old. We piled out of the car and walked down a set of wide cement stairs. Shedding shoes and socks, we stepped out on the soft, creamy tan sand of Pismo Beach. Marc and I ran to the water's edge, where small, foamy waves lapped the shore. The wet sand was gritty and cold on feet bottoms that had spent most of their life in shoes. The fog thinned, and then vanished as the pale sun rose higher. We walked south, following the curve of the sea, bending over frequently to examine bits of shell and shiny wet rocks.

We hadn't gone far when we saw a small, beige-colored clam marooned like a tiny boat above the wave wash line. We saw more castaways as we continued down the beach. Within five minutes we'd counted dozens. They'd been dug up by early-rising clam-diggers, and left behind on the surface of the hard-packed sand. They were under-sized and too small to be taken legally. The rules of clamming state the digger of such babies must re-bury them, because they can't dig through the surface layers of sand, and will die if exposed for too long.

Mom stopped and looked at the clams with a furrowed brow, then dropped to her knees and quickly dug a hole in the wet sand. She said we had to re-bury the small, rejected clams because they had a right to live their lives. They weren't being treated fairly and they needed our help.

So we went to work. We buried numerous pale, smooth-shelled clam bodies that day, covering them with several inches of cold, wet sand while waves rolled up over our toes, feet, and ankles. It all felt very, very good.

Pismo became a favorite destination, and clam rescue was always part of those trips. Some days were busier than others. We'd rush from clam to clam, trying to start them on their downward journeys before it was too late. Dad caught up to us on one of our busier days and saw despair etched across my mom's face as she looked at the hundreds of small clams scattered across the beach.

"Mom," he said. "Sometimes you just can't bury all the clams."

His words never stopped either of us from trying.

In sixth grade I was shipped off to science camp for a week. One of our days was dedicated to wildlife study, and that was the day my internal compass was set. Right after breakfast, the red-haired wildlife biologist, whose camp name was Flash, told us we'd be taking a long hike to Lake Cachuma. We'd travel through different habitat types and have a chance to see birds and squirrels, maybe coyote or deer. If we were really lucky, we might see a bobcat or a mountain lion. I hung on his every word. He told us to be quiet or we'd scare the animals away. We were to stay together and keep our eyes and ears open.

After a forty-five minute hike we emerged from a scrubby thicket of oak, manzanita, and deerbrush. As we continued on to the lake shore, we spotted an American coot lying by the water's edge. I squinted through my cheap, out-of-focus binoculars and realized, at the same time as many others, that the bird was alive, but couldn't move. Yards of twisted nylon fishing line were wrapped tightly around its legs, wings, and bill. Twenty twelve-year-olds were silenced by the bird's plight.

Flash looked at our wide eyes and tight faces and said, "Let's see if we can help."

He walked quietly up to the bird and squatted down next to it. He pulled a pocket knife out of his fishing vest, and then put his hand on the bird's back, murmuring softly. He carefully cut, untangled, and removed the coarse nylon line. Then he set that coot free.

Flash became my instant hero as the bird stood up on wobbly legs, shook itself, ran a few clumsy steps, and flew off over the water. We all cheered in unison at this life-saving magic.

My lifelong drive to protect the Earth's creatures and their habitat was fledged on the wings of that coot.

CHAPTER 2
Coming of Age in Wildness

Journal

The meadow grasses are past their prime, all golden brown and falling over. Shiny, dark brown milkweed seeds float off on the wind in silken fluffs. The narrow, winding deer path under my feet is marked by small, chocolate-brown M&M droppings. In a small pocket meadow, the slightest whisper of a tickle teases my arm. Up above, the sky is full of windborne travelers. A brilliant network of gossamer spider web fragments floats on a slight breeze across a backdrop of black granite and a denim lapis sky. Each web fragment carries its own tiny group of even tinier spiders—a new generation in search of a place to call home.

◆◆◆

In May of 1972, when I was not quite twelve years old, we camped in Yosemite Valley for the first of many times. Our Yosemite ritual held to a common pattern. The Saturday before we embarked, we packed sleeping bags, blankets, food, lanterns, chairs, clothing, and games into a rented camper. We woke early the following Sunday and embarked on the long trek through the Central Valley and up into the mountains. We started our vacations on Sundays, because most people were leaving the Valley when we arrived. On our first trip, the camper was a mere twelve feet long. The size and complexity of the vehicle grew in tandem with our level of sophistication as campers.

We always went in the spring. Marc and I were allowed to skip school for the week so our vacation could be one of relative quiet and solitude. Mom swore she'd never go to Yosemite Valley in summer, when "the hordes overran the place."

The drive was long and boring. Dad drove. Mom rode shotgun. Marc and I sat in the camper and broke the monotony by playing card games like War, or by making fun of the people in the cars we passed. We'd stop for lunch at a pullout or roadside picnic area. Mom made ham or roast beef sandwiches with French's mustard on white bread in the camper's tiny kitchenette. For dessert we had our choice of Ding Dongs, Twinkies, or HoHos. After lunch we returned to our stations and drove on.

By the time we reached the southern entrance to Yosemite National Park, we'd be restless and ready to be outside, but we still had another hour to go. The dialogue in the car was simple and predictable.

"Are we there yet?"

"Almost."

"I'm hungry. I'm thirsty. I gotta go potty."

"Sit still. We're almost there, I'm sure the tunnel is just around this next corner."

The long tunnel on the Wawona Road signaled the beginning of the end of the journey. When we finally reached the tunnel's entry arch, Marc and I scrambled to the upper berth over the truck's cab to look ahead. The drive through the long tunnel seemed as long as Catholic mass. Oncoming drivers honked horns, exhaust fumes seeped into the camper, and water dripped from the tunnel's ceiling. Finally, we emerged into bright sunlight, and once our eyes adjusted, the glorious panorama of Yosemite Valley unfolded in front of us, evoking sighs of relief and anticipation.

We descended the slope from the tunnel to the Valley floor, and passed Bridalveil Fall—a glorious free-leaping shout of white froth spilling over a sharp granite lip. We rarely stopped at Bridalveil, though; we were on a mission to secure a campsite and set up camp. Dad made a bee-line for the campgrounds at the east end of the Valley.

The Soul of Yosemite

We drove past Curry Village, and then turned right into our favorite campground—Upper Pines.

We selected a campsite with a great deal of care. Our annual vacation was precious, often the very best week of the entire year, so we had to be in the best location. According to Mom, this was as far away as possible from other people. We drove through loop after loop in the campground, in search of a site away from the entrance kiosk, and not too close to a restroom. Our favorite sites backed up to a small creek. The other Valley campgrounds, like Upper and Lower Rivers, had sites right next to the Merced River, but these were, by our standards, too crowded with rowdy people, radios, and rafts. The creek-side sites at Upper Pines were private and quiet because no one could camp behind us.

If other campers were in our favorite sites—which was cause for great disappointment—we'd settle for one in close proximity to the object of our desire and set up a vigil. As soon as one of our favorites was vacated, we'd run over and set up a lawn chair on the parking pad, clearly marking our territory until we could move the rest of our stuff.

We did the same things on most of our Yosemite Valley trips. We woke each morning to the timeless aroma of campfire smoke, accompanied by the brilliant blue flash and demanding chorus of Steller's jays. The fire of the morning sun lit the Valley's sharp granite rim as Mom cooked breakfast over the two-burner stove—eggs sunny-side-up, bacon, toast with butter, juice, and coffee for the grown-ups. We hiked, rode bikes, and went to campfire talks, immersed in Yosemite's sights, sounds, smells, and energy. Our lives merged with those of mallard and merganser, coyote and cottonwood, willow and water. We all slept deeply in the quiet night, cradled within the solid embrace of granite.

We saw our first bear on our second Yosemite trip.

"Hey, wake up, here comes Fat Albert!" My voice echoed through the camper in which my family had been, until that moment, sleeping. I'd been awake for hours, staring out the window by my bed into the dark mountain night. I just had to see him first. I had to be the one to announce the arrival of the infamous campground bear.

At the campfire program earlier that night the ranger told us about Fat Albert, a very large black bear who'd been frequenting the campground. In search of anything edible, he broke into cars by punching out windows and pulling off doorframes, and he'd ripped up a few back seats to get into car trunks. Several times during the night I'd seen movement just outside the glow of the campground bathroom light. Until now, the objects were hungry raccoons or sleepy campers with full bladders.

"Where?" Marc slid down from his sleeping alcove over the cab and rushed to my window.

"By the picnic table. He's sniffing at the stove. Dad, are you sure you put all the food away?" As the self-appointed junior ranger of the family, I made sure every speck of trash was picked up, all food put away, and all dishes washed as soon as a meal was over. And no one was to feed the animals, ever, under any circumstances.

The bear failed to find anything to eat. To express his displeasure, he sent the Coleman stove flying off the table with a single swipe of a large front paw. The saucepans, plates, bowls and silverware Mom had carefully stacked on top of the stove flew in all directions.

"Hey, that stove's brand new!" Dad threw off a light blanket and rolled out of bed, sporting a worn white t-shirt and briefs. He rushed to the back of the camper, opened the door, stepped down two metal stairs attached to the rig, and tripped over the cement curb behind the camper. Marc and I looked at each other, eyes wide, and burst out laughing.

"Dammit! I told you we shouldn't park so close to that damned cement bumper. Why do they have to put those damned things there anyway?" Dad grumbled as he stepped back into the camper.

Fat Albert wandered off to other campsites in search of Cheetos or Hershey bars, and Mom herded us back to bed. I curled up next to the window to resume my watch, but quickly nodded off.

I woke up first the next morning. In t-shirt and socks, I tiptoed to the camper door, pushed open the screen, and walked out into cool air under a cloudless sky. The bright, golden light of the morning sun illuminated the ridgeline to the northwest, silhouetting a perfect row of very tiny, very faraway trees with a glow that seemed to come from within. I studied the ground as I walked to the picnic table, looking for bear tracks to confirm Fat Albert had not been a dream.

Our moods dimmed considerably when it was time to go home. We packed the camper, climbed in, and sat in silence as Dad drove out of the Valley. For the first few miles, we all stared out the windows, hoping against hope for one last view of a bear, coyote, or deer. When we emerged from the tunnel, Mom and I, and maybe even Marc, sat in a silent wash of tears as we drove toward home, hearts breaking. I think Dad's tears were at the surface too, but he couldn't let them out.

I learned early in life to open my heart to the land and its inhabitants—the animals and plants, the rivers and lakes, the rocks and the clouds and the stars. The seeds my parents planted grew quickly into a tawny meadow of passion for wild places. Flanking that meadow now is an old-growth forest of belief that wild creatures and their homes are infinitely important and must be protected at all costs.

CHAPTER 3
Anchors

Journal

The Yosemite Valley I know and love is being destroyed. Why do I care so deeply? Because my roots are co-mingled in sand and cobble with those of the Valley's oak and pine, because my blood runs continuous with the flow of the Merced's crystalline mountain water, and because my psyche is lifted heavenward with the energies of those rising granite walls.

♦♦♦

My family continued its southern migration not long after our introduction to Yosemite. We moved from Orcutt to San Juan Capistrano, in southern Orange County. Life in Orcutt had been slow and steady. I spent my time riding my strawberry roan gelding, Shortcake, and just being a kid. When we moved south into the land of the rich and famous, I was catapulted into a turbulent adolescence. I started junior high school and found myself in a completely different world. My female schoolmates were into surfing or, more to the point, male surfers. If you didn't sport long, straight, blond hair, a lean, cute body, and a golden brown tan, you were no one. With my red hair, cowgirl thighs, and pale skin, I was no one.

To survive in this new world, I hooked up with a few others who also found themselves outside the inner circle and started down a path of intense rebellion and moderate self-destruction—a path of wildness.

For the next several years, I had little interest in anything except guys, beer, recreational drugs, and parties. I lied to my parents, ditched school, and shoplifted.

The one constant in my life over the course of those years was the family camping trips to Yosemite Valley. My brother Marc had moved away to go to college, so it was just Mom, Dad, and me. Occasionally, I was allowed to bring a friend. I had utterly rejected my parents by then, believing they were an embarrassment beyond belief with their uncool clothes, ridiculous comments, and incessantly applied rules, so I usually took off on a solo hike as soon as we arrived at our campsite.

On one of our trips, when I was fourteen, we walked to the amphitheatre in Lower Pines campground to take in the ranger-naturalist evening program. A young male ranger in a gray and green uniform showed slides and discussed the park and its wildlife. After the talk was finished I approached the ranger and spoke with him for twenty minutes about career opportunities in the parks.

I was hooked.

The next morning I rose early, before the sun hit the tops of the towering ponderosa pines surrounding our campsite. I quietly dressed, grabbed water and lunch, and slipped out of the camper. The air was cool, the sky clear. A few early risers were up and about, traveling bleary-eyed to the restroom, piling kindling to start a fire, or following a dog pulling eagerly toward the smells of the forest morning. I headed east, stepped on rocks to ford a small creek, and then moved quickly cross-country toward the trailhead to Vernal and Nevada falls.

It was early May. Dogwoods were wrapped in garlands of lime green and soft cream, and the Merced River was spring-dancing to the beat of melting snow. I hiked up the sloping trail to the bridge below Vernal Fall, stopping frequently to look down into the river canyon at the surging whitewater far below. No one else was on the trail. I was completely alone, just the way I liked it.

I walked to the middle of the bridge and leaned out over the foaming water. It tossed and turned like a restless sleeper in its granite boulder bed, and left in its wake dozens of tiny, transient waterfalls that cascaded down slick boulder faces. I hung suspended over the bridge railing for a long time. Generated by the crashing water, intermittent gusts of mist-laden wind swirled around my head and rippled through my hair. The only sights and sounds were of water, in all its wildness, moving and flowing ever downward, constantly seeking the path of least resistance.

The incessant buzz of thoughts in my head fled as I gave myself over to feeling. The raw, pulsing energy of the river melded with the flow of blood in my veins. I stood absolutely still, my feet solid and square underneath me, to fully embrace and embody this powerful union. At that moment I felt, for the first time, a direct connection to the Earth. I knew what it meant and how it felt to be grounded.

Through my selfish teenage armor, the Earth reached out and touched my soul. My attention turned outward as I realized the world was bigger than I was, and much more important. I had found an ancient and authentic wildness.

A flash of bright red among the trees caught my eye—a hiker. Wanting to be alone in my experience, I continued up the trail. Upstream, the Vernal Fall was at spring peak; a huge curtain of snow-white water plunged straight down to the rocky cradle at its base. Rainbows shimmered in the misty veil thrown up by the waterfall's pounding crescendo.

I slowly climbed up a steep rock staircase toward the top of the fall. Waves of tiny water droplets showered over me as the morning breeze gently pushed the falls my way. At the top, out of breath and soaking wet, I found a flat seat on the sprawling, sun-baked granite slabs. As I watched the river flow into the Emerald Pool above the waterfall, its waters resting for a moment before rushing over the lip and down, it hit me that my life mirrored the river, constantly in flux and always moving from place to place. But, the cradle within which the river flowed, the granite-walled Valley and her defining features—Half Dome, El Capitan, Glacier Point—stayed essentially the same. Reliable, consistent, and silently present, they observed without judgment the dramas that played out within their rocky embrace. This river, these rocks, and Yosemite Valley, were the friends, the anchors, the home I'd been searching for.

The first time I saw a rock climber I wanted to be one. I don't remember how old I was—maybe thirteen or fourteen. As we drove out of the Valley after one of our trips, we saw dozens of people standing or sitting in lawn chairs in the meadow near the base of El Capitan, a granite monolith that stretched 3,000 feet straight up from the Valley floor. Everyone faced north, and several people peered through binoculars at the blindingly bright rock wall.

Of course, we had to stop and look too. After several minutes of seeing nothing but rock, I walked out to the congregation and said, "What's everybody looking at?"

A man near me lowered his binoculars. "Climbers," he said, pointing at El Cap. "See that long, dark crack that looks like a skinny piece of pie? Go up from there about two fist widths, then go a bit to the right, just below that little ledge. There are two, and one of them is moving."

I located the pair, two miniscule specks of muted color transposed on the sun-baked slab, hardly distinguishable from shrubs and small trees clinging to the giant rockscape. One of them was moving very slowly.

My interest in climbing, and particularly in climbers, grew as I grew. I sought opportunities to stand close to them in line at Degnan's Deli, or sit next to them on the hard plastic seats of the Valley shuttle bus. I rode the shuttle more often than needed in hopes of basking in their presence. They knew they were cool. At that time, in the mid-1970s, their uniform usually included worn canvas shorts and tank tops or bare torsos, with feet encased in tiny, tight-looking shoes. Their rock-hard, deeply tanned bodies were wrapped in coils of brightly-colored rope, nylon webbing, and clanking hardware, like cams and carabiners, and they all emitted a similar aroma: a heady mixture of testosterone, sweat, and granite, often layered with the sweet scent of a recently smoked joint. The entire package was overwhelming, and undeniably intoxicating to my adolescent senses.

In the spring of 1976, my friend Valerie joined us for our Yosemite trip. We were fifteen years old, and much more interested in looking at and picking up guys than admiring rocks and rivers. During the drive up from southern California, I told Valerie Yosemite was a very good venue for such activities.

As soon as we arrived at our campsite, we changed into shorts and were off like a shot. We caught the shuttle bus as it was pulling away from the campground and got off in Yosemite Village. Following my usual routine, we each bought a small carton of Producer's orange juice at the Village Store, and then strolled past the deli and the Ansel Adams Gallery. We continued another half mile or so to Camp 4, the climber's campground. Valerie was happy to let me be the tour guide, and we made it to Camp 4 in record time.

We entered the campground and I quietly explained the first step in the pick-up game. "We need to casually stroll through the campground to see if there are any cute guys hanging around, and then we flash bright smiles at appropriate moments."

Small tents of blue, red, yellow, and orange dotted the landscape of the camp. Laundry dangled from almost every guy line. Stuff sacks of food and toothpaste hung from tree branches—in theory they were beyond the reach of bears, but bears were canny when it came to snagging human food. If the branch from which the food sack was suspended was too thin for them to crawl out and get the sack, they launched themselves in a great leap into the air and grabbed the sack with paw or claw on the way down.

Camp 4 was quiet as we walked down the path. We realized we were being watched as we approached the west end of camp, and were soon greeted with one of the more common lines: "Hey ladies, would you two care for a beer?" Of course we did, and in short order we were seated at a picnic table in chaos covered with banged-up, charred pots and pans, dog-eared climbing guides, ropes, harnesses, climbing hardware, and several empty Michelob bottles.

Mark and Rick were from Massachusetts, on a break from college. The four of us chatted over a beer, and then the unthinkable happened. They asked us if we wanted to go climbing with them the following day—a good reminder to be careful what you ask for. I had long dreamed of this day, wanting so badly to learn to climb, to be one of the climber chicks, and here, suddenly, was the opportunity. Valerie and I looked at each other, and she raised her eyebrows. I took this to mean it was okay with her.

"We'd love to." I replied.

"Have you ever climbed before?" Rick asked.

"Well, no." I said. "Not really."

They talked for a few minutes about where we could go, and finally settled on the Glacier Point Apron. We agreed to meet at their camp at 7AM the next morning. On our walk back to our campground, I made Valerie swear she would not breathe a word of this plan to my parents. They'd never let us go climbing with two men we didn't know who gave beer to fifteen-year-olds.

The evening was a bit strained because of the big secret. I mentioned to Mom that we were going to leave early the next morning to go on a hike to Vernal Fall. Mom said, "Fine. Be careful." It was only a small lie; the Glacier Point Apron wasn't far from the trail to the falls.

The next morning we grabbed granola bars and water bottles and left camp before the sun cleared the ridge. We caught the shuttle and arrived at the campsite at the appointed time. Mark and Rick were shoving harnesses and climbing hardware into canvas haul bags. Mark, the taller of the two at about 5'10", pushed a lock of long blond hair out of his eyes and handed me two heavy climbing ropes.

"Come on, let's get these loaded," he said, heading down the path toward the dirt parking lot.

"Wait," I said, as I scurried to keep up and fumbled to hold the ropes in place over my shoulders, trying to look like I knew what I was doing. "Can't we take the shuttle bus?" After all, part of the thrill of this adventure was showing off to the world that I was a climber chick.

"Oh, last night we decided to go somewhere else, and we need to drive there. We're going down the canyon to Elephant Rock. The river's low, so we should be able to get across easily enough." My little lie was growing by the minute, and I wondered if we were being really stupid and going to end up raped or dead somewhere. But I said nothing.

When we got back to the campsite, Valerie and Rick had finished cleaning up the site and putting stray food items away. I told Valerie about the change of plans. She shrugged her shoulders, "Okay, that's fine."

We piled into Mark's forest green VW bus and headed west, down the Merced Canyon. We crossed the river easily; it was a drought year and water levels were low. The approach to Elephant Rock was short, but entailed a scramble up a steep talus slope through prickly manzanita and deerbrush.

As we got close to the massive slab of granite, the elephant herself, I started to feel sick to my stomach. What had I gotten us into? This rock was massive, and it went straight up. How could we possibly climb it?

We arrived at the base of the rock, and Rick pointed out two cracks of varying width that ran from the ground up to distant points on the rock. He flipped open a climbing guidebook and pointed at each crack in turn. "That's the Crack of Doom, and that one's the Crack of Despair." Oh boy, I thought, maybe I'd just remain a climber groupie and forget the climbing part.

Before I could muster my courage to tell Mark and Rick that we'd made a terrible mistake and were very sorry, but that we would love to stay and watch, Mark looked at me and held up a piece of blue nylon webbing. A few carabiners and a piece of metal shaped like a figure eight clinked together as the apparatus swung my way.

"Here, this harness should fit you. Put your legs through these loops, bring this piece around your waist, connect it in front with this 'biner, and then hook this figure eight right here. Got it?"

I gulped and reached out to take the harness, stepped into the leg loops, pulled the apparatus up and around my waist as instructed, and then looked up for help.

"Here, like this," Mark said. Stepping closer, he took hold of the harness in front of my belly and clipped the hardware into place. "This is a locking 'biner. Twist this piece and it locks, and won't open accidentally." My stomach churned, at odds with my hormones, which really wanted Mark to stay closer and continue playing with my harness. I looked over to see Valerie also getting dressed for the occasion.

Within ten minutes we had learned the basics of belaying—serving as another climber's anchor, and holding him in case of a fall. Mark and Rick checked every rope, harness, carabiner, sling, and piece of protection several times to be sure they were affixed properly before anyone put hand or foot on the rock. They told us we should do the same whenever we went climbing, and if we felt our climbing partners weren't paying close enough attention, we should back off and not climb.

Mark led the first pitch. Rick belayed him while Valerie and I watched. Mark made his way slowly up the rock wall, calling our attention to where he was putting his hands and feet. I watched him like a hawk, trying to memorize where to step and where to hold on.

Then it was my turn. The crack ranged from about two to twelve inches wide and was intermittently filled with dirt and small ferns. I managed to get about thirty feet up with ease, keeping three points—either two hands and one foot or two feet and one hand—on the rock at all times, as instructed. I stopped to breathe, and then could not for the life of me figure out where to go next.

"Grab that small knob above your right hand." The directive came from below. "Then move your right foot up a few feet and jam your whole foot into the crack until it locks in."

"Right," I thought, as my right big toe began to slip off its hold on a one-inch wide ledge. And then, probably due to sheer terror, my left leg began to quiver uncontrollably, and I couldn't move. I found out later I was afflicted by a common climber's malady: "sewing machine leg."

"C'mon. You just gotta go for it. Don't think about it, just go for it," said the voice of the blond god Mark from above.

It felt like hours passed. I looked at that knob and prayed my foot wouldn't slip. I willed my left leg to stop its infernal shaking, took a very deep breath, and went for it. The remaining forty feet up to the narrow ledge where Mark was perched flew under my hands and feet. Heart pounding, I pulled myself up, turned around, and sat down next to him.

The eagle's eye view of the Merced River canyon was stunning—so stunning it took me several minutes to notice how tightly our bodies were crammed together on that little ledge. At that moment, it dawned on me that climbing was as cool as climbers.

Maybe cooler.

CHAPTER 4
Getting on with It

Journal

I smell sunlight on dried pine needles.
Let me live this simplicity.
Let me share this simplicity.
Let me drown in this simplicity.

♦♦♦

My family reversed its migration and moved north again when I was sixteen, in the middle of my junior year. We moved to Nipomo, a town of a few thousand people in southern San Luis Obispo County. Before the move I attended San Clemente High, the Ritz-Carlton of high schools, nestled in the affluence of southern Orange County. It was characterized by lean teenagers with perfect teeth, nattily-dressed faculty, dozens of clubs, and top of the line computers and lab equipment. I never fit into the dominant surf scene at San Clemente, but the atmosphere was relaxed and the classes were interesting.

After we moved to Nipomo, I attended a school that belonged in a television show called "Leave it to Beaver Meets Cops." All female students were required to complete a class called Marriage and the Family. We made grocery shopping lists and balanced checkbooks, and, over a twelve week period, planned our dream weddings. I bought a copy of Bride magazine, cut out pictures of the dress and silverware I wanted, and created a lovely collage. I designed invitations, picked out hairdos, and figured out the cost of my big day. I fumed every hour I sat in that class, and thought about a million better things I could be doing with my time.

In contrast to the wholesome curriculum, the campus was unsettled and dangerous. Gang fights—knives were the weapon of choice—and alcohol were the common denominators in an uncomfortable blend of cowboys, Hispanics, and jocks. The administrators viewed students as untrustworthy until proven otherwise. There were no free periods. Hall passes were required whenever a student was not in a classroom during class hours. Before I learned the rules, I was sent to the principal's office for sitting in my car during lunch break. I completed one semester and declared I would never return to high school.

"It's a complete and utter waste of my time." I told my parents. "I need to get on with it, get on with my life."

"Okay, fine," Mom said. "But you have to finish high school. Figure out an alternative plan."

With a lot of finagling I convinced key school administrators that I was ready for community college. I attended classes at Allan Hancock College and transferred credits to the local high school. My high school diploma came from a school where I never set foot in a classroom.

In my second year at Hancock, in spring of 1979, I enrolled in a week-long course on desert biology and geology. The classrooms were open-air, with lectures held under blazing blue skies and oceans of stars in the Mojave Desert. About fifteen students and three staff members loaded a flatbed truck and two Suburbans with camping gear and set out in search of wildflowers and fault escarpments in Death Valley National Monument and Anza-Borrego State Park.

My memories of the week blended and tumbled like grains of dune sand pushed by successive waves of hot wind. Mosaics of rock and flower exploded in vibrant color—rust, crimson, deep violet, pale lilac, sunflower yellow, and more shades of brown and gray than were ever seen in a Crayola box.

Natural hot springs lined with ancient stone and bottomed with primordial ooze replaced confining desks as we squished warm silt through our toes and discussed the finer points of alluvial fan development. The wind tested our mettle, sending forty mile per hour gusts to carry tents, sleeping bags, and odd bits of clothing aloft into neighboring campsites. Eyes, ears, noses, and mouths filled with fine, gritty sand as we scavenged rocks to hold everything down and built a picnic table fortress to keep from being sandblasted. Noses and lips burned cherry red.

Our multi-talented instructors fixed the blue Suburban when it broke down in the middle of nowhere. They were experts in camping and outdoor survival skills, and their enthusiasm about all things outside was contagious. They even made good spaghetti over an old, rusty camp stove.

We bounced over dirt roads with washboard surfaces and blazed over endless miles of pavement. We stopped everywhere to look at everything. Nothing escaped our scrutiny—from the jagged line of a small fault cutting through a marble-walled slot canyon to the delicate pistils of the vivid purple phacelia. I developed deep crushes on the two male instructors and I wanted to be just like Sally, the botanist. I wanted her life. I bought a red bandanna and pulled my hair back with it, just like she did.

After dawn broke on our last day in Death Valley I wandered away from the group and sat down in the middle of a sandy wash. A two-foot tall stem bearing a large golden sunflower called desert gold nodded softly in my direction. At that moment I wanted nothing more than to live and work in that desert—to be immersed in unfiltered sun and parched air, to revel in the silence, the raw beauty, the extremes.

Little did I know the universe had a similar plan.

CHAPTER 5
Anything but a Passive Observer

Journal

I want to cultivate reverence, help heal relationships between humans and the land and the more-than-human entities with whom we co-exist. I want to foster love and respect, craft visions for a healthy future for the land. I want love for the Earth to seep under people's skin, into their blood stream, to their hearts, lungs, and souls. I want to help them learn how to savor and appreciate the world, stop the damage, save the worms, the butterflies, the snakes, and the grizzly bears. I want more than anything to cultivate reverence.

On New Year's Day, 1982, I left my parent's house in Nipomo in my pea-green Ford pick-up and drove north on Highway 101 to Paso Robles. Enveloped in a warm post-holiday glow emanating from Mom's homemade caramels, turkey with mashed potatoes and gravy, and lots of Christmas carols, I realized I had come full circle; I was friends with my parents again.

I was twenty-one, and in my third year of college at Humboldt State University. Initially, I planned to major in wildlife biology. Within a few months, though, I realized Humboldt's wildlife program emphasized propagating wild animals so hunters could shoot them. I switched my major to Natural Resources Planning and Interpretation.

Instead of continuing north on Highway 101 to Humboldt's home town of Arcata, the land of redwoods, rain, and fog drip, I turned east at Paso Robles and headed for the mountains. A month earlier I'd been selected to participate in a ten week internship with the National Park Service. My destination was Lodgepole in Sequoia National Park, deep in the heart of the southern Sierra Nevada. I knew no one who lived in the area, had only a vague sense of what I'd gotten myself into, and was more than a little scared. My truck broke down in the middle of the broad, flat Central Valley, before I even got to the toe of the mountains. I paced the parking lot of a service station in the tiny agricultural community of Hanford, while skeletons of leggy weeds, candy wrappers, and styrofoam cups spiraled around one another in the cold winter wind. Two hours later I was on the road again. I crossed the bridge over the river Kaweah in the town of Three Rivers, and the road began to ascend. Once past park headquarters and the Ash Mountain entrance station, the road switched back into the mountains, climbing high into the wild white yonder. Before long I was driving on a layer cake of packed snow topped by a transparent, vanilla ice frosting.

The sun was descending behind a wreath of tall conifers when I arrived at Lodgepole. I found my assigned quarters at the end of a short road and knocked on the door of the adjacent apartment. My new neighbor welcomed me warmly and offered to escort me to my new digs. He told me Lodgepole was a great place to spend the winter, and to please let him know if I needed anything at all. He walked away and I was very alone.

I didn't sleep much that night. It was pitch black in the apartment. Every tiny noise of scurrying mouse or scraping tree branch turned into a crazy man trying to break in. When the window finally turned a pale shade of gray, I hauled myself out of the twin bed, got dressed, and appraised the apartment. My new home consisted of living room, kitchen, bedroom, and bathroom. They were all small, and furnished with tables, chairs, couches, and beds in various combinations of unremarkable blond wood and vinyl covered cushions. I learned later it was called "ranch oak," a signature feature of national park quarters.

After breakfast I shoved open the creaky front door, stepped out onto the tiny wooden deck, and was momentarily blinded by a brilliant white world topped by a crystalline blue sky. While I'd tossed and turned in my bed of nerves all night, snow had fallen in peaceful silence.

The sun crested the rocky ridge to the east, its dagger sharp rays splintering through snow-laden tree branches. Squinting against the brightness, I returned to the kitchen to grab sunglasses. When I stepped back outside, the glint of an aluminum snow shovel resting on the deck caught my eye. I saw what I hadn't seen the night before; the walkway between the parking area and my apartment was a snow tunnel, with walls about seven feet high. The walkway itself was buried under a foot of new, fluffy white powder. When I stepped on it, the snow compressed into almost nothing, but nonetheless managed to fill the gaps between my grey wool socks and the tops of my shiny new Vasque hiking boots. My truck was buried under a downy snow blanket, so I walked the quarter mile to the Lodgepole Visitor Center to report for duty.

The morning walk became a daily routine. It took me alongside and then over the Marble Fork of the Kaweah River, which gently gurgled through the small canyon where Lodgepole was nestled. The river meandered around granite boulders, small sand bars, and clumps of tired yellow-green sedge.

I rock-hopped across the water and walked up a slight slope to the hamlet of Lodgepole, which included a park visitor center and offices, gas station, campground, and a small, funky market. Lodgepole was the winter home of about twenty-five people, primarily law enforcement rangers, maintenance workers, interpretive naturalists, and a few retail salespeople. Giant Forest, a large grove of giant sequoia trees, was about two miles south. To the east, the park's high country wilderness beckoned.

My job as intern was to be an interpreter, which in Park Service jargon means a naturalist or environmental educator. I showed films, conducted slide shows, and took visitors on snowshoe walks and cross-country ski tours. I spent many hours behind the Visitor Center desk and chatted up visitors, sold books and maps, and answered a range of questions. We maintained a clipboard behind the desk to jot down the most memorable questions, which included: "How much of Crystal Cave is undiscovered?" "How far have we come?" and "When do you let the bears out?"

Snow fell all winter. Cross-country skis became my favored means of travel and the Giant Forest one of my favorite destinations. It was best after a heavy snow. Some of the massive trees were thousands of years old. Their rust-colored trunks rose straight up from winter snow beds, trunks bare of branches except at the very top, hundreds of feet up. Like veterans at a Memorial Day gathering, the trees stood stoic. Their deep, black scars hung like medals on their massive red flanks, telling silent stories of the flicker and scorch of past fires. The forest was so very quiet, resting in a silent hush until a lump of melting snow slipped off a branch and landed with a muffled thump, or a Douglas squirrel, in search of seeds, chattered as he ripped through the stem of a sequoia cone, sending it into freefall.

My internship required me to conduct an in-depth analysis on some aspect of park management. I chose the park budgeting process because I knew nothing about it. I attended several budget meetings with all of the park managers.

The meetings were my first exposure to upper level park management. Every year Congress allocates a certain amount of money to the Park Service and the parks each get a piece of the big pie. The program managers were tasked with deciding how to distribute Sequoia's slice, which had been reduced from the previous year.

I attended budget meetings every week, and they followed a similar pattern. The managers came together, and each one declared he or she needed more money, and could not possibly afford to cut anything from their programs. For the first several weeks the group was at a complete stalemate. Participants crossed their arms over their chests, tapped their feet, and identified ways other programs could sustain cuts, but never their own. I was surprised at the lack of cooperation, the failure of the managers to get down to business and address the budget cuts in a mature way. I expected more from my leaders—the people charged with safeguarding our nation's natural treasures.

After four or five such meetings, things began to change, almost imperceptibly. The managers proposed ways they could make very small cuts in their programs. I realized afterwards there was a strategy to their methods—anyone who went forward with proposed cuts to their program early in the process stood to lose more. As the weeks passed each manager analyzed their program in-depth to determine where the cuts would be least painful to both park and park visitors. Sequoia's managers were masters at this game.

I left the park to return to school before the final budget decisions were made, but this experience was my first exposure to a truth that I would run into over and over during my career—the U.S. National Park Service operated from a position of scarcity. There never was enough money to do what managers felt should be done. Not enough for resource management, not enough for maintenance, not enough for administration, not enough for rangers—just plain not enough.

Four weeks after I started the internship, I walked into my supervisor's office at the end of a busy Friday.

"We're going to ski up to the Pear Lake Ski Hut next week with a small group," he announced. "We'll be staying for three nights."

"Do you think I can do it?" I asked.

"I do." he said. I suspect he thought the energy of youth would make up for my lack of skill.

My fellow interpreters told me with relish how difficult the Pear Lake trip was. My dread mounted. The National Park Service web site described the hut as follows:

> *It is located 3/8 of a mile north of Pear Lake at 9,200 feet (2804 meters) and is reached by ascending a STEEP six miles of trail from Wolverton Meadow (7,200 feet). This advanced level ski/snowshoe*

trail offers a chance to explore the beautiful wilderness of the Sierra Nevada mountain range in the winter months. The hut sleeps ten people and is heated by a wood stove.

We left early on Monday morning. There were six other people in our group, all of them very experienced skiers. They divided most of my gear among themselves to lighten my load. After the first five minutes on the trail I discovered another reason they had taken my gear—so I would be able to get up after falling. The trail was icy and all too frequently my skis decided I was going the wrong way. I fell dozens of times. I fell on my butt. I did face-plants. Falling down was easy. Getting up again was hard, especially with a load on my back. I learned to sympathize with up-side-down turtles as I lay on my back in the snow, legs paddling, but gaining no purchase.

We climbed slowly up the trail. I was second to last, with my boss behind me. The trail went up right from the start, gradually at first, then steeper, and then even steeper. My companions ascended the slope by aiming straight uphill, adjusting their skis to points at ten and two o'clock, and duck-walking up. The trick to this technique, the herringbone, was to angle the skis just right so they didn't slide back downhill and split you in half, or worse. My legs were not strong enough for this maneuver, so I side-stepped all the way up that bloody hill.

The sun dropped below a snow-covered ridge just as we arrived at the hut. I unclipped my skis, leaned them against the side of the building, and went inside. The air was blessedly warm, permeated with the aroma of tomato, onion, and garlic simmering on the stove. I dropped my small pack on the last empty bunk, removed my boots, and lay back on the twin bed to rest a minute before dinner.

The next thing I knew, someone was nudging my shoulder gently. My boss stood over me with offerings—a plate of spaghetti in one hand and a slice of French bread in the other. I ate with relish and fell back to sleep immediately, unconscious until morning rays beamed through the window above my head.

The final six weeks of my winter in Lodgepole were a flurry of snow and wonder. On my last day I got a letter of recommendation from my supervisor. It said, among other things:

"She proved herself to be anything but a passive observer. She was encouraged to analyze critically the activities going on around her, and she did this in a productive and useful manner. She did not hesitate to ask significant and penetrating questions of those around her, and to pursue those questions further if the answers were not adequate."

I liked that.

CHAPTER 6
The Best Jobs in the World

Journal

There is nothing like lying naked on a flat granite boulder on a hot Sierra Nevada summer day, next to a large, deep pool framed by a whitewater river. When you get too hot you plunge into snowmelt that has warmed just a bit on its long journey down canyon—tumbling over rocks, between tree roots, under bridges, and past black bear dens, thirsty deer, and grassy, flower-filled meadows.

Sufficiently cooled, you haul yourself back up onto the rock like a wet seal, lay flat on your stomach, and rest your head on its side. The aroma of granite fills your nose and mind—a powdery essence that evokes the energy of age, time, motion, stillness, trees, birds, and caddis flies, as well as an amazing ability to roll with whatever might happen next.

♦♦♦

As I stepped out onto the cabin's small, wooden front deck and headed down to the corral, a big, dark bay mare burst forth with a loud whinny.

"Good morning, Sweets. Ready for another day, big girl?" I pulled a thick flake of alfalfa hay from an open bale and tossed it into her manger.

She snorted an affirmative answer and dropped her velvety muzzle deep into the hay, raising a small cloud of dust. I walked back up the hill to the old two-room cabin to fix my own breakfast.

Following my snowy internship, I spent three summers working as a mounted patrol ranger in Sequoia—if you could call it work. I rode Sweets two miles to and from work each day down an old fire road, always on alert for wandering bears. Most days I patrolled Lodgepole Campground and talked to campers. Sweets and I ambled through swarms of motor homes, cars, bicycles, and hikers. She got her nose petted while I answered questions and instructed campers to keep their food in the metal food storage lockers and their campfires in the fire pits. I resolved arguments, found lost children, and served other critical ranger functions, like removing a nest with six baby mice from the wheel well of a camper. When visitors were injured on a trail within a few hours ride, Sweets and I were called to carry them out.

I was the most photographed employee in the park. Years later when I taught outdoor education in northern Oregon, a visiting teacher kept telling me he knew me from somewhere, but couldn't remember where. One morning he showed up at breakfast and told me I was in his photo album, astride a dark horse. He echoed many others when he said, "You know, you have the very best job in the world." I agreed, but by the end of the third summer I was restless. The spirit of my friend the Pismo clam had taken up residence on my left shoulder, and the spirit of the Cachuma Lake coot on my right. They kept whispering to me that I had to save the world, that I needed to do more for the environment. Once again, I needed to get on with it. I decided to pursue the environmental education work my degree had prepared me for.

The next step on my path was a series of jobs as a seasonal interpreter, or naturalist. For two seasons in Kings Canyon National Park, just north of Sequoia, and one season in Death Valley National Monument, I regaled visitors with stories of the parks' wonders, and preached the need to preserve those wonders. I had become the ranger doing evening campfire programs, just like the one in Yosemite who had inspired me so many years earlier.

My connection to wild land and wild creatures continued to deepen each time I hopped from one granite boulder to the next to ford a raging spring-fed creek, or took a solo hike into a remote corner of the Mojave Desert. I lived among natural sounds—my ears rang sometimes just to fill the absolute silence of endless miles of open country. I slept in beds under canopies of giant sequoia trees and tasted brine-filled air swept up from salt-encrusted playas, delivered like a kiss to dry lips by a hot wind. I saw more stars than empty space in the night sky.

I was very deeply blessed.

Naturalist work provided endless incentives to learn more, to be able to share more about parks and their resources with visitors. And, as my knowledge grew, so did the sense of urgency I felt when I learned how imperiled many of the resources were—by air pollution, acid rain, invasive non-native species, and adjacent development causing habitat loss. At the same time, I had a growing sense I was preaching to the choir in my role as naturalist.

I acted on my instincts in 1987 when a work associate and friend told me about a project he was leading in Tuolumne Meadows the following summer. He encouraged me to apply for a position as a Biological Technician for Yosemite's Resource Management Division. I applied for the position, which involved restoring damaged habitat in high elevation forests and meadows. I was ecstatic when I got the offer. It was almost like going home.

CHAPTER 7
The Perfect Summer

Journal

Give me the splash and roar of a waterfall; peals of wild running thunder; the snarl and hiss of fresh, hot lava hitting cold ocean waves; and the cricket's chirrup as he leaps and flashes his lovely thorax at the world. Give me the flicker of wind among aspen leaves and the call of the chickadee-dee-dee-dee-dee.

♦♦♦

I left Death Valley before dawn. It was mid-June, and daytime temperatures had spiked to over one hundred degrees frequently over the past six weeks. I wanted to be out of the park before the sun crested the Funeral Mountains and started to heat things up.

My route took me up and down over low passes—terrain typical of the basin and range province—and then on into Lone Pine, a tiny town near the foot of Mount Whitney, the highest point in the contiguous United States. Morning sunbeams illuminated the uppermost band of the spiky Sierra Nevada crest as I pulled up to a T-intersection. The top of the T was Highway 395, which runs like a skinny snake along the base of the steep eastern flank of the mountains.

I turned right and drove north for two hours toward Lee Vining, one of many small settlements on the Sierra's east side. Just south of town a sharp left turn onto Highway 120 signaled the start of a steep, 3,000-foot climb to Tioga Pass. I reached the top of the pass, a high elevation saddle at 9,943 feet, and felt like I'd arrived at the top of the world.

Despite many previous visits to Yosemite Valley, I had never been over Tioga Pass and had no memory of Tuolumne Meadows. The drive to Tuolumne from the Valley took only a few hours, but the road was closed under deep snow the better part of most years, generally from late October through late May. Thus, the spring timing of our family vacations precluded side trips to Tuolumne.

"Hi!" I said to the swarthy male ranger on duty at the entrance kiosk, whose name tag said Ferdinand, "I'm here to start a new job."

"Welcome to Yosemite," he said with a bright smile as he waved me through.

I was filled with a deep sense of peace and safety as I pulled away from the kiosk. Since my first Park Service job in Sequoia, I had come to feel the same way whenever I entered any national park. It was as if all the parks were familiar somehow—I was safe there, I knew how to behave, and people there would take care of me. It was the way I suspected some felt about their home town. My feelings were linked to what is known in the agency as the "Park Service family."

During my seasonal trysts with Sequoia, Kings Canyon, and Death Valley, I heard from many park employees about this "family." It turned out "parkies" were bound together closely by common interests in parks and wild places, by life in remote locations that precluded a social life with anyone except other parkies, and by periodic events like accidents, floods, fires, or rockslides that required everyone to pull together.

My experiences with the family up to that time had been overwhelmingly positive. I was automatically a member wherever I worked. Additionally, when I went to other parks, I was welcomed into the homes of "parkies" I'd never even met before. I anticipated similar warmth in Yosemite.

The short drive from the entrance station to Tuolumne Meadows was a blurred mix of thick forests, rock, and meadows interspersed with small lakes. My mind swam with transient thoughts and images. Memories of heat waves rising from salt flats and sand flowing across dune fields were transposed onto views of vertical mountain edges and milky blue glacial lakes, all mixed up with my butterfly-infested stomach of anticipation.

Lost in reverie, I missed the turnoff to my new residence. I continued on to find a place to turn around. The forest thinned out and suddenly the majesty of Tuolumne Meadows opened up before me—a vast patchwork quilt of grasses, sedges, and wildflowers stitched around huge, sun-baked granite boulders. The Tuolumne River sparkled and shimmered in shades of blue, green, and brown as it meandered across the landscape, nourishing the mix of seasonal greens and the stands of leggy lodgepole pines that edged the wild garden. Once again I would be working in one of the most beautiful places in the world. I pulled into a parking lot near a small market and turned the car around to find my summer quarters.

I found the large parking lot for the Dog Lake Trail as described in the directions my new boss had sent. A small dirt road spurred off from the west end of the lot. I drove a few hundred feet down this dusty road and arrived at the residential area known as Bug Camp.

The camp was a circular cluster of half a dozen tiny, wood-framed, canvas tent cabins and one bathhouse scattered across a gentle, pine-forested slope. Patches of snow still lingered in the northern shadows of boulders and buildings.

My tent cabin was on the east side of the encampment. The dark interior smelled like old smoke and moldy canvas. The cabin had two ten-foot-square rooms; one served as living room, kitchen and dining area, and the second was furnished with two twin beds. The cabin had no closets, storage areas, or insulation. A small woodstove with a built-in cooking box generated heat. This "oven," combined with a hot plate, a cold-water sink, and a small refrigerator, was the kitchen. I shared this tent cabin with another seasonal technician.

We lived close to the elements in Bug Camp. One day a large black bear ran past the picnic table out front and grabbed the corner of a two pound bag of M&Ms in his teeth on the fly. I feared for his stomach.

For much of the summer, though, I didn't live in the tent cabin. I spent almost all weekdays in the backcountry just south of Tuolumne as part of a three-person team hired to work on Yosemite's first backcountry habitat restoration project. Our job was to eliminate backpacker's campsites in areas where camping was not allowed. We focused our efforts around three lakes: Elizabeth, Budd, and Lower Cathedral.

Elizabeth and Budd lakes were closed to overnight use in 1974 because of the cumulative effects of decades of use. Vegetation was pulverized or completely obliterated. Soil was compacted. Rocks were scarred from multiple campfires. Campfire rings and other site "improvements" like benches dotted the area around the lake like acne on a pretty face. The Park Service had decided to give the lake basins a rest. Thirteen years later, though, the old campsites had not shown much natural recovery—they still looked like campsites. This invited illegal use, so the Park Service stepped in to assist with the restoration process.

Camping was still allowed at Lower Cathedral Lake, but many of the campsites were very close to the lake shore, where the pressures of camping—walking, sleeping, cooking, washing, and general outdoor life—had taken their toll on the lake's edge and were affecting the quality of the water. Campers throughout Yosemite's backcountry are required to use sites that are at least a hundred feet away from all water—springs, creeks, lakes, ponds, and rivers. At Lower Cathedral we planned to eliminate sites within that buffer zone.

For the first week we made plans and got acclimated. On Monday of the second week, we donned our ranger uniforms, shouldered heavy packs filled with food, clothing, camping stoves, cookware, flashlights, first aid kits, and other backcountry necessities, and hiked to Elizabeth

Lake. In addition to packs, we carried shovels, tape measures, clipboards and pencils, compasses, and green plastic watering cans.

We left the trailhead and climbed steadily through a forest of lodgepole pines. Our unusual accessories, especially the watering cans, attracted numerous questions from passing hikers. We told them we were gardeners of the wilderness.

About a mile up, the route flattened a bit and paralleled the crystal clear waters of Unicorn Creek as it flowed from the lake above. The creek gurgled and splashed through a lush bed of grass and sedge. After a short slog through the lake's marshy outflow, we reached the lake itself—a blue-green gem nestled in a granite bowl and fringed by small meadows, shrubby willow thickets, and clusters of lodgepole, whitebark, and western white pine trees. The high point on the ridgeline, Unicorn Peak, kept steady watch over the fair Elizabeth.

Upon arrival at the lake, we set up our home away from home. Most nights we slept out under the vast star-studded sky. We pumped lake water through water filters for cooking and drinking, and used the lakes for soap-free bathing.

During the week we worked to erase all signs of campsites. We pulled apart fire rings and buried or scattered the charred rocks. If the rocks were too large to move, we scrubbed them to remove char marks. As I buried thick layers of residual campfire ash accumulated over decades, I wondered who had stared into those fires and what mountain memories still lingered behind their eyes.

Once the fire pits were gone, we dismantled and scattered log furnishings. We dug up compacted soil to help plant growth, and as a last step, we transplanted native plants from surrounding areas into the sites. We carefully mapped each site and noted the locations and species name for each planting. The corners of the sites were marked so they could be located in the future for follow-up monitoring. Our mission was to erase the scars and help heal the land.

Several weeks later we hiked into Budd Lake, also south of Tuolumne Meadows via a network of unmarked trails. The trek took a bit of route-finding as we scrambled over large granite slabs. Melting snow fed the lake, which sat in a glacial cirque—a roughly circular bowl of gray and white granite glazed to a high sheen by an icy potter, then hand-painted with a smattering of trees and pocket meadows. At about 10,000 feet in elevation, Budd was higher than Elizabeth, and patches of whitebark pine and mountain hemlock largely replaced the lodgepole pine stands.

Our third work site was Lower Cathedral Lake, almost four miles from the trailhead and a bit west of Budd. The trail was a very heavily-used and well-worn part of the John Muir Trail. It was a busy place, ringed by about 150 campsites.

"Hey Richard," I yelled at the project coordinator as I bent over to pull a clump of *Carex exerta*, a small sedge, up out of the ground. "It seems to me we're just displacing the impact here. We're transplanting healthy plants out of one area to plant them in these restoration sites. We're robbing Peter to pay Paul."

"Yeah," he answered. "It does seem like that."

"Wouldn't it be better to just de-compact soil in the old campsites and wait for native seeds to come in?" I asked. "Then the plants that were best suited to grow there would colonize and eventually take over."

"It probably would be better," he said, nodding. "But this is a Fee Demo project. Congress wants to see results from the money spent on this project immediately. We have to be able to get good before and after photos," he told me as he carefully dug up a small lupine.

"So if the plants we plant die after a year, it's okay because we have our before and after photos?" I said.

"Yeah, basically that's right," he said with a trace of resignation. "But I sure hope they live."

Congress authorized the Recreational Fee Demonstration Program, or Fee Demo, in the 1986 Interior Appropriations Act. The program allowed the National Park Service to retain a large percentage of the money generated through entrance and use fees for park projects. The new program was initiated in 1987, and the Tuolumne backcountry campsite removal was one of the first projects funded. These pilot projects had to appear successful to convince Congress of the program's merit, thereby ensuring the continued flow of money.

On most days the silence of the mountains was broken only by the click of shovel on rock and the scolding rattle and yelp of Clark's nutcrackers as they supervised our work from nearby lodgepole pines. Work days ended with dips in the lake, which were quick, as the lakes often were fringed with sheets of old winter ice. At mid-day on Fridays we made our way back down to Bug Camp, grateful to be hiking downhill. The allure of hot showers and pizza kept us moving.

One morning at Budd Lake I arose before my workmates, crawled quietly out of my sleeping bag, and looked a thousand feet straight up to the first rays of the sun as they blazed over the top of the rugged granite ridge to the east. The flutter of wing beats broke the silence as the local flock of ptarmigan passed mere feet over my head on their morning pilgrimage from rock alcove to lake. The rich scent of warming pine needles greeted my nose as I pulled my sleep shirt over my head and walked down to the lake. Memories of my backcountry summer were etched forever into my soul as I accepted the frigid lake's embrace.

CHAPTER 8
Finding My Niche

Journal

 I drove to the Onyx Mine yesterday on a very bumpy, rocky road. As I rounded a blind corner, the windshield filled up completely with the underside of a golden eagle. Huge wings beat in slow motion, sweeping the air in a cloud of energy. A solo raven took off right behind the eagle and chased him, striking at him repeatedly. The smaller, more agile bird soared up and dove to strike again and again. After the shock of surprise passed, I gagged on a truly foul smell seeping in through the window. I'd disturbed the birds as they'd fed, or, in the raven's case, waited to feed, on the carcass of a dead burro right next to the road.
 The desert wind has come again. It comes so fast and blows so hard.

◆◆◆

 At the end of my Tuolumne summer I returned to Death Valley to overwinter. I shifted from my earlier role as an interpretive naturalist to take on a variety of duties as a Biological Technician with the park's Resources Management Division. One day I'd hike solo across vast expanses of salt-encrusted playas and up rugged, rocky canyons in search of remote springs, and the next day I'd sit in a converted closet—office space was at a premium—organizing data on springs and wildlife.

As the last wildflowers waned in late spring, I was offered a chance to experience the desert summer as coordinator of the park's Youth Conservation Corps. For ten weeks, my small crew of hardy Death Valley residents, aged fifteen to eighteen, and I painted park signs, broke up unnecessary foot trails in the salt pan, repaired boardwalks, and drank gallons of Gatorade. The hottest day of the summer was 127 degrees Fahrenheit, which didn't feel that much different than 126 degrees, or 125 degrees. We worked from 6AM to 2PM, and then headed for the community pool.

As I sweated through the summer, I yearned for a Park Service position that would allow me to make a more significant contribution toward protecting natural resources. Conversations with my supervisor and co-workers convinced me I needed at least a Master's degree, if not a Ph.D., to be competitive.

In late September I applied for admittance into a Master's program in environmental science at Oregon State University. My letter of acceptance arrived a few weeks later. I worked at Death Valley until December, went home for Christmas, and then headed north for Corvallis, about ninety minutes south of Portland.

On New Years Day, 1989, heavy, gray clouds obscured the sky like a soggy wool blanket. The rain stopped shortly after noon, but Interstate 5 just north of Mount Shasta was a puddle. Sheets of water engulfed my gold Toyota Corolla and rendered me sightless as I passed caravan after caravan of tractor-trailer rigs. I cranked the stereo volume up high as the Indigo Girls told me in no uncertain terms that "...the sweetest part is acting after making a decision." I wondered when the sweetness would kick in.

Corvallis was graced with thirty-four consecutive days of rain as soon as I arrived. The weather was a shock after two years in Death Valley, but my re-introduction to academia was a bigger shock. For six months I slogged through courses like organic chemistry, trigonometry, and statistics. My advisor called these "deficiencies" in my academic background—in truth they were classes I had avoided like the plague in my undergraduate program.

The Soul of Yosemite

When summer came, I was more than ready to trade gloomy, cold classrooms for bright, warm mountains. I returned to Sequoia to be a naturalist in Lodgepole. At summer's end, I headed north again to the land of perpetual drizzle to continue my studies. My graduate program focused on three primary subjects—botany, statistics, and environmental policy. After much deliberation over my thesis topic, I decided to analyze the results of the backcountry campsite restoration I worked on near Tuolumne Meadows in 1987.

In spring of 1990, I was offered a temporary job as a GS-7 Biological Technician in Yosemite. This was a promotion, a step up in pay and responsibility from earlier jobs. In 1990, the GS-7 salary was between ten and twelve dollars per hour. The job, like my earlier position in Tuolumne Meadows, involved habitat restoration. This time it was even better though, because I would coordinate the projects, and could collect data for my thesis on weekends. Best of all, my duty station was Yosemite Valley.

It was late afternoon when I pulled into the parking lot of the personnel office in El Portal to check in and pick up the key to my summer residence. It was June 8, and my thirtieth birthday.

"Okay, here's your residence key," said the black-haired woman behind the desk after I'd filled out several forms in triplicate and had my fingerprints taken. "You'll be living in the first trailer in the trailer park. Do you know where the trailer park is? It's just down the road, back the way you came a bit."

"But wait," I said. "I'm supposed to be living in the Valley."

"That's not what my list says," she said as she swiveled away from me in her chair.

"But my supervisor told me…"

"Sorry, you'll have to take it up with her. You're assigned to the trailer. It's a three bedroom, and you have three roommates." She stared at me over her shoulder, as if daring me to challenge her, then stood up and walked into an adjacent room. I wanted to ask her if she'd ever heard of the Park Service family.

When she made the offer, my supervisor-to-be assured me repeatedly that I would live and work in Yosemite Valley. I was very clear on this point because it was so important to me. Fuming, I picked up the key and left the building.

As I drove to the trailer, I wondered who would be stuck sharing a bedroom. No one was home, but all three rooms showed signs of occupation, littered with backpacks, bicycles, hiking boots, and scattered articles of clothing. I dumped my scant belongings on an unmade twin bed in a room at the far end of the hall and left to take a walk.

It was a warm evening. There was no sight or sound of another human being in the trailer park. The air was filled with the buzz of cicadas, the occasional croak of a frog, and the unmistakable resonance of flowing water. I navigated carefully through dense walls of healthy, bright green poison oak as I followed the water sounds to the river's edge. This same river, the Merced, flowed through Yosemite Valley. At this lower elevation, the river was flanked by rocky banks and broken stands of cottonwood and willow, instead of the lush meadows encountered higher up.

I sat down on a large rock and stared at the river. I wondered if I'd made a huge mistake. I should have attained more in my life by age thirty than the opportunity to share a small bedroom in a cheap trailer with a stranger for a temporary job. I was thirty. I was old. And I was all alone on my birthday. I wallowed in a morass of self-pity.

Eventually, I pulled my head out of my mental murk and focused on the river. The water was in no hurry. Billions of drops of water all moved together, flowing effortlessly past the big square rock on which I sat. Each drop was on its own journey out of the mountains, headed for the Central Valley, never to experience this particular moment, or this particular place within the larger flow ever again. I once again saw myself and my life mirrored in Yosemite's water, and realized my best course of action was to emulate the river's easy flow—relax, take things a day, or even a moment, at a time, and, above all else, be kind to those with whom I shared the trailer.

I commuted from the trailer to my office in the Valley and back. The drive took thirty minutes. The road was narrow, and had very few straight sections. For much of the route, the river canyon—a deep chasm—yawned on the south side, while rock walls lined the north side. Many people who drove this route twice a day five days a week drove it fast; it was nicknamed the "El Portal 500". I survived the commute for a week, and realized that was my limit.

After much verbal wrangling peppered with a few mild threats, I was re-located from the trailer to the Rangers' Club, a two-story wood and stone, Swiss chalet-type structure built in Yosemite Valley in the 1920s. I occupied the back half of an upstairs bedroom that faced Yosemite Village and the Visitor Center. Located on the east side of the building, the spacious room had a private entrance, and lots of windows with views of massive, old black oak trees, creamy-blossomed dogwoods, and the occasional wandering mule deer or black bear.

I shared a kitchen and large living area with a dozen or so other people—rangers, interpreters, resource managers, park volunteers, and search and rescue experts. The Rangers' Club was a venue for quick friendships and lively conversation.

My office was in the Resources Management building, formerly the residence of the park Superintendent. The old two-story house sat at the edge of a black oak woodland. The back porch, the favored space for meetings, overlooked Cook's Meadow. Yosemite Creek ran behind the house, and the Merced River flowed by less than a quarter mile to the south.

My job was perfect. I was a restoration specialist, although my title was a bit less glamorous: Biological Technician-Revegetation. I planned and carried out projects designed to help heal damaged land in the Valley. Various actions that could be called habitat restoration had occurred in the Valley over the course of its 150 years as a park, such as discontinuing livestock grazing in meadows and prohibiting camping outside of designated campsites, but it wasn't until the late 1980s that the practice of restoration was formalized. The primary emphasis was re-establishing vegetation in denuded areas. We were on the cutting edge and we were excited about it.

That group of "we" included twelve people. I worked closely with two other restoration specialists. One was responsible for backcountry projects, and one also worked on Valley projects. Two other biological technicians lent critical support to the program, and a work crew leader and six-person crew did most of the hands-on project work. We were all young and full of energy, and our enthusiasm for the work was palpable. We focused most of our efforts on two habitat types: black oak woodlands and montane meadows.

My commute was much better after I moved out of El Portal—a five minute bike ride. The bike path wound through the Schoolyard Oak Woodland, named for its proximity to the Valley elementary school. The woodland was populated with geriatric oaks, their age evidenced by huge, gnarled trunks and heavy limbs. Many large branches, and several of the big trees in their entirety, had broken and fallen to the ground.

The oak community was a beehive of activity, particularly in the mornings. Piles of last year's leaves rustled as gray squirrels searched for acorns, and then chased each other up and down furrowed tree trunks, tails switching rapidly. Herds of mule deer browsed on low-hanging leaves, while Steller's jays and acorn woodpeckers greeted the day with screeches and trills. Coyotes rose from their night nests, stretched, yawned to expose big, sharp teeth, and trotted off in search of a vole or two for breakfast. The woodland was lively, but several important elements were missing: young, adolescent, and middle-aged oak trees.

The old oaks were stately and grand, and still produced acorns, homes, and cover for abundant wildlife, but new generations were not coming in to replace the senior members of the community. With this realization, the giant limbs and trunks of dead and dying oaks scattered across the ground took on a different, troubling aspect. Like bleached bones, the pieces of the old giants lay silent and still. A few broken limbs arced into the air, caught in time for a moment as they waved their farewells.

Some of the Valley's oak woodlands supported oaks of all ages, others did not. The Park Service recognized the latter areas could lose all their oaks if nothing was done, and set out to identify reasons for the lack of reproduction.

Some of the reasons were obvious. The soil around the trees was completely bare. All vegetation had been pulverized—trampled by millions upon millions of human feet, bicycles, and horses, and, in earlier days, automobiles. Other reasons were a bit more obscure, and included changes in the frequency of wildfire, competition with pines and firs, and browsing by deer and rodents. The Native Americans had lit fires every year in the dry season for perhaps several thousand years, which killed young, competing conifers, kept the forests open, and created a bed for oak germination and growth. This routine maintenance probably perpetuated the woodlands. Even in the absence of humans, ecologists estimated fires would burn every eight to twelve years. Ever since non-Natives arrived in the Valley in the mid-1860s, though, fires had been suppressed, and so had oak regeneration.

The Park Service initiated oak woodland restoration in Yosemite in the late 1980s, and we continued with the work in 1990. Initially, short fences were constructed around woodlands to keep people away. We collected acorns and grew oak seedlings, then planted them into the woodlands. Metal cages were set up around young trees to keep hungry deer away from tender young leaves. Some of the trees survived; many did not. The understory layer of bracken fern and grasses recovered when trampling stopped, but was still thick with invasive non-native plants such as wooly mullein, cheatgrass, stork's bill, bulbous bluegrass, and remnants of an old apple orchard.

Our second emphasis that summer was on meadow restoration in Sentinel Meadow—the first place from which newly arriving visitors could see Yosemite Falls. Most of the millions of Valley visitors stopped at Sentinel Meadow and many walked across it to the river's edge to take in the view. The effects of this popularity included miles and miles of crisscrossing trails and intense trampling. Meadow plants were killed, the flow of water through the meadow was impeded, and the damage was unsightly.

Our revegetation team eliminated most of the foot trails from the meadow, constructed a boardwalk to provide access to the river's edge, and built split-rail fences to channel visitors to the boardwalk. Several years later, *Sunset* magazine published a feature article on Yosemite Valley. The magazine's cover sported a sun-drenched photo of Sentinel Meadow, radiant in the glorious green of early summer. The boardwalk was prominent in the photo, with the snow white plume of Yosemite Falls providing a perfect backdrop. Resource protection, in the form of habitat restoration and revegetation, had become part of the scene.

I felt very good about our accomplishments, and consistently received praise and kudos from my boss and my boss's boss. I was overjoyed by the fact that the National Park Service was committed to protecting and restoring nature in Yosemite Valley, and was certain I'd found my career niche.

In early August an intense lightning storm hit the western slope of the mountains, and ignited several fires near Yosemite's boundary. The park was evacuated and closed, and most of us went off to fight fire. Little did I know, when I returned to work after the fires, that my incipient joy over my new career path would be suppressed faster, and more thoroughly, than the fires of 1990.

CHAPTER 9
On Fire and Getting Burned

Journal

In Yosemite Valley, I have found sanctuary in the truest sense. My body hums, my breath slows and deepens, and every part of me smiles. In a strange twist, though, I've always sensed a dark, brooding energy just beneath the surface of the Valley—a deep sadness; heartache; heartbreak. Perhaps this energy is rooted in the conflict and trauma that came with the Euro-Americans. Perhaps it's the result of something locals call Chief Tenaya's curse.

♦♦♦

It was mid-morning when I first noticed the cumulus clouds. I stepped outside every few hours to check on their progress. With each visit, the clouds took up more space in the sky. Summer thunderstorms are common in Yosemite. The towering cotton-ball clouds usually amassed east of the Valley over the Sierra Nevada crest, and occasionally pushed west far enough to shower the Valley. Infrequently, storms would start to develop farther west, over the foothills flanking the mountains. These anomalies made local residents deeply uneasy; too often they brought lightning. At higher elevations, conditions stayed relatively cool and wet into summer, but the foothills tended to be tinder dry by early July. On this seventh day of August, clouds filled the western sky.

In the middle of the afternoon, the huge mass of clouds released its pent-up energy. I left the Resources Management building and walked out to the middle of Cook's Meadow. Jagged bolts of lightning ripped through the sky, angling down to lick the ground below. Thunder cracked and rolled up the Merced River canyon, echoing off the Valley walls. All the action was to the west.

By 5PM, wispy plumes of smoke began to drift slowly above the forested horizon. After work, I jumped in my car with several co-workers and we drove west out of the Valley, then turned north on the Big Oak Flat Road for a few miles. I pulled into the Big Meadow overlook parking area, which provided an expansive western view.

Gray and white smoke columns billowed almost straight up in the still air, growing taller and fuller with each passing moment. A small crowd of visitors was lined up at the overlook to watch the fires, talking in hushed tones. As the sun descended, the smoke clouds turned delicate pastel shades of pink and orange.

There were no planes in the sky. It looked like no one was scouting or fighting the fires yet. I wondered when crews would mobilize. Later, I learned fifteen fires were ignited that afternoon, and thirteen small fires already burned in the park when the lightning storm hit. Yosemite's fire crews were overwhelmed.

Mesmerized by the towering columns of smoke, it dawned on me that I would probably be asked to fight fire. I had completed the training required to work on a fire crew earlier in the summer, but hadn't taken the physical fitness test. Many seasonal employees waited eagerly for the chance to participate in fire-fighting activities, for the adrenaline rush as well as the overtime dollars. On the drive back down to the Valley, I made plans to be ready to go when the call came for help.

It came the next morning. The wind picked up and several of the fires exploded, rapidly consuming highly flammable chaparral and forests with extremely dense understory vegetation—the product of decades of fire exclusion. I met up with my supervisor and we went to the fire station to take the fitness test. We would join the crew we'd been assigned to, known as NPS-1, later that afternoon. We passed the test, which entailed running one and a half miles in eleven minutes, forty seconds, or less, then went to the fire house for directions on how to find our crew.

We were sent north and west to Crane Flat, and up the twisty road that led to one of the park's main fire lookouts and bases of helicopter operations. The lookout perched on the side of a hill with a panoramic view of the fires to the west.

We parked the truck and walked out to join a small huddle of firefighters in yellow shirts and green pants standing at the edge of the paved helicopter landing pad. My heart leaped into my throat when I saw the fire. A gargantuan column of smoke swirled thousands of feet up into the sky, exploding into a brilliant white thunderhead at its upper terminus. It was a convection column generated by massive wildfire, and it grew larger with every passing second.

"You guys are here to hook up with NPS-1?" asked one of the fire guys.

"Yeah..."

"Okay, you need to just hold tight here for a few minutes, see what this is going to do. We've got a crew down there in the Foresta Meadow. This doesn't look good."

His tone was cool and measured. I was anything but. If there was a crew in the meadow below us, they were in trouble. The column of smoke was so huge and dense it obliterated the view of the meadow, which wasn't far below us.

"We may have to evacuate out of here, too. We're in the path," one of the fire-fighters added. My chest tightened.

The fire slowed a bit, and we were released from the helispot. Before we left, we learned the crew in the meadow was ours—NPS-1. A bulldozer operator assigned to the meadow had cleared a large safety zone in the middle of the meadow before the fire blew over. Everyone huddled in the dirt clearing as the fire raged around them. They all emerged unhurt.

We left Crane Flat and drove northeast to fire camp, which was in a large meadow complex at Camp Mather, a public facility owned by the City of San Francisco.

We arrived at the turnoff to the camp as the sun descended behind the fires, and drove slowly down the forested entrance road. As we approached the meadows, the forest dropped away and the view opened up into a kaleidoscope of light and motion—the fire-fighting industrial complex.

Dozens of overhead spotlights affixed to temporary poles illuminated the broad, flat meadows. Flashlights and headlamps dipped and bobbed in all directions, like fireflies on a humid southern night. People were walking everywhere, and everyone carried something— giant Costco-sized packages of toilet paper, sleeping bags, cardboard map tubes, backpacks, chain saws, and bright red gasoline cans. A herd of generators growled, busy powering lights, computers, radios, and other equipment. As I learned later while trying to sleep, the lights and generators, as well as the hustle and bustle, ran all through the night.

A small, poorly-planned city of tents rose up on our left as we entered camp—hundreds of small nylon enclosures designed to sleep two or three people uncomfortably, and provide a smidgeon of privacy within the madness, or at least the illusion of privacy. In vacant spaces between tents, sleeping bags were laid out on the ground like large, deflated caterpillars.

I felt like a refugee. We wandered through the maze of tents, looking for an open spot. We walked slowly and stepped carefully to avoid any occupied sleeping bags, and finally found a small clearing to set up our tents. I crawled in my sleeping bag to a sleepless night filled with images of smoke columns, bulldozers, and dirty firefighters.

The next morning we breakfasted on greasy scrambled eggs, cold toast, and lukewarm hash browns. By 8AM (*oh eight hundred* in the fire world) we climbed into a crew carrier, a rugged vehicle designed to carry firefighters and gear. We were now officially members of the NPS-1 crew. I hoped they weren't lightning rods.

Our assignment for the day was to cut line on the eastern flank of a blaze called the T-Grove Fire, near the community of Aspen

Valley. We drove down a network of dirt roads and pulled off onto a carpet of mountain misery, an aromatic shrub with a reputation for being exceptionally flammable because of the oil in its leaves. We each selected a tool for the job ahead—a shovel, a rake called a McLeod, or an axe-headed Pulaski.

After a short walk into the oak and pine forest, we got to work cutting fireline—essentially a quick and dirty trail intended to contain the fire. Containment meant a perimeter was established around the entire fire, a continuous boundary of linked fireline, rivers or creeks, or large expanses of barren rock. In theory, the fire would burn to the established boundary and stop. In reality, fires frequently jumped these petty obstructions. The slightest breeze could carry a stray ember aloft, over the line.

For several hours we raked and scraped all the dead and downed plant material off a three to four-foot wide line, then cut out and removed roots close to the surface. Crew members with chainsaws cleared trees and brush growing close to the line.

The fire was out of sight to the west, but the ominous crackle and snap of burning vegetation told us it wasn't far off. During the briefing, we'd been told this fire had burned slowly to the west the past few mornings. As morning turned to afternoon, though, air temperatures rose and winds reversed direction. In response, the flames grew and were pushed back to the east. Some of the land between us and the active fire had already burned—known as "the black" in firefighter lingo. During fire training we'd been told, "If you find yourself running away from a fire, if possible, run into the black." It was a safe zone if it had burned thoroughly enough and couldn't re-burn.

We cut fireline on flat ground for about three hours, gradually making an arc on a large circle. We took a short water and snack break just before noon.

Our crew leaders decided we would cut one last section of line quickly before lunch, because the weather of previous days indicated the wind was likely to shift back toward us after noon, in which case we would have to leave until the following day. If we could connect, or "tie in," our line with a creek just down slope, we could contain this flank of the fire. I was already weary from lack of sleep, crappy food, and much harder work than I was accustomed to, but adrenaline and fire are blood brothers. I was up for it. Not that it mattered; in fire training it was drilled into my head that fire crew members obey their leaders—it's essential for the safety of the group.

We started to cut line down a steep slope toward the creek, and I noticed the land west of us was no longer black. It was unburned oak and pine forest with a deep layer of very dry leaves and needles underneath. I stopped again for a quick drink and shoved the sleeves of my bright yellow, fire-resistant Nomex shirt up to my elbows.

At that moment the wind shifted. Smoke blew over our heads, and the snap and crackle got much louder. We stopped work and gathered on a small, flat clearing under a big oak tree. I looked at several of my crew members. When we made eye contact, it was clear we were all worried. Our crew leaders stood at a slight remove, talking quietly.

"I think we need to go," I finally said, at risk of being insubordinate. I couldn't hold back. I felt threatened.

"Yeah, hold on a minute." our crew boss said.

I was fuming. This was so stupid. It was clear to me we were in danger. Why weren't they doing something about it? I, for one, was not going to die in this fire. If they didn't direct us to go back up our line soon, I was going anyway, rules or no rules.

Then the fire crested a small ridge just west of us. A wall of flame about fifteen feet high and one hundred feet away rolled toward us. It was coming fast.

"Okay, we're out of here. Go! Quick! Up the line! Single file! Everybody! Now! Up to the black! Go, go, go!!"

I was closest to the lower end of our cut fireline, so was first in line for the retreat. I ran as fast as I could, struggling up the steep slope. The fire burned right next to the line. I watched flames totally consume a small oak, maybe eight feet tall, not two feet away from me. The heat blasted my face. The hair on my left arm was burning. I'd failed to pull my sleeves down before we ran. My lungs were bursting. The crew leader yelled at me, "Go, go, go! Faster! Come on, you have the whole crew behind you. It's hot as hell back here. Hurry, go, go, go!" I was smacked by a huge wave of guilt. I should have been in better shape. I should have been able to climb this hill faster. I was making all these people suffer. What if they died because of me? My heart was exploding in my chest.

And then I crested the hill and was in the black, the rest of the crew right behind me. While we ran, the fire wrapped itself beneath the lower end of our line and escaped to the east.

We set out again the following day to try to gain control of the opposite flank of the irascible T-Grove Fire. We ended up in a situation almost identical to the one of the day before. We were cutting line downhill to tie in to a creek, the wind shifted, and we had to scurry out of harm's way. Everyone was much more cautious, however, and we didn't put ourselves at risk as we had the day before. After this third consecutive day of being exposed to extremely dangerous conditions, the NPS-1 crew was demobilized and scheduled for post-traumatic stress debriefing.

The Yosemite fires of 1990 continued for several more days, ultimately burning about 23,000 acres. After the smoke cleared, we returned to our regular jobs. Everyone on the resource management staff was given post-fire writing assignments. We were led to believe that after big wildland fires, the government opened up a bottomless coffer of money for post-fire rehabilitation. To secure some of this money, I was asked to prepare short proposals and estimate costs for three projects: an inventory of all firelines, so the disturbed land could be rehabilitated, a plan for restoring damaged ecosystems in Foresta, a community within park boundaries that had burned, and a research project on the effects of the fires on natural resources.

We received assignments on Friday. Our deadline was the following Tuesday. The Chief of Resources told us he had jotted down his thoughts on some of the proposals to help us get started.

I arrived at the office on Saturday morning to work, and discovered the Chief had made notes on the Foresta restoration proposal. I read his ideas, and saw he wanted to transplant black oak trees from the Wawona Road corridor to Foresta. He wanted to buy a tree spade, a large, expensive piece of equipment, to do the transplanting.

I saw two significant problems with this proposal. First, the Wawona Road and Foresta were separated by many miles and a few drainages, which meant it was likely the oaks in the two areas were genetically different from each other. Restoration ecologists believed mixing up gene pools could cause problems, because the trees were adapted to their own local conditions. In general, it was not considered a good idea. Second, many of the burned oaks in Foresta would resprout on their own. Their regeneration would be slow, but would occur naturally. I felt the proposal to transplant the oaks was ecologically unsound and unnecessary.

The Chief wasn't working that day, and was to be out of town several more days. I asked my supervisor what I should do. She agreed with my conclusions and told me to delete the Chief's ideas and write an appropriate proposal. I completed my work and left for a much needed day off.

The proposals were submitted the following week to the national fire office in Boise, Idaho. After they went out, I was told by a co-worker that the Chief was furious with me for deleting the oak transplanting part of the Foresta proposal. He wanted to purchase a tree spade from the post-fire rehabilitation account that he could use later on other non-fire projects in the park. The oak transplanting was his justification for the purchase. It didn't matter if the proposal was ecologically sound or not, he wanted a tree spade. I felt I had done the right thing and didn't give it much thought.

The following Friday dawned crystal clear and beautiful—paradise topped by a lapis blue sky. The meadow grasses had turned out in autumn tones of yellow and orange. They bowed and dipped to a soft breeze as I rode by. I parked my bike, walked into the office building, and was met immediately by my boss.

"The Chief wants to talk to you," she said and looked away.

I walked into his office. He stood up from his desk chair with a smile, walked over and closed the door behind me, then returned to his desk and sat down.

"Barbara, these are the times that try supervisor's souls," he said with a dramatic sigh.

I stopped breathing. I knew exactly what he would say next.

"I'm letting you go."

Despite my prescience, I was stunned to silence. He went on for a long time. He told me I was too strong-minded, and that at times he wasn't sure if he was running the division, or if I was. He accused me of "collusion and conspiracy," and said I was organizing and encouraging other people in the division to oppose him.

He used the Foresta proposal as an example of where I had gone wrong. I was insubordinate because I didn't include the oak transplanting in the proposal. And then he told me I'd been too scientific in my approach to the Sentinel Meadow project. I had worked closely with the park's wildlife biologist—also a statistician—to develop a valid study to identify the best way to eliminate unnecessary trails in meadows. Once we determined the best method, we could use it in other meadows. The Chief supported this approach fully while we were doing it, but when it came time to fire me, he said I should have just rototilled all the trails and not spent time and money on the study.

And then he said, "You are too preservation-oriented in your view towards resource management. That may have been okay in Sequoia, but Yosemite is different."

I left his office and hurried out the back door of the building, holding back the tears until I got outside. I walked across Cook's Meadow to a giant old elm tree that stood in the center of the meadow, sat down on a gnarled twist of roots, and sobbed. Had I really done anything wrong? Did I deserve this? A warm breeze dried my tears as I searched my soul. No, I'd done nothing wrong. In fact, I'd worked harder and accomplished more during that summer than ever before in my life. I was fired for not being a good soldier, for questioning the Chief's actions, for thwarting his plans.

I returned to the office, packed up my things, and rode my bike back to the Rangers' Club. I found out later that day I was not the only one to be terminated. Two co-workers, smart, dedicated people who also coordinated habitat restoration programs, were "let go" on the same day. It appeared Yosemite's Chief of Resources Management was threatened by employees with intelligence, drive, and integrity.

The Chief's words—Yosemite is different—echoed through my head for weeks. Just how different didn't become clear for many years, though, not until I returned to Yosemite a third time to live and work.

CHAPTER 10
Steep Learning

Journal

I selected the following piece to read at Rod's memorial gathering:

"Eventually, all things merge into one, and a river runs through it. The river was cut by the world's great flood and runs over rocks from the basement of time. On some of the rocks are timeless raindrops. Under the rocks are words, and some of them are theirs.

I am haunted by waters."

-From A River Runs Through It *by Norman Maclean*

♦♦♦

Like a giant sequoia tree after a major fire, I had deep scars when I left Yosemite in September of 1990. I returned to Corvallis and finished my graduate program in spring of 1992. Despite my termination, I was offered another temporary job in Yosemite. This time the work involved monitoring and assessing the effects of wildland and prescribed fire on vegetation and wildlife. I was heartened to know there were people in Yosemite who still respected my work and credentials, but I wasn't sure I was ready to return.

In the midst of my decision-making process, I was offered another job, as a botanist with a small consulting company in Tiburon, California. It was a permanent job with a larger salary and full benefits.

I was torn. I wanted to return to the land of my heart, but still felt bitter and self-righteous. The decision was easy when the consulting company called and offered me even more money to arrive on duty a week early, as well as reimbursement for moving expenses. My attention shifted to the private sector.

I hated my new job from the start. The firm had a reputation for integrity and high quality work, but most of the projects focused on development. In most cases, our crews of highly trained and dedicated "ologists"—biologists, ecologists, archeologists, and hydrologists—surveyed, measured, and mapped all features of various tracts of land for federal, state, and local agencies and private developers. We carefully documented locations of rare plants, wetlands, endangered wildlife, and historic and prehistoric sites. Then the bulldozers came. Pipelines were laid, power lines were erected, and roads were built, effectively wiping the precious resources off the maps we'd just created. We worked on a few conservation-oriented projects, but the bread-and-butter jobs that generated revenue were large, linear development projects. I wanted to quit almost immediately, but was worried about damaging my credibility and my resume. I made the decision to stick it out for at least a year.

At the end of the first year, my supervisor resigned and I inherited his projects. Swept up in a whirlwind of work and responsibility, as well as a salary increase, I moved to the company's main office in Santa Cruz and stayed on for another three years, until a series of bad financial decisions took the business down. Before the bankruptcy was final, another consulting firm offered me a sweet deal as a program manager. I made the move and took my projects with me.

My ego was delighted with my consulting successes. My self-image peaked when I was flown on a private jet to attend a meeting, put up in a penthouse suite, and wined and dined while wearing an expensive peach-colored dress. But a brooding black cloud of compromised values, represented by the ever-present clam and coot, never stopped hovering close to my head. It took a plant the size of a quarter, a rude awakening, and cancer to remind me of who I was and what I valued.

The Soul of Yosemite

The proposed natural gas pipeline was 229 miles long, and stretched from Reno, Nevada to the Oregon border. The route bisected vast, undeveloped open lands, characterized by sweeping sagebrush-clad desert, rocky, rolling juniper woodlands, boggy wetlands flanking the Pit River, agricultural fields, and the volcanic panorama of the Modoc Plateau.

I supervised crews of botanists through three consecutive growing seasons of pre-construction vegetation assessments for the pipeline project. This work involved walking the entire length of the route to survey and map plant communities, rare plants, invasive non-native plants, and sensitive habitat types such as wetlands. Our objective was to determine precisely what would be damaged by pipeline construction. The land was biologically rich and diverse. We documented 35 different rare plant species that occurred in 306 discrete populations.

"These things are all over the place this year," my co-worker announced one afternoon as he leaned over to study a small tufted plant in the middle of a volcanic gravel field. The plant of interest was Lilliput lupine, a low-growing member of the pea family that rarely had a diameter larger than a quarter. In California the plant was known to occur only in Modoc County. It also grew sporadically in Nevada, Oregon, and Idaho. We were conducting our second year of surveys, and the comment reflected the fact that the diminutive plants were much more numerous than they had been the previous year, probably because of abundant rainfall earlier that spring.

As we looked around at the extent of the plants, a Ford pickup rumbled over the gravel and crushed many of the plants. The driver pulled right up to us and stopped. He got out of the truck, but left the engine idling.

"Waddya lookin' at?" His voice was gruff.

"This plant. This little lupine," I answered. "Is this your land?"

"Yup. What's so special about this plant?" he asked with a frown. He kept his hands in the pockets of his blue jeans while we talked.

"It's rare," I said, "and protected by the State. We're counting to see how many are here, and then we'll map the population."

"Hmph," he grunted as he turned his back on us. He walked to his truck, got in, and drove away, leaving us in a cloud of dust.

The next day we returned to the Lilliput lupine site to finish mapping. Before we even got out of the truck, we could see the entire population had been erased from the land. Apparently, the land owner didn't want rare plants on his property, had perceived that their presence would curtail his freedom to do whatever he might want to do on his land in the future. He'd used a common technique to clear them away—he'd dragged a piece of chain link fence behind his truck, back and forth over the population, to ensure they were all uprooted.

I was horrified. These tiny plants were wiped out because we'd found them while conducting surveys for a proposed pipeline. No one knew they existed here before we did the surveys. Our actions led directly to their demise.

Karma, however, played the last card in the Lilliput lupine story. The plants were past flowering when the land owner scraped them away, and their seeds were mature. Lupine seeds germinate at a much higher rate when their seed coats are scarified—abraded or scraped. The technique used by the land owner was a very effective seed coat scarifier. During our third year of surveys, we counted more plants on the site than we had in the first or second years.

The air in the Bureau of Land Management conference room in Susanville was hot and stale. Numerous project meetings were held there because the proposed pipeline route bisected a lot of the Bureau's land. The topic of this meeting was environmental impact mitigation.

It was obvious that the natural gas pipeline project would have substantial impacts on the environment. Nonetheless, there was no question it would be built. The pipeline company was involved in long, complex permitting processes linked to environmental laws like the Clean Water and Endangered Species acts. With the help of professional consultants like us, the company navigated successfully through these processes. For the vast majority of development projects proposed in the United States, getting permission was time-consuming and expensive, but permission was almost always granted.

Impact mitigation was a key element for most projects; the pipeline project was no exception. After detailed surveys were conducted, like the rare plant inventory, and all the deleterious environmental impacts of the project were identified, mitigation measures were established to reduce the severity or duration of the impacts. For example, if the pipeline project bisected a wetland, mitigation measures could include narrowing the right-of-way where the line crossed the wetland, or restoring the wetland after the pipe was in and covered. The state and federal land management agencies affected by development projects were very influential in the types of mitigation measures that would be applied.

There was little small talk at the meeting that afternoon. The representative from the California Department of Fish and Game got right to the point.

"We expect all rare plant populations that are disturbed will be restored on-site after the pipe is in and construction is complete," he said. He looked around the room at the assembled participants.

I was mystified. Rare plants were usually rare because they were very specific in their habitat requirements. Some grew on pure sand, others in seasonally saturated soils. Some had critical biological relationships with other plant species and only occurred where those plants grew. Once the pipeline trench was dug and the soil upturned and mixed, the habitat conditions would be completely altered. We might be able to re-establish a few of the rare plant species documented along the proposed route, but I felt sure many of them would never grow on the pipeline corridor again, at least not in our lifetimes. The guy from Fish and Game had to know this—he was a botanist.

I raised my hand and said, "Do you really think that's possible?"

The room was silent. My clients, representatives from the pipeline company, watched and waited. We'd discussed this issue at length before the meeting, and I had told them I thought trying to re-establish all of the rare species would be throwing money away.

"No, I don't," was his reply.

Everyone in the room breathed a sigh of relief. After a few more meetings, all parties involved agreed that the pipeline company would purchase land in other areas of California that supported rare plants, and ensure the land was protected in perpetuity. This "off-site" mitigation would offset the impacts of the pipeline on rare plants.

I felt victorious. My clients would make the land purchase and walk away, instead of spending unlimited time and money trying to restore rare plants on the pipeline right-of-way.

Within a few days, though, I realized it was a lose-lose situation for the plants themselves and the land they grew on. I began to understand that mitigation, no matter how good it appeared on the surface, never truly protected land and natural resources. If development projects were approved, the land and its inhabitants always would lose ground, regardless of mitigation measures. In this case, all the beautiful and rare plants we'd mapped along the route would be lost. Protecting a different area off-site was good, but would never make up for the net loss of the plants we had so carefully documented.

It dawned on me for the first time that although the United States had some of the strongest environmental laws in the world, those laws were not adequate to protect resources.

It was 5:30PM and hot, even for June. I sat at my desk in a small office near the American River in the community of Fair Oaks, just east of Sacramento. I was waiting for my boss, Rod, who was on his way back from a meeting in Reno. He was president of the second consulting firm I worked for.

Rod and I had worked together on several projects over the past few years and became friends in the process. Four months earlier his live-in girlfriend and her two children moved out. Mine was the shoulder he cried on after the break-up. We spent many evenings at a Mexican restaurant just a short walk from our office.

"I'm okay with it, really," he said repeatedly as he ordered another bottle of expensive Chardonnay.

At about 5:40, Rod walked into the office, dressed in his usual blue jeans and white, long-sleeved cotton shirt and accompanied by a blast of hot air. He walked into my office space, put his well-worn leather briefcase down on the floor, and sat down with a deep sigh.

"I've got a problem," he said. I looked up and saw tight lines around his blue eyes. He was almost always upbeat, a "glass half full" kind of person, but that afternoon something was wrong. I assumed the meeting had gone badly, that we were over budget, or the Department of Fish and Game had threatened to shut the project down again.

"I've got cancer. The doctor called me on my cell phone to tell me. Can you believe that? He calls me on the phone to tell me I have cancer."

The world blurred, and suddenly the air-conditioning in the office was making me way too cold. Goosebumps rose on my bare arms.

"Oh my God," I said. "What did he say?"

Rod had noticed a small lump on the right side of his neck several weeks earlier, but we figured it was a swollen lymph node, or a cyst of some sort.

"The biopsy was positive. It's cancer. The big problem, though, is it's not the primary source. It came from somewhere else. They're not sure where. I have to get more tests done." He was speaking clearly, rationally, while I felt like the top of my head was about to blow off.

I was silent for a moment as the news sunk in, and then I asked, "What do you want to do? Right now, I mean." We'd been planning to drive to Santa Cruz that evening, to spend the weekend at my house. "Do you still want to go to Santa Cruz?"

"Yeah. Let's do that. I need to stop by my house first to get some clothes and things. Let's go."

I switched off the lights and set the air conditioner thermostat to eighty degrees. We walked out and I locked the door behind us. The air outside was beginning to cool down. It promised to be one of those glorious Sacramento evenings, made for sitting outside, eating and socializing by the pool long into the night, lulled by warm, soft air. I had a deep and visceral memory of those warm summer nights as I spent most of the first ten years of my life in this little town of Fair Oaks. During subsequent visits to the area, I swore I would never return. Go figure.

We walked in silence across the parking lot to Rod's fire engine red GMC Jimmy. He handed me the keys and we got in, each of us lost in our own thoughts. After a quick stop at his house, we joined the slow but steady migration of cars heading out of town on a Friday evening. At the house he'd packed a few items of clothing, toiletries, and six bottles of good wine. "I expect I'll be doing a little drinking this weekend," he said.

As we swung south and I accelerated up the on-ramp onto Highway 99, he said, "We need to remember to get gas." A glance at the gauge confirmed his statement. He pulled a corkscrew and a bottle out of his duffel bag. A well-practiced turn of the screw had the dark green bottle open and the pale liquid cooling his throat in what seemed like seconds. He looked over at me and grinned, "Try not to get pulled over, okay?"

We were quiet for much of the first hour. I drove, he drank. He'd almost finished the first bottle when the vehicle choked a few times, then stopped. We were out of gas.

"Shit." I said. "I'm sorry. I completely forgot." I was mortified. I'd never before run out of gas.

We walked to a gas station and were soon on the road again. Within seconds, bottle number two was open and flowing.

At about 9PM we pulled into the dirt driveway that led to my home—a cabin in the tiny town of Felton, in the mountains above Santa Cruz. The sun had not yet set, but it was fully dark, as the cabin was nestled in a grove of towering coast redwood trees. Originally the cabin consisted of only one room made of solid redwood, built in the 1920s. Successive occupants added a bathroom, a small kitchen, and a bedroom. It had been home for about two years.

I led Rod up to the front door and walked into the cabin, flipping on the light switch. He made his way directly to the bed, and flopped down on his back, fully clothed. With a last look at me he closed his eyes, drunk to the world. I brought our things in from the car, put a kettle of water on to boil, sat down on the couch, put my head in my hands, and cried.

The doctors determined the cancer started at the back of his tongue and metastasized to his lymph nodes. After a series of intense radiation treatments, they declared him cancer-free. Nine months after the initial diagnosis, a follow-up scan revealed cancer in his lungs. Chemotherapy came next, along with a host of alternatives ranging from shark cartilage and Essiac tea to organic foods and meditation. Three months later, on June 8, 1997—my thirty-seventh birthday—an unrelenting, searing headache sent him to the hospital. The cancer had invaded his brain. It paralyzed the left side of his body before they could stop its growth. His ex-wife and I brought him home, set up a hospital bed in his family room, and cared for him. Three months later Rod and I said our goodbyes.

"What happens if I disappear off the face of the Earth while you're gone?" he asked in a dry, cracking voice. I was preparing to leave for a critical work meeting in Montana. We'd argued about my going. I didn't want to; he wanted me to.

"Well," I said, trying to stop my quivering chin and stem my tears. "I'll really miss you. But I know I'll see you again farther down the line."

"You really think so?"

"I do."

"I hope you're right."

Rod drew his last breath the night before I was to return home.

CHAPTER 11
You Can Go Home Again

Journal

In the dream a large piece of my body was missing. A one-foot-square piece of my chest, from just below my chin down the left side of my body was gone. There was no skin, no covering. One could look right in and see my insides. There was no physical pain, no injury or trauma, just a big exposure. In the dream I asked a friend what was happening to me. "Oh," she said, "You have nothing protecting your heart."

♦♦♦

"I'm scheduled for an interview at Point Reyes, for the Park Service job I told you about. But I don't think I want to go." I pushed open the front door of the project office in Susanville, which fronted the main highway through town. It was a sunny May afternoon, but a chilly wind powered down from the mountains. I zipped my blue fleece jacket up to my chin.

"Oh, you should go," said my co-worker, John, as he caught up with me on the sidewalk. "I'd hate to see you leave, but go for the interview. It doesn't mean you have to take the job, it'll just keep your options open. You can see what it might be like to work there. I love Point Reyes. It's beautiful country."

Instead of sleeping that night, I pondered John's counsel. Maybe it was time for a change. Six years earlier I left the Park Service to try something new. Initially, I hated consulting, but was held captive by ever-increasing levels of responsibility and pay. And then Rod entered the picture.

I accepted Rod's job offer because of the salary and his infectious excitement—he was fun to work with. Since his death nine months earlier, I'd continued to work for his partners, but it wasn't the same. He was the life of the company, its founder and primary motivator. It was obvious to everyone: No one could take his place.

Without Rod, I was left with a hole in my heart, a big salary, and the numerous undesirable aspects of consulting: intense competition for projects, seventy-hour work weeks, and month after month of living in motels and eating restaurant food. The worst part, though, was the emphasis on economics; the resources always suffered. Biologists in non-consulting positions often referred to consultants as "biostitutes." In many cases, the label fit.

I knew it was time to get back on track and find employment more aligned with my values. Maybe it *was* time to return to the National Park Service, where the agency mission and goals dove-tailed closely with my own. I took my friend's advice and drove west for the interview.

The Resources Management office was in an old white house at Bear Valley, where a scattered group of historic ranch buildings served as headquarters for Point Reyes National Seashore. A herd of four white-tailed deer—two does and two fawns—grazed on the raggedy lawn that fronted the office building. The sharp call of an osprey pierced the surface of the otherwise quiet morning. I looked up to see the large white-bodied bird circling near the deep green upper branches of a Douglas-fir. A cool, gray fog, with its attendant mist, blanketed the entire area.

I was met at the front door of the building and escorted to the Chief's office in the far corner of the house. My interview attire was mixed. I'd worn my power dress, which had been fine when I'd left sunny Susanville. Blasted by cold, damp ocean air as soon as I stepped out of the truck in Point Reyes, I realized the only wrap I had was a dirty Gore-Tex rain coat. As I went to remove my coat before sitting down on a black padded chair, it struck me that my unorthodox attire was perfect for the Park Service.

The interview questions were easy. The job seemed tailor-made for me. My experience of the past six years as a supervisor, a rare plant specialist, a weed warrior, and an adept project manager was exactly what the seashore needed.

After the interview, I drove west from park headquarters and up Inverness Ridge toward Limantour Beach. Persistent fog draped the steep ravines like a chiffon cape, and danced in wisps through tree tops. I reached the ridgeline and began to descend to the coast. In the space of a few seconds, the sun's rays penetrated the thick wet blanket and burst through in a welcoming shout. Shrouds of mist rose from forest and shrub-covered hills as if pulled from above by unseen hands. A long stretch of pale cream sand lay before me, etched with white foam and backed by a slate-grey and blue ocean.

I dropped down the hill to the sea. Shafts of sunlight peeked through remnant patches of fog and illuminated the waves, creating a multitude of bright shiny mirrors, like a sequined veil that rose and fell with the swells. I knew at that moment I would take the job if it was offered. I was ready to move on, to stop being chewed up by the corporate machine, to stop compromising my integrity.

Within a few days the offer came. I would be the seashore's Plant Ecologist, responsible for over 90,000 acres of wild land about an hour north of San Francisco. Four weeks later I moved into a dilapidated old house in Inverness, at the edge of park land. I returned to the safety of the fold: to the Park Service family.

Point Reyes was new to me. To get acquainted, I took long walks on wind-swept open beaches, through towering forests of coast redwood and Douglas-fir, and across fog-enshrouded coastal prairies punctuated by the haunting bugle calls of elk. My work was satisfying and my co-workers phenomenal. Place, purpose, and people came together to provide me with a sanctuary in which to heal.

"Tough job, eh? I still can't believe they pay me to do this." Kim pushed a reddish-blond lock of hair out of her eyes and reached into a day pack for a bottle of sunscreen. It was lunch time. We'd chosen a spot near a sheer cliff overlooking the ocean for our break. The sun was high overhead. We were at the very edge of the land—steps away from a vertical drop of several hundred feet to sand, rocks, and sea. Gulls circled and cried below.

The top of the towering bluff sported incipient populations of the rapidly-spreading non-native iceplant. Early that morning we hiked six miles in to remove the plants by hand. The best way to curb the spread of such weeds was to uproot them early, when their numbers were low.

On paper I was Kim's supervisor, but she was the heart of the Point Reyes vegetation program. She kept me on my toes. When I first started work at the seashore a few months earlier, she arranged for me to accompany her to survey a site known to support a nasty invasive plant called giant plumeless thistle. She was trying to eradicate the plant from seashore lands and had to visit each population every year to ensure success.

We drove a short distance from the office along the west edge of Tomales Bay, and then parked the truck and struck out on foot. Within the first hundred yards, the barely discernible trail disappeared completely. I followed Kim through a waist-high mix of grasses and shrubs. After a few hundred yards we dropped to hands and knees when the vegetation became too dense for walking. Suddenly I realized the dominant plant in the thicket surrounding me was poison oak. I wondered if Kim was testing the mettle of her new supervisor.

Most vegetation management work at Point Reyes focused on three inextricably linked elements: habitat restoration, rare plants, and non-native invasive plants. The restoration work usually involved removing non-natives, often to improve conditions for rare plants. Our focal habitats included wind-swept coastal dunes, vertical ocean-front cliffs, and streamside riparian areas.

One unique species on our protected list was the endangered annual Sonoma spineflower, a member of the buckwheat family that grew a few inches tall and produced tiny pale pink flowers. It lived on open coastal prairies and was known from only one small site at the seashore. It grew nowhere else in the world. To help the species along, we harvested and sowed seed in nearby areas that seemed to have soil conditions that would favor the plant, and we successfully established two new populations.

Two other rare species under our care were dune inhabitants. Beach layia, also called beach tidytips, was a tiny, fleshy-leaved sunflower with blooms of small white ray flowers surrounding a central cluster of yellow disk flowers. Tidestrom's lupine, or clover lupine, was a pea family member that produced blue or lavender flowers. Both species were federally endangered, and their dune habitat was being overgrown by introduced European beachgrass and iceplant. Once the non-native invaders were removed, though, the two natives came right back into the sites.

Most aspects of my job at the seashore were very rewarding. It was easy to secure funding for projects because the needs were so great. Lots of imperiled native species were being replaced by a host of rapidly spreading non-natives. Loss of native habitat and species was inevitable unless immediate action was taken. There was, however, one case where securing funding was much more difficult than it should have been.

Point Reyes supported almost 300 different species of non-native plants, many of them highly invasive. One of the most pernicious and damaging was cape ivy, a creeping sunflower family member. It was a lovely plant by aesthetic standards, with shiny green, inch-long, star-shaped leaves and tiny yellow flowers. The problems arose when humans removed cape ivy from its native lands in South Africa and brought it to the United States.

Originally planted in containers or as a landscape plant, cape ivy adapted to conditions in its new home like a seasoned expatriate.

It easily escaped from domestic habitats and spread into wildland settings, in part because it left its natural predators behind in South Africa. Cape ivy detectives determined it arrived in the eastern United States in the 1850s, and wasn't transported to California until the 1950s. By 1997, though, it grew on at least a half million acres in the Golden State.

Cape ivy severely disrupted natural plant and animal communities. Aptly named "the Kudzu of the West," it spread exponentially, and produced dense impenetrable mats as it climbed up tree trunks and over the tops of shrubs. Huge, thick jungles of pure cape ivy were on the march. Problems were compounded because cape ivy was common in riparian areas along streams and creeks and in other wet areas, which provided critical habitat for numerous native and rare species. To make matters even worse, researchers determined the plant was toxic to spiders and some mammals, and could harm aquatic organisms.

Removal of cape ivy was a high priority management action, and, in 2002, I coordinated development of a proposal to remove it from the seashore and from the neighboring Golden Gate National Recreation Area. The proposal was submitted for internal Park Service funding.

The project was expensive—we requested $800,000—because the plant grew in dozens of scattered locations. Much of the cost was associated with the time it took to get to the sites. Many were in remote areas with no trails, crews had to hike cross-country over rugged terrain and vegetation had to be cleared just to get to the cape ivy. Riparian sites often were on steep slopes, and very dense stands of tall shrubs like poison oak and stinging nettle blocked access. Removal, too, was tricky, because new cape ivy plants could grow from half-inch stem fragments. Every bit of plant material had to be removed or killed.

We proposed to do most of the removal by hand. Some sites would be grazed by goats, and herbicide would be applied to a few areas. Removal by hand had been tested and worked well. We'd conducted a trial using goats and they, too, were very effective. Apparently, they loved the taste of cape ivy and pulled it up by the roots, like long strings of spaghetti.

We proposed minimal herbicide use because numerous federally listed species lived in or near the cape ivy: the endangered California freshwater shrimp, mission blue butterfly, and San Bruno elfin butterfly; and the threatened California red-legged frog, coho salmon, and steelhead. At least seven rare plant species also occurred near cape ivy. Herbicide application could harm these listed species.

We contacted the United States Fish and Wildlife Service about using herbicides on cape ivy and they expressed concern, stating the agency was "leery" of such applications and that there was a general lack of information on the effects of herbicides on the listed species in question. National Park Service policy stated the highest level of protection must be given to native species in natural areas, and pesticides were to be used only after all other alternatives had been considered and found to be inadequate. Additionally, previous experience indicated when cape ivy was removed without herbicides, native species rapidly re-colonized. Sprayed sites were likely to require expensive hands-on revegetation to get natives to return.

Despite sound reasoning and agency policy, however, the proposal came under attack because of herbicides. Criticism of herbicide use on park lands is common, as park neighbors often don't want pesticides sprayed where they live, work, and play. But we weren't criticized for proposing to use too much herbicide; we were slammed for proposing to use too little. And the criticism didn't come from outside the Park Service, it came from within.

The plan's critic worked for the Integrated Pest Management Program. He claimed the project was poorly designed, which resulted in unnecessarily large costs per acre. He felt expenses could be substantially reduced if more herbicides were used. Funding for non-native plant removal was limited, and projects had to be cost-effective.

He sent his critique to a National Park Service Deputy Director in Washington D.C. In response, I was asked to further explain our rationale for limiting herbicide use, and had to point out that much of the project's expense was due to the complexity of cape ivy removal.

Ultimately the proposal was funded and little herbicide was used. I later learned proponents of herbicide use called those who exercised more caution "chemophobes." Alternately, those less in favor of herbicides called those who advocated them "nozzleheads," in reference to the nozzles used in herbicide application.

For four and a half years, I worked to protect and restore native plants and habitats at Point Reyes. Every morning of those years, I rolled out of bed and looked forward to the day and the work ahead. The plants and I thrived at Point Reyes, but I yearned for Yosemite.

"Will you marry me?" The proposal came over drinks in the small bar at the Station House Café in downtown Point Reyes Station. The proposer was Tom, a man I'd met in 1983 when I worked as a horse patrol ranger in Sequoia National Park. We didn't know one another well at that time, but I worked on one of the fire crews he supervised that fall. Then our paths diverged for fifteen years.

When I moved to Point Reyes in 1998, Tom was working at the National Park Service regional headquarters in San Francisco. We collaborated on fire management projects in Point Reyes and soon realized our interest in one another went beyond hazard fuel reduction and fire return intervals. He proposed to me in February of 2002.

"Can you ask me again in three months?" I answered. "I need more time to think about it." I'd never married, and, at age 41, I found it a frightening prospect.

Three months later, to the day, he took me to Manka's for dinner. Perched on the forested east slope of Inverness Ridge, Manka's was an intimate, very expensive dinner house patterned after an old hunting lodge.

"Okay," he said after our salads were delivered. "Now will you marry me?"

"Can you ask me again over dessert?"

I took my first bite of vanilla crème brûlée, looked up at him, smiled, and said, "Yes."

I pushed open the front door of the house as the late afternoon sun cascaded through skylights set in the high, open-beamed ceiling. The shafts of light illuminated dust-bunnies on the pale, knotty pine floor. I flipped through the mail and dropped Tom's portion on the kitchen table. A white-flowered *Dendrobium* orchid in a blue and white ceramic pot sent a light sweetness into the air.

We'd moved into the roomy house in March. It was tucked into the slope of Inverness Ridge in a Douglas-fir and coast live oak forest. I drove a five minute commute to the office at Bear Valley, but Tom drove to and from Oakland every day—over an hour each way. We were working to find jobs in a different park so we could leave the commute behind.

I went outside and watered the vegetable garden, and was on my way back to the house when Tom drove into the carport. He stepped through the front gate and walked down the gravel path toward me. A small grin lent a slight curve to his mouth.

"Hi honey. I got the job in Yosemite. That is, if you still want to go." He tried hard to pretend neutrality, but his inner grin shone through in his eyes, and erupted into a big smile.

"Hallelujah!" I yelped. "Yes, yes, yes, I want to go!" I ran across the yard and hugged him for all I was worth.

"Oh, and the job comes with a house in the Valley," he added. He raised his eyebrows and waited for my response.

"Oh my God!" I hollered. "Can we go right now?" I was ecstatic. All my dreams were coming true: the perfect husband *and* the perfect place to live.

For weeks nothing could wipe the huge grin from my face. I sang and danced through the rooms of our house, high on the sweet joy of anticipation, ready to return home—once and for all.

PART TWO

BEARING WITNESS

Embody your values.

-Terry Tempest Williams

CHAPTER 12
The Lorax, the Flood, and the Top 15+2

Journal

A fluffy-tailed gray squirrel perches on a stout branch on the large redbud outside the bedroom window. Morning sun slants behind him as he rapidly peels the tough outer skin from an acorn to get to the tender flesh inside. Who will look out for these guys? Who will be their advocate? Who will make sure they have a healthy, safe place to live their lives, bear their young, and fulfill their evolutionary destiny?

♦♦♦

Tom moved to Yosemite and started work in July. I stayed in Point Reyes until October to tie up loose ends. After I finished packing, I drove down Bear Valley Road past park headquarters one last time and turned right on Highway 1. With heavy heart, I waved goodbye to the mucky tidal marshes and golden coastal prairies. My job at Point Reyes had been a good fit, and I received tremendous support from my co-workers and the community. I was sad to leave, but my spirits lifted quickly as I aimed my truck east, toward the mountains.

I arrived in Yosemite Valley in late afternoon. The orange glow of the low autumn sun saturated the scene. The rich carmine of dogwood, milk chocolate of oak, and lemon yellow of maple were splayed over a canvas of deep cobalt sky. The river meandered slowly around root crowns of cottonwoods and willows, and gold and brown meadow grasses nodded acknowledgement to the coming winter. When I pulled into the gravel parking space in front of our house, a thick-furred coyote backlit by twilight trotted across the yard. I smiled and sighed. I was home.

Our new house on Lost Arrow Road was built in the 1920s. It was small, two-storied, and built of wood and stone. Downstairs included a dining room, kitchen, master bedroom, and living room with a river rock fireplace. A steep staircase led to a bathroom and two small bedrooms with ceilings sloped to fit the roof lines. The neighborhood belonged to a historic district—a cluster of fifty or so houses near the Valley's north wall, set among ponderosa pines, incense-cedars, black oaks, and dogwoods. Yosemite Creek was a stone's throw to the west, passing through on its way to the Merced River. The creek was flanked by a small meadow.

Mule deer, coyotes, robins, and ravens were frequent visitors. Gray squirrels chased one another up and over the picnic table out front, and Steller's jays scrabbled for anything edible in the dirt below the kitchen window. Black bears also prowled the neighborhood in search of food. My next door neighbor cautioned against leaving doors open. One Sunday morning, she baked several batches of cookies and brownies for an elementary school bake sale, and transferred the goodies to her dining room table after they cooled. She pulled the last batch from the oven, and headed toward the front yard to do some weeding. Wanting to admire her culinary handiwork, she passed through the dining room on her way out and saw her cat, Helena, in the dining room, eyeing the baked goods. But Helena had grown a lot since morning. The image suddenly snapped into focus, and my neighbor realized the "cat," which stood about three feet away, was a small bear with a golden-brown pelt similar to Helena's coat. Retaining her usual relaxed demeanor, my neighbor said, "And what in the world are you doing in here?" The bear responded by sauntering slowly out the back door, which had been left open for Helena's convenience.

The front of our house had a northerly aspect, and every time we stepped out, the glory of Yosemite Falls greeted us. A ten-minute walk took us to the bottom of the falls. During peak spring runoff, torrents of melted snow tumbled over the sharp lip of the Valley wall, dropped 2,425 vertical feet in great white plumes, slammed into a bed of rock, and then joined the twisting cascade dance of Yosemite Creek. The windows of our house rattled to the beat.

I was offered a biologist position with the Park Service soon after we arrived, with a start date in mid-December. When I discussed the position with the hiring official, he said, "I want to hire someone who can play hardball for the resources."

"I can do that," I answered.

"I've gotten that impression from people I've spoken to about you."

My job title was Liaison. I would serve as the main communication link between two park divisions: Resource Management and Project Management. In most national parks, employees worked in "divisions," such as maintenance, visitor protection, interpretation, resource management, or administration, and each division was managed by a "Chief." The term "division" was a vestige of the military roots of the National Park Service. Prior to the creation of the Service in 1916, the parks were managed by the United States Army.

I was part of the Resource Management Division, which is tasked with protecting all natural and cultural entities—called resources—in Yosemite. Natural resources included air, water, wildlife, plants, soils, dark night skies, natural soundscapes, hydrologic features, and geologic formations. Cultural resources included important historic and prehistoric components: archeological sites; cultural landscapes; and historic sites, structures, and buildings.

Yosemite's Project Management Division, as the name suggested, administered all park projects, which mainly included infrastructure development and maintenance. I was surprised to learn Yosemite had an entire division devoted to project management, and believed it was the only park in the entire system with such a division. The words of my former supervisor echoed once again: "Yosemite is different."

My primary responsibility as liaison was to ensure all resource concerns related to all park projects were identified and considered during project planning, and to be sure impacts were minimized when the projects actually happened. For example, if a new utility line was planned, the Park Service was to make every attempt to avoid sensitive areas such as meadows and oak woodlands. If they couldn't avoid impacts, they were to apply mitigation measures to reduce the impacts. Using the utility line example, if there was no choice but to site the line through a meadow, the impact could be mitigated by carefully removing meadow sod before trenching, keeping the sod well-watered during construction, and then replacing it after the lines were buried.

The work was very similar to work I'd done as a consultant, but I was comforted by the fact that the Park Service was more committed to protecting resources than my former clients had been. I was confident resource protection would be the highest priority.

When Tom and I arrived in Yosemite, the Park Service was planning numerous large development projects, many of which were linked to a major flood that swept through the Valley in 1997. I was one of several liaisons hired to ensure all elements and functions of the park, such as human safety, visitor enjoyment, traffic flow, and resources, were not compromised by the many multi-faceted projects.

I couldn't believe my luck. The position was perfect. I would be paid to protect the integrity of rich, loamy meadow soils, salt and pepper granite, gray squirrels and black bears, oak trees and azaleas, rivers and creeks, Native American village sites and gathering areas, and historic artifacts and memories. Like Dr. Seuss's protagonist, I was the Lorax. I would speak for the trees.

There was an additional bonus to the job offer. I had ten weeks to move in and reacquaint myself with the Valley before I started work. I unpacked our belongings and created a nest in our new house. At the same time, I watched a young doe build a nest of her own under an incense-cedar west of the house. She returned to bed down in it night after night.

I wandered the Valley from end to end during my brief hiatus. In early November, six inches of rain fell in a forty-eight hour period.

Every vertical crevice in every granite face hosted its own waterfall. In December, snows dressed the Valley in bright white. My journal read:

> *It is so incredibly beautiful. I can't even begin to describe it. Snow has put a new face on everything. It's a blessing and a miracle that I am living here. Thank you.*

Yosemite Valley was everything I remembered, but one small shadow lurked in my new life. Although Tom and I knew several people who worked in the park from previous Park Service postings, I was lonely when he left for work every morning. The Valley lacked the feel of the close-knit Park Service family I had come to expect. The warmth and acceptance exhibited to newcomers did not arise instantly, and people socialized in more exclusive circles. I thought this was due to sheer numbers—approximately 1,500 people lived in the Valley during the busiest part of the tourist season. These included employees of the Park Service, as well as various concessionaires and cooperators, such as the medical clinic staff and their families. With time, I hoped, the "family" would embrace us.

At 7:30AM on December 16, before the sun struck the Valley rim, I walked a quarter mile to my new office for my first day of work. The office was upstairs in a historic building at the west end of Yosemite Village, one of the Valley's commercial hubs.

The morning was winter quiet. Trees, grasses, rock ledges, roads, cars, and buildings were tucked under a fluffy blanket of new snow. As I walked past the Valley's small historic cemetery, the silence was broken by the wing beats of three ravens passing overhead.

I arrived at the office and two liaisons from other divisions immediately swooped me up, loaded me into a government truck, and took me for a thirty minute ride down the narrow, twisting road to El Portal. Forests of pine and incense-cedar, snow-covered meadows, and frost-rimmed ponds sped by as we rounded curve after curve. I stared out the window and hoped for a glimpse of a deer, coyote, or bear.

The Soul of Yosemite

El Portal, nestled in the long shadows of the Merced River canyon, is home to about seven hundred residents, and is the site of park headquarters, a massive, several-storied sprawl of buildings and workshops, referred to by some as "The Gulag." Just east of the buildings, large, cement sewage treatment ponds process the by-products of park visitors and residents. At the time, many of the park's resource managers worked in offices near the ponds, and referred to their location as "Sewer View." This very un-park-like place was the setting for my first Monday morning project management meeting.

The meeting room was upstairs in the main administration building. When we arrived, I saw about twenty people seated behind long tables organized in a U-shape, talking and fussing over personal planners. Ten more people stood around in small clusters, deep in conversation. Stark fluorescent lights buzzed overhead.

At 9AM, everyone took a seat. One by one, people identified as project managers stood up and described the status of their projects. I wrote furiously in my notebook, awash in a flood of names, project titles and locations, updates, meetings, workshops, timelines, and deadlines. For two solid hours the air in the room was unmoving and thick. Feet tapped. Pens and pencils clicked. Brows furrowed. Before arriving at Yosemite, I had heard employee morale was very low, and many people felt overworked, but I sensed the body language at the meeting reflected deeper issues.

The agenda focused on a suite of projects called the "Top 15+2." I never understood why they weren't called the Top 17, but I quickly learned things didn't always make sense in Yosemite. The Top 15+2 were the park's highest priority projects, which rose to the top of the list in the wake of the 1997 flood.

Through the winter of 1996 it seemed the snow would never stop falling. Throughout the central Sierra Nevada, the lovely white blanket reached an average depth of twenty feet by year's end. Skiers were ecstatic. On New Year's Eve, while Yosemite residents and visitors reveled, a subtropical storm system called the "Pineapple Express" streamed their way. While they slept and dreamed of ski lifts and hot chocolate, warm rain fell quietly on the thick layer of snow.

The rain continued into New Year's Day. By nightfall, the El Portal Road, the main access road to Yosemite Valley, was closed due to flooding. Yosemite Lodge was isolated by the swirling waters of the Merced River and Yosemite Creek, both engorged by the combination of rain and rapidly melting snow.

On January 2, all three roads into Yosemite Valley were closed. The water continued to rise, and the speed of the flow increased. Torrents surged down rocky canyons and gushed through the steep-sided, mile-wide Valley, stranding approximately 900 visitors and 1,200 employees. Roads, campgrounds, trails, signs, fences, vehicles, and the bottoms of buildings disappeared under water. A gauging station measured the Merced River's flow at 24,600 cubic-feet per second at the flood's peak, which occurred on the night of January 2. Hydrologists estimated more than 1 billion tons of water flowed into the Valley in one four-hour period.

On the third day, the flood tapered off. By sunset on January 3 everyone who needed to leave was able to drive out of the Valley on the Wawona Road to the south. Yosemite National Park was closed for ten weeks.

As the water receded, layers of nutrient-rich sediment were left behind to nourish meadows, forests, and woodlands. The flood was a natural event. Floods have washed Yosemite Valley clean for eons. Since 1864, when the Valley was first granted park status, five major floods—in 1867, 1871, 1937, 1950, and 1955—as well as countless minor ones, have come and gone. One of Yosemite's Wildlife Biologists summed it up well after the 1997 flood when he said: "Why is the park here? It is to let natural processes prevail. This certainly was a big natural process."

The flood was natural, but it damaged human-made structures and significantly disrupted park operations. The only "problem" with the flood was its effect on human developments that happened to be in its way.

Yosemite received about $200 million to recover from damage associated with the New Year's Flood. The majority—$176 million—came from an emergency appropriations act authorized by Congress. Park managers were excited by the possibilities. The influx of money provided a tremendous opportunity to complete many improvement projects they had long wanted to do, but could not afford.

At my first Monday morning meeting, I learned about twenty-two major projects: Curry Village Employee Housing, Utilities Master Plan, East Valley Improvements, Crane Flat Environmental Education Campus, Cascades Dam Removal, South Fork Bridge Replacement, Architectural Design Guidelines, Camp 4 Improvements, Indian Cultural Center, Lodge Redevelopment, Northside Drive Re-route, Out-of-Valley Campgrounds Study, Shuttle Bus Stop Construction, Intelligent Transportation System, Shuttle Bus Purchase, Lower Yosemite Fall Project, Rivers Campground Restoration, Camp 6 Parking Lot Improvements, Visitor Center Renovation, Ahwahnee Hotel Roof Replacement, North Pines Campground Utilities, and Yosemite Creek Sewage Lift Station. The Lorax was going to be very busy.

Later that day I learned the Top 15+2 projects were only the tip of the iceberg. The park received funding for 210 flood recovery projects, almost all of which were to be completed by 2003. When I arrived at the tail end of 2002, most projects were still in the planning phase, and much of the money had been spent. But it hadn't been spent on projects. It had been used for additional, unexpected planning efforts driven by a long string of lawsuits. A few co-workers informed me that a small group of "radical environmentalists" was preventing the Park Service from making much needed improvements to the Valley.

I couldn't wait to hear the rest of the story.

CHAPTER 13
Radical Environmentalists

Journal

    Yesterday afternoon I walked down Lost Arrow Road and turned left just before the government stables. The area was abandoned; the horses had gone to their winter home in the Central Valley. I walked uphill toward the Valley Loop Trail, which skirted the Valley's north edge behind Yosemite Village and the park's maintenance yard. I traveled over a mosaic of old, patchy snow and bare, wet soil, and kept my eyes to the ground to keep from tripping over rocks and roots.
    As I approached the trail, I looked up and was surprised to see a doe curled up about twenty feet ahead. The light was low and her milk chocolate coat blended so well with the rock and dirt background, I almost missed her.
    I wondered if I could walk by without disturbing the doe. She rose to her feet when I was about ten feet away, but didn't run. When she stood up, I saw another doe lying right behind her. A third stood off to one side. Six ears twitched, but no one took flight.
    I walked past the three deer. Deep, dark, liquid eyes followed my progress. When I glanced farther up the hill, I realized there were deer everywhere. I counted ten large does, three bucks with full racks, one young, single-point buck, and three yearling does. Most of the animals lay next to rocks or trees scattered across the slope. A few stood and pulled at tired-looking shoots of grass, or nosed through fallen leaves to find acorns.

I continued up to the main Valley Loop Trail, turned around to face the herd, and sat down on the ground with my back against a rock. I watched them. They watched me. After a few moments they resumed their business. A few nuzzled the ground and chewed acorns. One buck reached back to scratch an itchy flank, another rubbed his antlers on the trunk of an old oak, while a third sniffed at a doe's behind, causing her to leap and run away.

While I sat and watched, one of the young does approached me from behind, ever so slowly. When she was about four feet away, she stopped, dropped her head, and ate a few leaves. Completely enchanted, I basked in the quiet nearness of deer.

◆◆◆

My first weeks as liaison were filled with meetings, workshops, and piles of project files. I carpooled to El Portal every Monday morning, and spent the remainder of most weeks in my Valley office or on project sites. Early on, I met with the person who filled the liaison role prior to my arrival, to transfer information. He handed me several boxes filled with notebooks, documents, and files and said, "I'm so glad you're here. I've had enough."

His comment should have served as a warning, but I missed it.

My Valley office was upstairs in the park's administration building. It was spacious, and often I had it to myself. I shared it with the Chief of Resource Management, who spent most of his time in El Portal.

One afternoon, I took a break from sorting files and walked into Yosemite Village to pick up the mail. The village was the Valley's social hub, with a large general store, hamburger stand, sporting goods store, hair salon, art center, ATM, gift shop, deli, pizza place, ice cream parlor, Ansel Adams photography gallery, wilderness center, visitor center, Native American museum, and government and concession offices.

As I entered the village, the sheer face of Half Dome, one of the Valley's signature granite monoliths, dominated the horizon. The scene was backed by an azure sky and framed by crisscrossing black oak and pine branches. In the foreground, to the right of Half Dome, a small table was set up with a banner across the front that read: "No more development in Yosemite Valley." I walked over to see who was exercising their First Amendment rights.

It turned out to be the "Friends of Yosemite Valley," one of the primary plaintiffs in the ongoing Yosemite litigation—the "radical environmentalists" themselves. I walked to the table and flipped through assorted handouts and asked a few questions of the woman sitting behind the table. In short, she claimed the National Park Service had a development agenda for Yosemite Valley, and was deluding the public into believing the agency was restoring nature.

I decided it was time to investigate the lawsuits and draw my own conclusions.

With the help of my co-workers, I pieced the long, complicated story together. The roots of the lawsuits extended back to September of 1980, when the Park Service released the *Visitor Use, Park Operations, and Development Plan for Yosemite National Park*. The 81-page document was designed to set the direction of park management and to guide managers as they worked to protect the park. It was one volume of a three-part *General Management Plan*; the other two parts addressed natural and cultural resources.

The *General Management Plan* grew out of an extensive public involvement process that began in the 1970s. About 60,000 individuals, organizations, and government agencies received planning information, and about 20,000 of these actively participated through workshops, meetings, workbooks, and written correspondence. The plan covered the entire park—nearly 750,000 acres at that time—but Yosemite Valley was its main focus. Managers and the public recognized that the Valley, the beloved heart of the park, was being destroyed by too much development, too many cars, and too many people. The trend of destruction had to be reversed.

The first four paragraphs from the plan's Introduction, presented below, clearly outlined the intent of the authors and the numerous members of the public engaged in the planning effort.

"Yosemite Valley is but a mile wide and seven miles long, yet this tiny place on the face of our planet is a premier masterwork of the natural world. It is of incalculable value to those who seek it and is cherished in the consciousness of those who know it only through works of art and the written word. Yosemite Valley and the sweep of Sierra wilderness that surrounds it possess superlative scenic grandeur and are a constant test of our wisdom and foresight to preserve them as a treasure for all people.

Yosemite is now at a crossroad. During a century of public custodianship of this great park, many decisions have been made, all well intended, which have resulted in a march of man-made development in the Valley. Today, the Valley is congested with more than a thousand buildings—stores, homes, garages, apartments, lodging facilities, and restaurants—that are reflections of our society; the Valley floor is bisected by approximately 30 miles of roadway which now accommodates a million cars, trucks, and buses a year. But the foremost responsibility of the National Park Service is to perpetuate the natural splendor of Yosemite and its exceedingly special Valley.

The intent of the National Park Service is to remove all automobiles from Yosemite Valley and Mariposa Grove and to redirect development to the periphery of the park and beyond. Similarly, the essence of wilderness, which so strongly complements the Valley, will be preserved. The result will be that visitors can step into Yosemite and find nature uncluttered by piecemeal stumbling blocks of commercialism, machines, and fragments of suburbia.

Implementation of this general management plan will be the first big step in carrying out this intent and a distinct turning point in the management of the park."

The plan had five broad goals: to reclaim priceless natural beauty, markedly reduce traffic congestion, allow natural processes to prevail, reduce crowding, and promote visitor understanding and enjoyment.

The authors acknowledged Yosemite Valley was too valuable to use for administration, maintenance, parking, or other commercial services that didn't contribute directly to a quality park experience. Facilities that supported such uses and services would be removed. In addition, nature would be restored and the natural processes of park ecosystems—specifically floods and rock fall—would prevail. Prescribed fire would be used to restore vegetation and habitats.

Regarding visitors, the Park Service was to ensure overcrowding did not interfere with visitor enjoyment or threaten park values. Visitor use levels were established, and facilities such as day parking and overnight accommodations would adhere to those levels. The amount and variety of information and interpretive programs would increase to help ensure a visit to Yosemite was "a lifetime treasure."

The plan's primary objectives were, first and foremost, to preserve resources, and second, to make those resources available forever for public enjoyment, education, and recreation. The over-arching emphasis was protecting and restoring natural ecosystems, scenic resources, and cultural resources, both historic and prehistoric. Public use also was emphasized, but only if it was compatible with resource protection.

On one hand, the plan was visionary. On the other hand, it simply echoed the National Park Service's mandate. The key provision of the 1916 Organic Act, which created the service, stated the new agency was to "promote and regulate the use of the Federal areas known as national parks, monuments, and reservations hereinafter specified by such means and measures as conform to the fundamental purpose of the said parks, monuments, and reservations, which purpose is to conserve the scenery and the natural and historic objects and the wild life therein and to provide for the enjoyment of the same in such manner and by such means as will leave them unimpaired for the enjoyment of future generations."

As I reviewed Yosemite's *General Management Plan* and considered the Park Service's Organic Act in terms of Yosemite, I was struck by the realization that one of the reasons Yosemite was "different" was because it first became a park way back in 1864, when the federal government ceded the Valley and the Mariposa Grove of giant sequoias to the state of California. This "park" was born fifty-two years before the National Park Service was created. Development and use of the new park took precedence over resource protection from the very beginning, before much thought was given to the fact that inappropriate or excessive use would preempt protection, and damage or destroy resources.

Cast in this light, the 1980 *General Management Plan* marked a very significant turning point in Yosemite's history. For the first time since 1864, managers made a strong commitment to protecting Yosemite Valley's unique and priceless resources—protection was to take precedence over use.

As I dug deeper into Yosemite's management history, I discovered a second bright light, an earlier visionary effort to set park management priorities firmly on the side of nature. This flame of inspiration was contained in a report written by Frederick Law Olmsted in 1865, one hundred and fifteen years before the *General Management Plan*. But Olmsted's nascent flame never had a chance to illuminate Yosemite. In fact, it barely flickered before it was extinguished. By all accounts, it was snuffed out by narrow economic considerations.

In September of 1863, at the age of forty-two, Olmsted journeyed from the east coast to California to serve as Superintendent of the Mariposa Estate, which comprised seventy square miles of land in the foothills west of Yosemite. The estate, formerly owned by General John C. Fremont, supported 6 mines, several mining camps, a railroad, and about 7,000 residents. It was reputed to be rich with gold. The work assignment was a bit of a departure from Olmsted's past roles as writer; construction superintendent, then architect-in-chief of New York's Central Park; as well as Executive Secretary for the U.S. Sanitation Commission, predecessor to the Red Cross.

While Olmsted explored his new domain, climbed into mine shafts, examined veins of ore, and worked to improve morale, the seeds of the United States National Park System were germinating. In an unprecedented move, on July 1, 1864, in the midst of the Civil War, President Abraham Lincoln signed the bill ceding Yosemite Valley and the Mariposa Grove to California. The lands were to be held in the public trust for "use, resort, and recreation" and were to be "inalienable for all time."

Six weeks later, on August 12, Olmsted saw Yosemite Valley for the first time. He was impressed by the individual features in the Valley—the chasms, cliffs, streams, meadows, trees, and bushes—but his writings indicate he was even more compelled by the Valley in its entirety, the way all the features flowed together in a seamless tapestry of beauty. "The union of deepest sublimity with the deepest beauty of nature, not in one feature or another, not in any landscape that can be framed by itself, but all around and wherever the visitor goes, constitutes the Yosemite the greatest glory of nature."

In late September, California's governor, F. F. Low, produced a list of individuals selected to serve on a commission to administer the new park lands. Frederick Law Olmsted was on the list. He quickly took the lead in park planning and hired a team to survey and produce maps of the terrain.

Soon after assuming management of the Mariposa Estate, Olmsted realized the financial condition of the holdings was not solid, and the situation deteriorated further over time. In July 1865, a new set of trustees stepped in to manage the estate, and they made it clear Olmsted would no longer be paid for his work.

Olmsted made plans to return to the east, but delayed his departure to manage personal financial interests, finish a few projects, and promote his plans for Yosemite. On August 9, 1865, he met with several fellow commissioners, as well as a few politicians and journalists, at his camp in the Valley to present his *Preliminary Report on the Yosemite and Big Tree Grove*, which was to be the foundation for management of the grant lands. Olmsted clearly identified two key priorities that were clearly echoed fifty-one years later in the National Park Service Organic Act: preservation and use.

"The main duty with which the commissioners should be charged should be to give every advantage practicable to the mass of the people to benefit by that which is peculiar to this ground and which has caused Congress to treat it differently from other parts of the public domain. This peculiarity consists wholly in its natural scenery.

The first point to be kept in mind then is the preservation and maintenance as exactly as is possible of the natural scenery; the restriction, that is to say, within the narrowest limits consistent with the necessary accommodation of visitors, of all artificial constructions and the prevention of all constructions markedly inharmonious with the scenery or which would unnecessarily obscure, distort, or detract from the dignity of the scenery."

Olmsted identified two considerations he felt should not escape attention. First, he knew native plants would be lost and "interesting objects" would be defaced, obscured, or destroyed if not carefully protected. He mentioned the "common weeds of foreign origin" that choked out native vegetation in the Atlantic states as an example of what could happen in Yosemite. The second consideration addressed the impact of present and future visitors on the new park. He knew visitors would take a toll on park resources, and when he considered the future, he knew someday visitors would be counted in the millions.

"...in permitting the sacrifice of anything that would be of the slightest value to future visitors to the convenience, bad taste, playfulness, carelessness, or wanton destructiveness of present visitors, we probably yield in each case the interest of uncounted millions to the selfishness of a few individuals."

"An injury to the scenery so slight that it may be unheeded by any visitor now, will be one of deplorable magnitude when its effect is multiplied by these millions. But again, the slight harm which the few hundred visitors of this year might do, if no care were taken to prevent it, would not be slight, if it should be repeated by millions. At

some time, therefore, laws to prevent an unjust use by individuals of that which is not individual but public property, must be made and rigidly enforced. The principle of justice involved is the same now that it will be then; such laws as this principle demands will be more easily enforced, and there will be less hardship in their action, if the abuses they are designed to prevent are never allowed to become customary but are checked while they are yet of unimportant consequence."

Olmsted believed strict laws governing visitor behavior were required to protect the Valley. He wasn't adverse to visitors. On the contrary, he requested funding for a stagecoach road to access the Valley, a loop road to go around the Valley, and five cabins to be let to tenants who would provide one room to serve as a resting place for visitors free-of-charge. Tents and camping gear would be available for visitors to rent. But, as Alfred Runte put it in his book *Yosemite: The Embattled Wilderness*, Olmstead "firmly believed visitation without uncompromising standards of behavior would defeat the very purposes of park preservation."

In a more philosophical vein, Olmsted believed scenic places like Yosemite Valley held tremendous value to society because they invoked or engaged the "contemplative faculty." He said a person's "attention is aroused and the mind occupied without purpose, without a continuation of the common process of relating the present action, thought or perception to some future end." Places of scenic beauty encouraged the visitor to be in the moment, in the now, to be fully present with no thought of past or future. Olmsted saw great value in that quality.

A few days after he read the report, Olmsted left Yosemite Valley for San Francisco. He trusted his co-commissioners would carry the plan forward to the state governor and legislature for approval. But commissioners Josiah Dwight Whitney and William Ashburner, who also were members of the California Geological Survey, feared Olmsted's plan for Yosemite would compete for limited legislative appropriations, and would affect funding for their own work. They took their case to the governor.

Olmsted departed for his home on the east coast in October. In November, the governor sent a message to the legislature that said no Yosemite report had been made.

Most of Olmsted's prescriptions for Yosemite Valley were never adopted. The roads he envisioned were built, but the most important part of his plan—his eloquent expression of the need to hold the Valley truly inviolate, inalienable, to keep it natural and largely undeveloped—never saw the light of day. Olmsted, one of Yosemite Valley's strongest advocates, resigned from the commission on October 23, 1866. Although he later returned to California, it is believed he never returned to Yosemite Valley.

In lieu of Olmsted's vision, Yosemite's commissioners emphasized tourism in California's first park. They encouraged more and more people to visit the Valley, and promoted more development and amenities to make those people happy.

In 1952, nearly ninety years after Olmsted presented his ideas, his biographer, Laura Wood Roper, turned up an almost complete copy of his report: the bright light that could have guided Yosemite Valley down a completely different path, a much less commercial, much less destructive, much more natural path.

Roper's discovery came far too late.

CHAPTER 14
Legal Actions and "The Yosemite Way"

Journal

I don't think humans can manage wild places. The web of life is too intricate and complex, too far beyond our understanding. Instead I suggest we take care of the planet by managing ourselves, by taking responsibility for our actions, and by recognizing that every single action we take has an effect. These effects are much greater than we will ever be able to understand.

It's critical that we all remember how to revere, honor, and care for the wild Earth. If the places we are most likely to fall in love with on this Earth, like Yosemite Valley, lose their wildness or disappear altogether, how will we remember how to care?

♦♦♦

Yosemite's 1980 *General Management Plan* strongly echoed Olmsted's intentions and put forth a lofty vision for Yosemite Valley's future, but it didn't provide details on how to manifest that vision. Progress on implementing the plan proceeded very slowly; little change occurred in the Valley for well over ten years.

In 1992, the Park Service developed plans to replace and upgrade visitor cabins at Yosemite Lodge, and to build new housing for concession employees. Nothing came from these plans. Late in 1996, the Park Service released a different employee housing plan that called for a substantial increase in the number of dormitories near Yosemite Lodge. Once again, nothing happened. Concurrently, managers were drafting a general plan for all of Yosemite Valley: the *Valley Implementation Plan*. As 1997 dawned, however, the New Year's Flood rendered all plans null and void. The depth and extent of water in the Valley exceeded all flood lines used by park planners. It was time to return to the drawing board.

The park was in complete chaos after the water receded. The flood wiped out or buried miles of roads and trails; battered bridges and fences; tore apart or deposited silt and debris in hundreds of buildings and campsites; swept picnic tables, trash cans, and tons of garbage into the river; and damaged utility lines.

Despite the magnitude of the event and its aftermath, managers came under immediate, intense pressure to re-open the park to visitors as quickly as possible. While re-opening the park would benefit visitors, the primary motive was to minimize disruption of revenue streams; concession operators and other business owners dependent on Yosemite tourism didn't want to lose money. The Park Service acted fast to repair and replace damaged accommodations and employee housing, and to fix a broken highway.

On June 12, 1997, an Emergency Supplemental Appropriations Act was signed which provided $176 million for flood recovery projects. Because it was a Congressional appropriation, even more pressure came to bear on park managers; they had to spend the money quickly or risk losing it. At the same time, the park secured another $21 million to implement Valley transportation projects. This windfall was an incredible sum for an agency long accustomed to pinching every penny.

Park managers scrambled to prepare and approve plans to get work done. In April 1997, less than four months after the flood and even before the appropriations act was signed, the Park Service released a brand new *Yosemite Lodge Area Development Concept Plan*. The plan included 5 new, 3-story dormitories for 336 employees and 12 new four-plexes to accommodate 190 visitors. Northside Drive, a main park road, was to be relocated from the north side of the lodge to the south side, where it would run adjacent to the Merced River. The site chosen for the new dorms and four-plexes was undeveloped land north of the existing lodge—a sun-drenched, mixed oak and conifer woodland bounded on the north by granite walls and sporting an assortment of large boulders. The new dorm site also happened to be just east of an historic climber's campground called Camp 4, a Mecca for rock climbers from all over the world.

Not everyone liked the new plan. In May 1998, the Park Service was sued. The list of plaintiffs read like a Who's Who of the rock climbing world, and included Fred Beckey, Jim Bridwell, David Brower, Yvon Chouinard, Warren Harding, Lynn Hill, Chuck Pratt, Royal Robbins, Galen Rowell, and many others. The American Alpine Club, The Access Fund, the Cragmont Climbing Club, and Friends of Yosemite Valley also were on the list. Plaintiffs claimed the new development would destroy the integrity of Camp 4, and that the Park Service did not comply with environmental laws during the planning process. In August, the Sierra Club filed a separate suit over the lodge plan that focused on the unacceptable environmental impacts associated with building in undeveloped woodland habitat and moving Northside Drive closer to the Merced River, into the floodplain. The first lawsuit did not gain traction; the second did.

The plaintiffs in the second suit claimed the Park Service didn't comply with either the Wild and Scenic Rivers Act or the National Environmental Policy Act. The latter, known as NEPA, requires federal agencies to prepare Environmental Impact Statements for major actions that could significantly affect the environment. If the agency is unsure if project impacts could be significant, a less detailed Environmental Assessment may be prepared first to determine if a more extensive Environmental Impact Statement is needed. Environmental Assessments also describe project need, present alternatives, and evaluate impacts.

In theory, the first step in the process is for the agency to identify a problem, issue, or need. Then, the agency works with the public to develop a range of alternative ways to solve the problem, analyzes and compares the alternatives, and determines the best course of action. Selection of an alternative is based on considerations of effectiveness, cost, and type and severity of environmental impacts.

In 1978, the Council on Environmental Quality published regulations for implementing NEPA that stated the alternatives section was the "heart of the environmental impact statement." Agencies were directed to "rigorously explore and objectively evaluate all reasonable alternatives," and "devote substantial treatment to each alternative considered in detail, including the proposed action, so that reviewers may evaluate their comparative merits." They also were directed to include a "no action" alternative, which represented the status quo.

For Yosemite Lodge, the issue was deteriorated and flood-damaged infrastructure. But, the lodge plan wasn't accompanied by an Environmental Impact Statement, nor was it part of any larger, Valley-wide plan. The *Valley Implementation Plan* was still in development. The Park Service wrote an Environmental Assessment for the lodge plan, but failed to present or analyze any alternatives to their proposal. Plaintiffs asserted the Park Service hadn't adequately assessed impacts of the development. A federal district court judge found in favor of the Sierra Club.

In response, the Park Service resumed efforts to complete a regional plan for the entire Valley. The earlier version, the *Valley Implementation Plan,* transmogrified into a new master plan, the *Yosemite Valley Plan,* which included hundreds of small, medium, and large-scale projects. Park employees worked feverishly to finish the plan and get flood recovery work started, unaware that another lawsuit waited around the next bend.

The winding road from El Portal to Yosemite Valley runs adjacent to the Merced River. The 1997 flood washed the road away in many places. When the Park Service prepared to repair the road, they saw an opportunity to upgrade the route by making it straighter and widening each of the two lanes from nine and a half feet to eleven feet.

Before road work began, Mariposa County sought an injunction to stop the $33 million reconstruction on economic grounds. The County claimed excessive road closures during construction would hurt local businesses. The injunction was not granted and the work commenced.

Actions to stabilize and widen the road bed had a substantial impact on the river, as well as on riparian and woodland habitat along its banks. Crews blasted boulders and rock formations with dynamite to create the new corridor, and added soil fill, rip rap, and concrete to stabilize the road bed.

Early in 1999, the Sierra Club and Mariposans for Environmentally Responsible Growth sued to stop the road project to protect the river. Their case focused on the Merced's Wild and Scenic River status, which was granted in 1987. At that time, the Park Service had three years to complete a river management plan to protect water quality, native plants and wildlife, recreational opportunities, and other river values. The plaintiffs asserted the management plan was nine years overdue, and should have been prepared prior to road widening and improvement. Additionally, the plaintiffs claimed the project was done without adequate assessment of environmental impacts.

The courts agreed, and road construction stopped in July 1999, but not before the Park Service was deeply involved in three of four segments. The court ordered the Park Service to write a wild and scenic river management plan, and gave the agency a year to complete it.

The court's decision presented park managers with a conundrum. The all-inclusive *Yosemite Valley Plan* should have been written *after* the river plan, because the Valley plan was supposed to conform to provisions of the river plan. At the time of the court order, the Valley plan was almost complete, but the river plan hadn't been written. Park personnel hurried to write a river plan.

The *Merced Wild and Scenic River Comprehensive Management Plan Environmental Impact Statement*—3 volumes and about 1,300 pages—was released in August, 2000. The *Yosemite Valley Plan Supplemental Environmental Impact Statement*—6 volumes and almost 3,000 pages—was released on November 13, 2000.

However, Friends of Yosemite Valley and Mariposans for Environmentally Responsible Growth sued again, claiming the river plan was invalid and wouldn't protect the river. The Federal District Court judge ruled the plan sufficient. The plaintiffs appealed to the Ninth Circuit Court of Appeals, who agreed with the plaintiffs. Parts of the plan that required attention included the boundaries of the protected area, called the River Protection Overlay, near El Portal, and carrying capacity. How much and what kinds of human use could the river withstand without being damaged?

The Park Service produced a revised plan in 2005. The plaintiffs still were not satisfied. They felt the Park Service once again failed to adequately address the human carrying capacity of the Merced River and its associated values. They sued and won again, despite an appeal by the Park Service.

Park planners started work on their third attempt at a river plan.

The litigation was a hot topic of conversation when I arrived in Yosemite in December of 2002. Park employees frequently discussed the lawsuits during work hours, coffee breaks, and lunch, as well as on their own time. When upper level managers discussed the lawsuits, they defended the Park Service's position vigorously, even though the courts continued to decide in favor of the plaintiffs. Occasionally, Park Service representatives even resorted to name-calling. In a newspaper article, they dismissed the plaintiffs as "a fringe group" pushing a radical agenda.

Many of my co-workers, on the other hand, sent mixed signals when they talked about the lawsuits. With some I couldn't tell if they sided with the Park Service or the plaintiffs. Others openly supported the plaintiffs in private conversations, but wouldn't speak out publicly for fear of reprisal. In mid-January I suspended my investigations into the litigation story. I had a wedding to plan.

Friday, the 31st of January, dawned clear and cold. I rose early after a mostly sleepless night to take a walk, to relax a bit and clear the cobwebs from my head. My shoulders felt like they resided directly beneath my ears. The past few weeks had been hard. I tossed and turned all night and did laps up and down the stairs of our house to burn off excess energy before I could sleep. I'm not sure if I was more worried about the wedding or being married.

Dawn sat gently on the sloping shoulders of the eastern horizon when I left the house. To the south, a soft, gray mist hovered above a blanket of snow laid down a few days earlier on Cook's Meadow. I caught a twitch of movement in the oak woodland about ten feet to my right.

Four coyotes were entwined in a dog pile under a copse of downed oak branches. Their thick, chestnut brown and beige winter coats blended seamlessly into a tapestry of fallen leaves, dead grasses, and snow. The coyotes woke, stood, stretched like yogis, and yawned to reveal sharp white teeth. Native American cosmology identifies coyote as the trickster, and I wondered what this pack presaged for my future with Tom.

At risk of inviting mischief, I invited them to the wedding, telling them it would be just across the river at the chapel, 10AM sharp.

By the time we arrived at the chapel, the sun had climbed above the eastern ridge, framed by a brilliant, cloud-free blue sky. I glanced up toward Yosemite Falls. Sunlight beamed across the Valley and illuminated the waterfall's ephemeral mist. Together, water and sun presented us with the perfect wedding gift: a brilliant rainbow arch shimmering over the dark gray chasm.

After the ceremony, Tom and I made our way down the aisle. In keeping with tradition, we pulled a long rope that hung next to the organ and rang the chapel bell, announcing to the world that we were newly wed. Then we stepped outside into bright sunlight. In the meadow across the road, a lone coyote sat on his haunches in the snow. He tipped his head back and howled his congratulations. I ran down the stairs, pulled off my veils, and howled back.

Back at work, I was immediately carried off to the weekly project management meeting in El Portal. A pattern in my weeks emerged that included five or six mandatory meetings, and three or four environmental and design documents in need of review. The latter were two to three inches thick, and invariably there were short deadlines attached to them. The pace never slowed. I scrambled to keep up. Every one of my co-workers complained about workloads. I was not alone.

The days flew by. Frustration swept in and refused to leave. It was my nature to be meticulous in my work, and I cared so much about Yosemite Valley. I wanted to be sure all the potential impacts of all projects were carefully identified and described, so they could be minimized as much as possible. I relied on my cohorts in the Resource Management Division, the wildlife biologists, botanists, cultural resource managers, and specialists in air and water quality for their professional expertise and input on the impact of the projects. But they, too, were seriously overworked, with barely enough time to do quick reviews of the larger projects. Many of the small projects got little or no attention. The frantic pace and lack of attention to details did not bode well for the resources we were charged with protecting.

"I don't want to be a whiner," I said to my supervisor one Friday afternoon. "But I can't keep up with the pace. There's too much happening all at once."

"I know," he said. "Don't worry. It's the 'Yosemite Way.' Just do the best you can."

CHAPTER 15
Waging War

Journal

I am so angry I can hardly see straight.

When I arrived in Yosemite late in 2002, big plans were afoot for Curry Village and the entire eastern part of Yosemite Valley. In late January of 2003, soon after entering on duty as resource management liaison, I attended a workshop focused on those plans. After preparing a large mug of tea, I sat down at the back of the meeting room and watched the project's design contractors set up easels, maps, and displays.

Today's Curry Village—once known as Camp Curry, and originally Camp Sequoia—was the creation of David A. Curry and his wife Jennie, two former schoolteachers. Initially, the pair's goal was to provide a low cost option for overnight visitors. The camp was modest when it opened in 1899, with seven sleeping tents and a large dining tent. Bed and board cost about two dollars per night.

The camp grew rapidly. By the end of the first summer, the Currys had hosted more than 290 guests and added 18 more tents. Within a few years, hundreds of tents dotted the landscape. Once the Currys recognized the tremendous economic potential of their fledgling camp, they aggressively pursued every opportunity to increase accommodations and services. Their repeated demands for permission to expand frequently put them at odds with park managers. David Curry earned a reputation for never taking "no" for an answer. If managers denied his requests, he appealed directly to the Secretary of the Interior, the Congress, and the public.

With dogged persistence, the Currys managed to do most of what they wanted. In 1915, they blasted numerous large boulders in the camp area to make way for trails and 300 new tents, bringing the total number of tents to 540. In 1919, at the height of the tourist season, which corresponded with high water in the Valley, the septic facility couldn't handle the volume. Raw sewage ran over the ground and into the river. Sewage and pollution problems were not unique to the Curry's facility; similar problems occurred in many places in the Valley.

By 1922, Camp Curry supported forty-eight cabins, in addition to the tents. Through the 1920s, in addition to lodging, bath houses, and dining facilities, the camp had telephone and telegraph stations, a garage and repair shop, a gas station, a sawmill, and a cabinet shop. A pool and billiard room, dance pavilion, soda fountain, movie booth, clubhouses, and general store provided diversions for visitors.

By 1930, Camp Curry had 102 rooms in cabins with baths and heat, 87 rooms in cabins without heat or running water, and 425 tent cabins. More comfort stations, bath houses, and an amphitheatre sprang up by 1931. According to Alfred Runte in *Yosemite: The Embattled Wilderness*, the Currys were "masters at elevating unnecessary luxuries to needs," as they argued for an ever-growing menu of services. Visitors "needed" items like candy, cigars, auditoriums, and swimming pools. Thus began what Runte called the "legal exploitation" of Yosemite Valley, a pursuit that continues to this day.

As 1999 came to a close, 100 years after its inception, Curry Village supported 628 tent cabins, cabins, and lodge units. Five establishments served food: a cafeteria, a pizzeria, a Mexican food take-out, an ice cream and coffee place, and a bar. Stores provided groceries, camping supplies, sporting goods and gifts. Guests could rent bicycles and rafts, or use the swimming pool or ice skating rink. The village also had a post office, information and reservations buildings, and employee housing.

The January workshop agenda included major redevelopment of Curry Village and the east Valley campgrounds, including reorganization of roads, traffic circulation patterns, and existing campgrounds; construction of new campgrounds in undeveloped areas; and new facilities for camp check-in, showers, and laundry. Dozens of large and small decisions were on the table, such as whether or not the Curry ice rink should stay, or be removed or relocated; the configuration of parking spaces, campsites, and footbridges for a new walk-in campground at Upper Pines; the "need" for new campsites to accommodate larger RVs; and the size and location of the new Curry Village general store, slated to be the "size of a Safeway."

The Park Service also intended to construct a new residential complex near the base of the Valley wall at the western edge of Curry Village. The proposed development included twenty-seven dormitories, parking lots, access roads, an employee wellness center, offices, a post office, and maintenance and storage facilities. The dorms would house concession staff—non-Park Service employees who worked in lodges, restaurants, bars, gift shops, and other visitor service operations. As many as 1,500 people lived in Yosemite Valley in the summer; more than 1,000 of them were concession employees. The flood had damaged or swept away some concession housing, and much of what remained was substandard. For some reason, though, this massive new residential complex was not discussed at the workshop.

I walked home that afternoon under a leaden sky and pondered the magnitude of the changes proposed for the east Valley. How did they fit with the goals of the *General Management Plan* to remove unnecessary infrastructure in the Valley and redirect development outside of the park? The expansion and construction of new campgrounds disturbed me, as did construction of the dorm complex. If the concession company didn't operate so many facilities—lodges, camps, grocery and gift stores, bars, raft rental and horseback riding complexes, and so on—fewer employees, and therefore less employee housing, would be required. What had happened to the Park Service's intent to downsize, to reduce development in the Valley? As I considered the facts, I realized that downsizing had never been part of the history of Curry Village. It was all about growth, and had been for over 100 years.

Soon after the workshop, I approached the Curry dorm project manager.

"Could I get a copy of the EA for the dorm project?" I asked, referring to the Environmental Assessment.

"There isn't one. Compliance was covered in the EIS for the YVP." In Yosemite-speak, this meant the project's environmental impact information was contained in the all-inclusive *Yosemite Valley Plan Supplemental Environmental Impact Statement* released in 2000.

"Where can I find a copy of the Yosemite Valley Plan itself?" I asked. Normally, when an Environmental Impact Statement is as large and complex as the one that accompanied the Yosemite Valley Plan, a separate implementation document is produced that clearly describes the selected alternative, all the actions that will be taken, and a timeline.

"There is no Yosemite Valley Plan, per se," she said. "You just have to wade through the EIS to find what you need."

The wading turned out to be more like slogging through waist-deep mud, as I combed through the 6 volume, 3,000 page "plan" to find the dorm project. It was described in one sentence: "Two new dormitories (up to three stories and 217 beds) would be constructed west of Curry Village adjacent to the Curry Village Historic District."

It was time to visit the proposed construction site. Perhaps it was already disturbed by development, in which case the project's impacts would be minimal. But no, the site was a lovely, shady, undisturbed black oak, incense-cedar, and ponderosa pine woodland tucked in close to the Valley's south wall. Several narrow, cobble-filled drainages wove through the site. In winter and spring, the shallow channels carried melt water from the Valley rim near Glacier Point to the river.

As I walked farther into the woodland, I saw numerous clusters of winter-weary, heart-shaped leaves scattered over a bed of granite pea-gravel, mixed up with last year's pine and oak litter. The leaves were a teaser: Later that spring, hundreds of bright yellow wood violets would light up the forest floor like tiny candles.

I was shocked. The Park Service was going to construct a huge new residential development complex on this lovely undeveloped patch of land in Yosemite Valley to house concession employees? And to add insult to terrible injury, it appeared park managers planned to do it with virtually no environmental impact analysis or public input process.

At the next opportunity, I discussed the project with a top level park manager, and expressed my concern about natural resource damage. He smiled and nodded. Desperate to gain traction, I said I thought the park might get sued if a separate Environmental Assessment was not completed for the dorm project. I was told there wasn't enough time to do assessments for all the projects that had to be completed, and the Park Service had to try to push through some projects without additional impact documentation. The dorm project was a test to see if the Park Service could implement Yosemite Valley Plan actions without additional compliance—and not get sued.

That night, the clam and the coot came to visit me. They weren't happy.

In March, I received an e-mail message that said the *80 percent Draft Environmental Assessment for the Curry Village and East Valley Campgrounds Project* would be delivered to me the following day. The assessment covered all the project elements discussed at the January workshop. This was the last draft that would be circulated for review before the final Environmental Assessment was produced.

This review was critical. If design changes were needed, they had to be made right away. Once I received the document, I needed to review it and prepare comments related to resource impacts, get five resource specialists to review the assessment, consolidate and approve everyone's thoughts, ideas, and comments, and then enter all feedback into the park's master project database. The database itself was problematic; it was still in the formative stages, and procedures used to process comments changed frequently.

The draft document didn't show up the following day; it took a week. All comments were due the following Tuesday. I had four days, two of which were my days off, to develop, solicit, consolidate, and submit comments on a project that promised to have major environmental impacts. And deadlines for comments were hard deadlines, because every project was on a super fast track. The project managers, many of them consultants under contract to the Park Service, were on tight schedules. If my division's concerns and comments weren't consolidated and submitted by the deadline, they wouldn't be considered.

Park managers had created a situation that was doomed to fail. Once again, undeveloped land in Yosemite Valley would become heavily developed, and native vegetation, soils, wildlife, and water would be irreparably harmed.

The Environmental Assessment did not include the dorm project. The reason for the omission was clear: The Park Service wanted to build the dorms as quickly as possible. If they included the project in the assessment, which they should have done based on NEPA provisions, dorm construction would be subject to delays associated with public involvement and planning revisions. The Park Service probably also felt litigation was more likely if the dorm project plans were made public. At that point, managers feared lawsuits lurked behind every tree. As it turned out, their fears were justified, but the plaintiff's targets were much larger than the Curry dorm project.

If I deleted job stress and concern for Yosemite Valley's natural resources from the equation, March was a lovely month. The Valley was poised on the sharp edge of spring. Yosemite Falls leaped from the rim in a thunderous froth, the meadows shimmered under a thin new veil of emerald silk, and the robins and juncos gathered twigs and shredded bark to line their nests. In the midst of this vernal splendor, I was preparing for a planning workshop on redevelopment of Yosemite Lodge.

The Lodge was established in 1915 by the Desmond Company (later the Yosemite National Park Company) on a site once used by the U.S. Cavalry, which oversaw management of the Valley from 1906 through 1914. In 1890, a large park (the original Yosemite National Park) was created, which encompassed the state-administered Yosemite Valley and Mariposa Grove. The cavalry was assigned to manage the new park. In 1905, the grant that deeded the Valley and the Grove to California was rescinded due to mismanagement, and the cavalry assumed responsibility for those lands as well. Prior to the army's arrival, the site of today's Yosemite Lodge supported the largest, most important Native American village in the Valley, known as *Koomine*.

The original lodge consisted of refurbished army facilities, and included 115 redwood cabins, numerous canvas cabins, 2 bath houses, 2 frame toilet buildings, and a car shelter. Other facilities included a cafeteria, dairy, laundry, hospital, barber, tailor, public bath house, recreation room, two linen rooms, warehouses, a telephone and ticket office, and employee quarters. A stage, dance pavilion, swimming pool, and tennis court provided entertainment options.

It turned out that management of tourists and sightseers was beyond the scope of duties of U. S. Cavalry personnel and they were relieved of their assignment in 1914. Responsibility for Yosemite was turned over to civilian rangers. In 1916, the National Park Service, newly created within the Department of the Interior, assumed management of the park. The birth of the Park Service, however, didn't change the situation in the Valley. The two-pronged emphasis on development and ever-increasing visitation that began in 1864 continued unabated. In 1918, a zoo was established in the lodge area that housed mountain lions, bears, deer and other animals. Around 1919, Leidig Meadow, immediately southwest of the lodge, supported an oval racetrack and an airplane landing field.

Over time, infrastructure at the lodge expanded to include roads, parking areas, sidewalks, paths, a pony track and shelter, an oil and gas station, dental facilities, warehouses, and a pump house. As the years passed, many of these facilities were de-constructed, re-constructed, or moved.

In 1939, the North Road (later re-named Northside Drive) ran right through the Lodge complex, immediately south of the current registration area. This segment was considered one of the most dangerous parts of the Valley's road system. In 1954, the Park Service rerouted the road to run north of the lodge instead of through it.

A dramatic post-World War II increase in visitation drove the Park Service to rebuild Yosemite Lodge completely in 1956. Little change occurred over the next forty years, until the New Year's Flood of 1997 swept away parts of the lodge, and flooded much of what remained standing. The central lodge complex, which included the reception area, shops, and dining areas, was redesigned in 1998.

When I attended the March 2003 planning workshop, the lodge had 245 rooms and 4 larger "family" rooms for up to 6 people. It offered an upscale restaurant, a cafeteria, two gift and sundry shops, a post office, an ice cream stand, a swimming pool, and a bike rental stand. To add to the congestion, low-quality temporary employee housing had been erected west of the lodge after the flood. This residential area earned the name "the train wreck" for its aesthetic qualities.

Yosemite Lodge needed an upgrade. Most accommodations were old, and the flood had damaged many of the units. The lodge project was one of the largest of the Top 15+2, with a price tag of about $30 million.

The workshop day dawned clear and sunny. The medium-sized conference room at the Lodge was sandwiched between a store and the Mountain Room Bar. I walked in as park employees and the lodge design consultants settled into their seats, and I studied the project map laid out on the central table while waiting for the meeting to start.

The project included construction of new lodging units and reception areas, and a rerouting of Northside Drive from north of the lodge to the south side. The new route would run right next to a side channel of the Merced River, an area fringed by boggy wetlands supporting cottonwoods and willows that flooded during spring snowmelt. This made no sense. The new road frequently would be under water. The channel bank would erode and creep slowly toward the new road. Eventually, the Park Service would have to reinforce the bank with rip rap or concrete to prevent water from under-cutting the road. Runoff and floodwater flowing over the new road would carry engine oil, transmission fluid, bits of rubber, and other contaminants into both river and wetlands. Additionally, the road would block the natural flow of water through the wetlands, which were critically important to wildlife and protected by law.

The Park Service wanted to move the road because lodge visitors and tour bus patrons had to walk across Northside Drive, a busy road, to gain access to Yosemite Falls. The crossing posed a safety concern and caused traffic to back up on busy summer weekends. I was seated next to my boss at the workshop, and leaned over to ask him in a whisper if the park had seriously considered alternatives to the road reroute, such as putting up a crossing light, or building a pedestrian overpass, which would avoid most of the natural resource impacts associated with the reroute. He said yes, other options had been considered and rejected.

I found it ironic that Northside Drive historically ran south of the lodge. The road was moved north in 1954 for safety reasons. Now the Park Service wanted to move it south again—for safety reasons.

At a lull in the conversation I mustered up the courage to voice my concerns. I leaned over the conference table and stated, "I'm concerned about the location of the new road, and the possible impacts on the..."

"The decision to re-route the road has already been made." A top level park manager cut me off quickly, and then said, "Now, let's move on to the layout of the new registration area."

It struck me then that I'd been hired as a figurehead. Relative to both the East Valley and the Yosemite Lodge projects, it seemed nothing I said made any difference. All significant decisions already had been made and were set in stone. And all of those decisions had been based on the extremely limited and grossly inadequate environmental impact analysis done for the *Yosemite Valley Plan Supplemental Environmental Impact Statement*. It was clear that my ideas and concerns, and those of my cohorts in the Resource Management Division, would be incorporated into project planning only if doing so didn't result in any appreciable change in existing plans. If the Lorax spoke for the trees, but no one bothered to listen, was she simply wasting her breath?

On March 19, 2003, the United States declared war on Iraq. At about the same time, I fully awakened to the fact that another war was being waged—on the resources of Yosemite Valley. The entity inflicting casualties in both wars was the same. In my job as Liaison, I was caught in the crossfire.

CHAPTER 16
Convolution, Obfuscation, Desecration

Journal

On a plateau high above Yosemite Falls, not visible from the Valley below, Yosemite Creek gathers volume and momentum, oblivious to the looming precipice—the sharp edge of the north wall. Without warning, the creek's rocky bottom disappears, sending the water into a breathless, free-wheeling leap of faith before gravity takes over and jettisons it straight down toward the Valley floor, almost half a mile below.

At the end of the free-fall, the creek careens down a rock-filled channel, tumbling, spinning, splashing head-over-heels in the eternal twisting cascade dance of Yosemite Creek. The water then dives under the bridge and away. A stone's throw downstream of the bridge, the creek splits into several braided channels and swings south toward the Merced River, like capillaries branching from arteries, carrying life to thirsty extremities.

◆◆◆

Yosemite Falls, among the tallest waterfalls in North America, are the most heavily visited feature in Yosemite National Park. Official estimates say 2 million people visit Yosemite Falls every year. I think this estimate falls far short of reality. In summer, as well as many spring and fall weekends, the Yosemite Falls experience is like Disneyland. People mill like ants over roads, trails, and viewing areas, and everywhere in between. Dogs and bicycles add to the confusion and congestion.

In 2002, when Tom and I moved to the Valley, the developed area near the base of Yosemite Falls supported an old, usually overwhelmed parking lot and shuttle bus stop. Numerous tour buses of all shapes and sizes rumbled in and out, belching large, black clouds of noxious diesel exhaust. A small, heavily-used, usually dirty restroom stood near the northwest corner of the lot. Garbage cans overflowed and streamers of toilet paper and banana peels mingled underfoot with pine needles and cones.

The main trail to the bottom of the Lower Fall, which was paved, departed from the parking lot near the restroom. A ten to fifteen minute walk delivered visitors to a paved viewing area and a sturdy bridge that crossed Yosemite Creek, just south of the base of the Lower Fall. On a busy summer day, this trail hosted thousands of visitors.

A stroll across the bridge during peak snowmelt provided a sensory feast; the force of falling water choreographed its own grand finale. The roar of water shut out all other sound as it slammed into solid granite boulders. The interplay of water and rock churned up a pulsing wind that picked up and carried aloft heavy curtains of water droplets, dousing bridge walkers in a frigid shower, and threatening to push them off the bridge. During the crossing, everything extraneous to the moment was rendered mute, washed away by cool wind and cold water.

A second trail—a dirt path—led from the east edge of the parking lot to the same bridge. This eastern route was longer than the western trail and provided an opportunity for a more leisurely meander through a forest filled with ponderosa pine, incense-cedar, western azalea, and black oak. The route traversed several historic wood and stone bridges that spanned cascades and pools, areas favored by mallards. A short side trail led to a historic plaque marking the site of John Muir's cabin. The cabin was long gone, its precise location not known with certainty, but millions of visitors visualized the cabin nestled in this Eden, alongside a rippling stretch of Yosemite Creek, with an unparalleled view of Yosemite Falls. Deer, squirrels, and birds were abundant as they went about the business of finding food and water.

The majority of visitors chose the more direct western trail to the Lower Fall bridge, which left the experience along the eastern trail quieter and more contemplative. The old east trail was one of my favorite places. It was very close to Yosemite Falls, the beating heart of Yosemite Valley, yet still retained a remnant of the inherent wildness that existed in a few secret pockets in the eastern part of the Valley.

Magic at Yosemite Falls reached its peak on certain spring nights when the moon was full. As Yosemite Creek struck the granite of the Valley walls, the impact of water on stone threw shimmering veils of mist high in the air. The tiny water droplets caught and refracted beams of moonlight, culminating in a tryst of light and water that melted into a divine arc of shifting color, into the rarest of the rare—a lunar rainbow.

For many years, the Park Service wanted to clean up and overhaul the developed area near the base of Yosemite Falls. The parking lot was an eyesore, the restroom small and dilapidated. In addition, area bridges and trails suffered substantial damage from the 1997 flood and needed repair. The solution, the Lower Yosemite Fall project, was promoted as a way to restore the area to a more natural state and enhance the visitor's experience of the Valley's premiere waterfall. The project included parking lot removal, a new restroom and shuttle bus stop, and improved trails and footbridges. The price tag for the facelift was about $14 million. Unlike the other Top 15+2 projects, most of the money for the renovation was donated to the park by the non-profit Yosemite Conservancy (formerly the Yosemite Fund).

Established in 1988, the Yosemite Conservancy raised money from private donors to finance a variety of park projects, including visitor center exhibits, wildlife surveys, trail repairs, and production of maps and videos. Individuals, foundations, and large corporations such as Bank of America, ChevronTexaco, and Delaware North (the parent company of Yosemite's primary concession operator) donated small and large sums. The Lower Yosemite Fall Project was the Conservancy's largest undertaking to date; the organization contributed over $12.5 million.

Planning began officially with a workshop in 1992. In 1995, the Park Service agreed to work jointly with the Yosemite Conservancy to accomplish the work. But before planning was complete, the flood of 1997 turned park management on its head.

Soon after I became liaison late in 2002, the Park Service and the Yosemite Conservancy chose contractors for the Lower Fall Project, and initiated development of detailed construction drawings. The piles of paperwork I received when I arrived to start work included *The Lower Yosemite Fall Project Environmental Assessment*, the project's National Environmental Policy Act document, which was released in December of 2001.

The assessment looked substantial. It was about an inch thick and 280 pages long. It turned out the assessment was long on words, but short on content. The document presented two action alternatives and the "No Action" alternative. The only substantive difference between the two action alternatives was the restroom location. All other project components, including parking lot removal and subsequent site restoration, seating and picnic areas, the new trail system, and the new bridges along the eastern trail, were identical in both action alternatives. I thought I had the wrong assessment. There should have been more alternatives. Perhaps a different or more recent version existed.

I called the project manager. "Is there more than one EA for the falls project? I have the one dated December 2001."

"No, there's only one. That's it."

"But there aren't any alternatives, except for the bathroom," I said.

"The Lower Fall project was fully analyzed in the Valley Plan EIS," was the reply.

A wave of déjà vu washed over me. I'd encountered the same situation with the Curry dorm project. Unlike the dorm project, though, an Environmental Assessment, albeit an incomplete one, had been prepared for the Lower Fall project.

As mentioned earlier, federal agencies often prepare Environmental Assessments as a first step to determine if a project could have significant environmental impacts. If the answer is yes, the agency is required to complete a more comprehensive Environmental Impact Statement. Sometimes, though, the sequence is reversed; the agency prepares a large, regional plan with numerous individual actions, with an accompanying "programmatic" Environmental Impact Statement. Environmental Assessments are produced later to provide details on individual actions within the larger plan. This process is called tiering.

For Lower Yosemite Fall, the Park Service initially described the proposed project in the massive *Yosemite Valley Plan Supplemental Environmental Impact Statement*. Later, the agency produced an Environmental Assessment to provide additional details on the project.

I once again pulled the six-volume *Yosemite Valley Plan Supplemental Environmental Impact Statement* off the shelf, in search of information on the Lower Yosemite Fall Project. The document analyzed four action-packed alternatives as well as the No Action alternative. The Lower Fall Project was described in two long paragraphs. This cursory treatment wasn't unusual for Yosemite Valley Plan projects because the plan incorporated more than 250 separate actions, many of them major. The plan couldn't contain details for that many projects, and the Park Service indicated its intent to do follow-up Environmental Assessments for complex or potentially controversial projects.

The cursory project description was to be expected, but as I read further I was shocked to discover that the Lower Fall Project was included in almost identical form in all four of the action alternatives. The only differences were related to the location of the new restroom, on either the west or east side of Yosemite Creek, and whether the east side trail would have four or six bridges. This lack of true alternatives meant the project as described was going to happen, regardless of which action alternative was selected. It was a foregone conclusion.

The Park Service's "preferred alternative" in the *Yosemite Valley Plan Supplemental Environmental Impact Statement* placed the new restroom east of Yosemite Creek. After releasing the document, though, the Park Service learned the site was of special significance to Native Americans in Yosemite.

The mystery was solved. The follow-up Environmental Assessment was prepared to address this concern. The only "alternative" considered in the assessment was the one that placed the new restroom on the west side of Yosemite Creek. The Park Service, of course, called this their "preferred alternative," and selected it for implementation.

In summary, the Park Service, in concert with The Yosemite Conservancy, developed a plan for the Lower Yosemite Fall area. Their plan was inserted into all four alternatives in the *Yosemite Valley Plan Supplemental Environmental Impact Statement*, which presented a very brief description of the project and its impacts. The Park Service then discovered the restroom location had to be changed, so they prepared the *Lower Yosemite Fall Project Environmental Assessment* to address this issue. As part of the assessment, the Park Service purportedly identified all environmental impacts associated with the Lower Falls project. The impact assessment appeared rigorous at first glance; eighteen different impact categories ranging from geology to energy consumption were evaluated. But a careful reading revealed numerous shortcomings and oversights.

The National Environmental Policy Act requires consideration of both short and long-term impacts. The Lower Fall Project assessment glossed over short-term, construction-related impacts, such as soil disturbance, vegetation damage, disruption of wildlife, noise, exhaust, and closed trails. The document downplayed these impacts, and claimed they would be substantially minimized through mitigation measures.

Regarding long-term impacts, the assessment stated eight of the eighteen resource categories would experience adverse impacts. Nine categories would benefit from the project. The last category, an odd grouping of geologic resources, geologic hazards, and soils, would be subject to both beneficial and adverse impacts over the long haul. Wildlife, air quality, noise, archeological resources, ethnographic areas (of special significance to Native Americans), and cultural landscapes were among the resources that would be adversely affected.

The assessment ranked all impacts according to their severity: negligible, minor, moderate, or major. Many of the rankings grossly understated the significance of impacts. For example, impacts to wildlife were deemed negligible—not measurable or perceptible—despite the fact that the eastern trail would be "hardened" and thousands of people, some with bicycles and dogs, would use that trail on busy summer days, as opposed to the dozens to hundreds of daily visitors who used the trail before the changes. It's highly likely that every species of wildlife living in or using the area would be affected, from bark beetles to bats to black bears, and that the impacts would be substantial.

According to the assessment, ethnographic areas and cultural landscapes would suffer moderate adverse impacts. The project area was a former Native American village site, and supported several plant species of significant cultural value. I later learned many Native Americans with ties to the Valley were adamantly opposed to the Lower Fall Project. Before I arrived, they had staged protests to voice their concerns.

Resources that stood to benefit most from the Lower Yosemite Fall project were social resources: scenery (because trees would be removed to open up views), the visitor experience, park operations (because the restrooms would require less maintenance), and recreation. The bias inherent in this project was very clear.

In conclusion, the assessment stated the Lower Yosemite Fall project would not have any "significant" environmental impacts. This point was the key. If the assessment concluded the project could have significant impacts, the Park Service would have been required to prepare a detailed Environmental Impact Statement, which would have been costly and time-consuming. Additionally, it's likely that the process would have revealed more environmentally-benign alternatives—options the Park Service and the Yosemite Conservancy may not have wanted to consider.

After reviewing the environmental assessment, the Regional Director of the National Park Service signed a FONSI, or Finding of No Significant Impact, for the Lower Yosemite Fall Project. This green light signaled the start of a project that did, in fact, significantly alter natural and cultural resources, as well as the experience of visitors, in the area around Yosemite Valley's great falls. The changes were not for the better.

Once I finally unraveled the intricate web of planning surrounding the Lower Yosemite Fall Project, it was clear to me that the Park Service designed the project before they completed the *Yosemite Valley Plan Supplemental Environmental Impact Statement*. In planning language, they "pre-selected" the design and didn't rigorously consider alternatives. They crafted the planning process around the project, instead of vice versa. In other words, they developed the Lower Fall area the way they wanted to. And the way they wanted it developed may have been, in large part, the way the Yosemite Conservancy wanted it developed.

Site preparation for the Lower Yosemite Fall Project began in April 2003. I was assigned to monitor the work to prevent or minimize environmental damage. Over the next few weeks, I learned that all of my fears for the continued sanctity of this most glorious piece of land were justified.

On one of my first days as monitor, I set out for the Yosemite Falls parking lot under a deep blue morning sky streaked with thin, high clouds. Variable weather had prevailed through the spring season; sunshine mixed with rain showers mixed with snowstorms. The pale streaks in the sky indicated another change was coming. The Valley was spectacular that morning; the dogwoods were in full bloom, and the falls leaped from the rim in a gala of thunder and froth.

When I arrived at the parking lot, about twenty people stood on the bike path that flanked the lot. All eyes were focused on a stately ponderosa pine that towered above its neighbors in the mixed conifer and black oak forest. The tree was at least five feet in diameter, about one hundred feet tall, and dominated the island of land near the east end of the lot.

Two men walked up to the tree. One carried a chainsaw with a bar about fifty inches long. The other wielded a sledge hammer. In one smooth move the sawyer yanked the starter cord. The saw whined as its spinning teeth bit into the tree's heartwood. Wood chips and sawdust flew. The sawyer cut four large, side-by-side wedges from one side of the tree, then walked to the opposite side and cut a thin, flat slice just above the wedges.

The section of parking lot where the tree was expected to fall had been prepared in advance. A long line of logs, tractor tires, and brush piles waited in a row along the projected fall line to soften the impact, to keep the tree from shattering when it slammed into asphalt. The massive pine would be worth more at the mill if it didn't break.

The crowd grew. The sawyer pulled the saw from the tree and stepped back. His partner shoved three metal wedges into the thin slice and raised his sledge hammer. The metallic ring of metal on wood echoed through the otherwise silent forest as the wedges were slammed deeper into the cut. The pressure slowly split the tree's heart, forcing it to give way.

The giant quivered for a second, and then began its descent. Time stretched into eternity as gravity teased the tall tree earthward. Its fibrous body groaned as its tremendous weight shifted. The rate of fall accelerated as the tree approached the horizontal, and then it slammed into pavement, tires, and brush with a resounding crash. Limbs, cones, needles and bark flew in all directions. When the pieces finally came to rest, silence enveloped the forest once again.

The big tree lived its life within sight and sound of Yosemite Falls. It survived repeated fires and floods, but it couldn't stop a bureaucracy bearing a chainsaw, couldn't survive the National Park Service's Lower Yosemite Fall Project, couldn't stand in the way of a new restroom.

A few days later, I stood in the rain near the west bank of Yosemite Creek and watched a logging contractor step out of his pickup and climb into the cab of a monstrous fat-tired loader. At a turn of the wrist, the big machine belched a black cloud and rumbled off the pavement onto the forest floor. The contractor was intent on the task of the morning: to haul several large ponderosa pine logs out of the forest to the logging truck that waited in the parking lot.

The man's job was complicated by the fact that Yosemite Creek flowed between the logs and the parking lot. The contractor had cut the trees down the day before, and told me he planned to drive across the small footbridge that spanned the creek, hook up to the logs, and drag them back across the bridge to the parking lot. But, it turned out the bridge was not sturdy enough to hold the weight of the truck or the logs. So, the Park Service forester overseeing the contractor devised an alternate plan. The contractor would drive the loader across Yosemite Creek to a log, hook it up to the loader, and then pull it back through the creek to the parking lot. The loader would cross the creek twice to retrieve each of several logs.

I couldn't believe it. During my six years as a consultant, I was faced with numerous similar situations where a large vehicle needed to cross a creek in order to get a job done. In none of these situations would any agency—the Forest Service, the Bureau of Land Management, the state resource agencies of California, Nevada, or Oregon—ever allow a contractor to drive a large vehicle across a creek like Yosemite Creek, one with soft, steep, vegetated banks, flowing water, and soils wet from recent rain and snow. And yet the National Park Service, the guys with the white hats, thought it was okay to do this to Yosemite Creek, when they, of all agencies, should be upholding the very highest standards of environmental protection.

There had to be a way to avoid the removal.

"Can we leave the logs on site to decompose naturally? I asked the park forester. "They'd provide cover for wildlife and nutrients for future trees."

"No," he said. "The logs have to be removed, they're a fire hazard."

This was not true. The logs were large. Small trees, branches, pine cones, and other "fine fuels" constituted fire hazards, not large logs.

I had no way to know I was wasting my breath. I didn't know, and the park forester did not tell me, that the logs effectively belonged to the contractor. He had bid low on the logging contract, with the understanding that the government would sell the logs to him at a very low cost as "excess government property." He would haul the trees away and sell them to the mill at a profit. This way, he was able to bid less for the contract. The National Park Service saved money by selling Yosemite's trees cheaply. I believe the logs in question were worth about $1,200.

The loader operator's partner stood beside me on Yosemite Creek's west bank. As we watched the driver descend into the creek channel, his partner leaned close to me and said quietly, "I'm really surprised the Park Service is letting us do this. You know, drive across the creek to get these logs. If this was Forest Service land, they'd never let us do it."

He went on to tell me the National Park Service was much more flexible than other agencies when it came to environmental safeguards.

My stomach clenched with anger and fear.

The loader rolled over the edge of the bank and down into the creek bed, gouging deep tracks in soft, wet soil. The big tires rolled across the creek bottom without incident, but on the far side the driver was unable to climb up the bank to get out. Too many fallen limbs and branches blocked his way. The sandy creek bottom was too soft. My stomach twisted again as the driver tried repeatedly to accelerate out of the channel. With each attempt, the tires cut deeper. Rocks flew, soil churned, water muddied.

I was frantic. The damage was appalling.

"He needs to get out, now!" I yelled to the park forester, who then signaled to the driver to stop. The contractor turned the rig around and started to exit up the bank he had gone down.

And then things got worse.

As the loader angled upward, I watched an iridescent black sheen appear under the vehicle and ripple across the surface of the creek. The oil quickly spread and floated downstream. I ran a half mile to the ranger station to find someone with a hazmat kit who could clean up the spill.

The loader could not be driven out of the creek bed; it eventually had to be winched out. But park managers weren't concerned about the spill. I was told, "It was just a small spill." Later that week, I was reminded clearly of just where the Park Service's concerns did lie: I was reprimanded via email by the park's contract officer for impeding the contractors in their work.

And then, just when I thought things couldn't get any worse, they did.

CHAPTER 17
Honesty and Integrity Need Not Apply

Journal

I am numb. I feel uninspired by Yosemite Valley. Is that really true? Have gross mismanagement, the caste system in park management, and the blatant disregard for ecosystem health dulled Yosemite's shine for me? These things should make me angry, depress me, but not diminish my passion for this place. They should inflame it even more. The Lower Fall Project just kills me. Instead of canyon wren and robin song, I hear heavy equipment. It's all so wrong-minded.

October is almost over. I've been living here for over a year—a very long year. Watching the Park Service tear up the Valley wears heavily on me. Today I heard a National Public Radio commentator say, "We are fighting terror..." I am fighting a different kind of terror.

◆◆◆

The days lengthened. Spring turned to summer. Meadow grasses shot skyward in a frenzy of emerald. Baby mallards paddled in tight lines behind mama ducks in quiet, olive-green river eddies.

Through early summer I encountered an ongoing stream of situations where Park Service actions damaged resources in the Valley. Heavy equipment, cement trucks, bright orange plastic fencing, road detours, and construction workers became more common than squirrels, jays, and deer. To make matters worse, gaps, oversights, and poor choices in park planning emerged like earthworms after a heavy rain.

The Lower Yosemite Fall project began in earnest after the Park Service removed the trees that happened to be in the wrong place at the wrong time. Contractors tore out the old parking lot first, and chaos ensued immediately. Repeat Valley visitors accustomed to parking in the lot, and those reading maps showing the lot's presence, arrived at Yosemite's premier attraction to find a barricade across the entrance. Confusion set in. Traffic backed up. The Park Service deployed signs and personnel to direct visitors to a different lot.

To make matters worse, the daily entourage of large tour buses continued to pour into the falls area. Before the project, bus drivers idled in the parking lot while their day trippers took their photos, and then moved on. Other drivers disgorged their loads and parked overnight in the lot while their patrons enjoyed a more leisurely stay. The Lower Fall Project plan indicated tour buses would load and unload passengers in a new transit center to be built at an unspecified future date. In the interim, buses were to load and unload on the shoulder of Northside Drive—the busy main road, and the only route out of the Valley. When it became obvious this system would not work for reasons of safety and traffic congestion, a new area for loading and unloading was quickly identified at Yosemite Lodge. New sidewalks were paved and signs were erected to reduce visitor confusion.

The Park Service then scurried to pave a new parking lot west of the lodge to accommodate buses overnight. Although the land that became the lot was formerly disturbed by lodge activities, it was unpaved. The asphalt was poured and improvements made without any environmental compliance process. This incident highlighted another major Park Service planning problem: sequencing.

The *Yosemite Valley Plan Supplemental Environmental Impact Statement* included over 250 separate actions or projects. It mentioned the importance of implementing projects in a logical sequence, but this consideration probably was an afterthought; sequencing was covered in the last of the six volumes—in Appendix M. During my tenure as liaison, park planners invested considerable time in developing a draft "spider diagram" to guide appropriate and effective project sequencing. The diagram illustrated all linkages between and among all projects. As far as I know, the diagram was not completed beyond the initial draft, nor was the public ever engaged in its development.

Additionally, the Park Service started, but never completed an actual "Yosemite Valley Plan." People interested in what was happening in the Valley were referred to the plan's six-volume Environmental Impact Statement. Similar to the spider diagram, considerable time and money were spent to draft a Yosemite Valley Plan, but the plan never was finalized or released.

Were these failures by the Park Service to complete and distribute the spider diagram and Yosemite Valley Plan intentional? The actual order in which projects were undertaken seemed to be based solely on economics. Projects were done if they were funded and if they contributed directly to visitor services. In other words, projects that provided revenue, either directly or indirectly, to concession operators or other park-related businesses came first. Other considerations, like restoring habitat, protecting resources, and minimizing disruption to visitors seemed secondary, as park managers set out to "improve" the park and please local politicians, Congress, wealthy supporters of the Yosemite Conservancy, and large corporations with a stake in Yosemite Valley. There were exceptions, such as the removal of Cascades Dam below Yosemite Valley, but these exceptions were few.

By day, I watched the Park Service wreak havoc on the Valley. By night, my frustration leaked out as I shed gallons of tears. My saline well ran dry at 2AM one September morning. I could no longer participate in the desecration of Yosemite Valley; it was destroying me. I resigned from my job as liaison, but agreed to continue to work part-time on two tasks.

For the next five months I monitored construction at the Lower Fall and worked on a framework for addressing visitor carrying capacity for the Valley. I hoped I could at least minimize environmental damage at Yosemite Falls, and help the Park Service build a solid program for Yosemite to balance visitor use and resource protection.

I was wrong on both counts.

As soon as construction started at the Lower Fall, I realized my earlier conclusions about the inadequacy of the project's Environmental Assessment were spot on. The document didn't describe the project accurately, the disclosure of impacts was incomplete, and the significance of impacts was substantially played down. Short-term construction impacts, which were barely described, were much worse than I anticipated. Trails were closed for long periods, noise from pumps and construction equipment was incessant for months, native plants were run over and trampled, soil, including the bed and banks of Yosemite Creek, was churned up and displaced, and a deer fell into a large excavation that was dug for a bridge footing.

The assessment didn't mention the tons of cement and concrete that flowed into Yosemite Creek's meanders for bridge and boardwalk footings. It didn't describe the seventy medium to large trees cut down to make way for new bridges, trails, and restroom, and to improve views of the falls. The assessment stated dirt trails that wandered through the forest east of Yosemite Creek would be "hardened"—a benign term that obscured the truth as effectively as the invisibility cloak hid Harry Potter. The cloak dropped away, though, when construction workers paved a network of trails covering more than a mile. One-inch thick, five-foot wide corridors of asphalt replaced the former dirt trail.

Workers erected concrete-reinforced boardwalks to connect several trail segments. Fences and signs sprouted up to keep visitors on the new trails. A massive wood and stone shuttle bus stop took shape and new trails bisected a site of Native American cultural significance. The Environmental Assessment provided a tidy project description that omitted the lurid details that ultimately defined the project. The Lower Fall Project was a major urbanization effort thinly disguised as environmental restoration.

It was heart-breaking.

The weeks passed and the work progressed. Temperatures pushed into the 90s. The zealous splash dance of Yosemite Creek slowed to a sedate and fluid waltz, and the contractors prepared to build the new bridges. Construction materials arrived on huge trucks, and I understood for the first time just how large and obtrusive the new bridges would be, and how much they would interfere with the hydrology of Yosemite Creek. The Environmental Assessment described seven "pedestrian" bridges, indicating six of the old stone and wood structures that spanned the creek's meanders would be "rehabilitated," and one new bridge would be built. This description sounded reasonable and relatively low impact, but it was far from accurate. All of the bridges were completely re-built, supported by huge steel I-beams and fifteen-foot square cement footings that extended ten feet down into the bed and banks of the creek—structures that would impede the flow of water through the Yosemite Creek drainage for as long as they existed.

"Why do the bridges need to be so big and bombproof?" I asked the project manager.

"They were designed to support emergency vehicles," was the reply. This certainly was not in keeping with the Environmental Assessment, which stated the existing pedestrian bridges were to be "rehabilitated." Ironically, several years after the project was completed, park employees indicated the bridges were not adequate to support emergency vehicles after all.

The Yosemite Creek drainage is extremely dynamic. Water flow varies significantly in volume and pattern from season to season, and from year to year. The braided channels shift position frequently in response to changes in the creek bed. Trees uproot from banks, and water spins into the gaps left behind and erodes the bank. Trees fall across the creek, rocks pile up, and water is blocked or diverted, forced to find a way around the obstructions.

In late winter and early spring, Yosemite Creek also forms a wondrous substance called frazil (pronounced "frazzle") ice, a milky mixture of water and ice crystals that coalesces in late winter and early spring. Under certain weather conditions, water from the falls cascades down, comes into contact with very cold air, and forms ice crystals, which mix with the water to create slush. The resulting river of pale gray, frozen curds then flows down canyon. The frazil ice isn't solid enough to stop flow completely, but it congeals enough to create mushy dams that force the water to change direction. According to Donald E. McHenry, a Yosemite park naturalist writing in the 1954 edition of *Yosemite Nature Notes*, "The stream carried within itself the means of its own diversion." The spongy, frozen stuff piles up and occasionally reaches depths of twenty feet near the base of the falls. It sometimes overtops bridges, or lifts them from their footings.

Yosemite Creek's dynamic tableau of rock, water, and ice changes perpetually under nature's paintbrush. Construction of expensive "permanent" bridges in the Lower Fall area makes no sense. The creek will abandon bridged channels in favor of new courses. Will the bridges be relocated when this happens? Or will the Park Service redirect flow back under their uber-bridges? Floods and frazil ice will pull up pavement and knock down structures. In the winter of 1964/65, frazil ice reached a height of thirty-five feet, destroying everything in its path. Despite professional recommendations to the contrary, though, park managers were set on making the bridges, boardwalks, and trails as permanent as possible.

When I recognized the magnitude of the environmental damage that would result from the new construction, I raised my concerns with co-workers. They said that during earlier planning phases, many park employees had argued strongly against the over-engineered bridges and boardwalks, as well as the paving, but park managers refused to scale them down. I convinced a lead park planner, who now works in a different park, to try once more to get the project design changed. He, too, failed.

Although overwhelmed with sadness by the urbanization of Lower Yosemite Fall, I retained optimism that my efforts on another park program would prevent similar damage in the future, would perhaps even reverse the development trend. With a small team, I embarked on a journey to design a cutting edge management strategy for the park based primarily on the following question: How many people can visit and recreate in Yosemite without damaging natural and cultural resources, or damaging the quality of other people's visits?

The task before us was unprecedented. The Park Service recognized the critical importance of balancing use with preservation—it was, after all, their primary mission—but the agency never seriously embraced the idea of user capacity. In part, they ignored the issue because, in many parks, numbers of visitors remained low, and crowding and resource degradation were not problematic, yet. But, as I continued to learn the hard way, Yosemite was different. Through the 1980s and early 1990s, park visitation climbed to over 4 million people per year. The 1997 flood set the numbers back, but they crept up again over time.

There is one notable exception to the overall lack of user capacity measures in national parks. In the backcountry of many parks, particularly in designated wilderness areas, backpackers must obtain permits for overnight use, and parks limit the number of people allowed in at one time. The Park Service understands the need to protect resources and ensure a high quality visitor experience in the backcountry, but they don't extend this philosophy to front country areas like Yosemite Valley. While I was working in Yosemite, I noticed the topic of limiting the number of visitors in the Valley made park managers squirm with discomfort.

Yosemite's 1980 *General Management Plan* addressed user capacity when it directed managers to permit only those types and levels of use or development that did not significantly impair park natural resources, and that were compatible with preserving and protecting scenery and cultural resources. But the plan didn't define terms like "significantly impair" or "preserving and protecting," nor did it provide details on ways to accomplish these objectives. It established visitor use limits, but they were derived solely from the number of facilities—campsites, lodging units, and parking spaces—present in the park in 1980. The limits were not linked in any way to resource impacts or visitor experience, and would not necessarily ensure protection of those values.

Yosemite's managers took a few preliminary steps toward addressing user capacity in the late 1990s, when they conducted studies to determine levels of crowding at popular Valley sites. They surveyed visitors to solicit opinions on crowding, and on park amenities like food service and facility cleanliness. In some years, the park did "manage" visitor use levels. When traffic slowed to gridlock in the Valley, rangers stopped incoming traffic until cars were moving once again. In the late 1980s, the Park Service took action in areas where visitor use had severely damaged resources. They erected signs, fences, and boardwalks to protect meadows, oak woodlands, and river banks, but the agency didn't take any steps toward developing a comprehensive user capacity program until forced to do so by the courts.

In the Yosemite Valley Plan and the Merced Wild and Scenic River Comprehensive Management Plan, both completed in 2000, managers committed to developing and implementing a program to manage visitor use by 2005. Both plans stated that a user capacity program designed by the National Park Service called the Visitor Experience and Resource Protection framework, or VERP, would be used.

Described as an ongoing, iterative process, VERP provided guidance on how to determine desired resource and visitor experience conditions, establish standards to maintain those conditions, and identify actions that can be taken if standards are exceeded. The Park Service made it clear VERP did not limit numbers of visitors or establish quotas, although such measures could be adopted if necessary.

The commitment made in the Yosemite Valley Plan was not legally binding, but the Merced Wild and Scenic River Comprehensive Management Plan was a different story. When plaintiffs sued over the 2000 river plan, they claimed the VERP framework wasn't adequate to protect river-related resources. In 2003 and 2004, the United States Court of Appeals for the Ninth Circuit agreed, and told the Park Service to rewrite the plan and improve their approach to user capacity.

The VERP program for the Valley and the Merced River was supposed to be operational by 2005, but very little work had been done on the program when I joined the team in 2004. Because the Park

Service's highest priority was to satisfy the courts at that time, efforts focused on the Merced River corridor where it ran through the Valley. In the future, the Park Service planned to expand the VERP program to other park areas.

The task before us was huge and complex. In a perfect world, a user capacity program would be based on clearly defined relationships among all types and levels of park use, and the impacts of such use on resources. The information required to define such relationships precisely, however, is very difficult to obtain. Pertinent questions include: How many people can picnic on a river bank before the river bank is damaged? What constitutes damage? How many people can picnic on that river bank at one time and still allow everyone present to have a high quality experience? What constitutes a "high quality experience?"

Two large hurdles arose immediately: We lacked the scientific and technical data needed to accurately link visitor activities and resource impacts, and many of the definitions we sought were highly subjective. For this reason, VERP had to be an open-ended and ongoing process. As the park generated more data every year about resources and the impacts of use, the program could be modified to reflect the new information.

We began by evaluating existing information on park resources, visitation levels, and the ways in which resources and the experience of visitors could be degraded. Then we attempted to identify the variables of concern, but found the number of elements related to natural and cultural resources, and the qualities that contribute to visitor satisfaction, seemed endless. What should the Park Service measure—aquatic insects, mosquitoes, deer, bears, lichens, oak trees, clean air, dark night skies, clean restrooms, solitude? We lacked the unlimited time and money required to monitor every element on the list, so we had to identify a subset that represented all the resources and all the attributes of a quality experience. VERP referred to these representatives as "indicators."

To ensure we considered all possible indicators, and selected a truly representative subset, we conducted a brainstorming workshop. A multi-disciplinary group of scientists, resource managers, wilderness managers, VERP experts, naturalists, and administrators convened for two days and identified dozens of potential indicators, such as water quality, abundance of litter, soil erosion, vegetation loss, and number of unplanned, or social, trails in the Valley. The initial list had about sixty attributes that could be measured to see whether conditions were deteriorating, staying the same, or improving. By the end of the workshop, the group produced a refined list of characteristics to be measured.

The next step involved determining desired conditions, or standards, for each indicator. This task required decisions on how much resource damage or deterioration, and how much crowding, was acceptable.

All park use has an impact. Everyone who drives, or even walks, into Yosemite affects the park. Our cars emit pollutants, we eat food brought in by trucks emitting diesel fumes, we use bathrooms and leave waste behind, we walk on meadow grasses, and our presence affects wildlife behavior. To maintain the park in a truly unimpaired condition, the Park Service would have to close the gates and walk away. Clearly, this alternative is not acceptable, nor does it comply with the purpose of the parks: to allow use without damaging resources.

Some damage to resources is inevitable, but the Park Service faces a difficult challenge. The agency must decide how much damage and degradation is acceptable; they must specify standards of quality for each indicator. If standards are exceeded, managers must stop further deterioration, take steps to reverse the trend, and improve resource conditions. For example, if stream bank vegetation is an indicator, the standard might be loss of no more than 10% of native vegetation in any one area. Once loss exceeds 10%, a management action to reduce impacts, such as fencing, would be implemented.

Ultimately, because so much of the program involved subjective criteria, the quality of Yosemite's VERP program required a strong commitment from upper-level managers to protect resources and the quality of the visitor experience.

A few weeks after the workshop, the park's level of commitment was made painfully clear. Park managers announced that no money would be forthcoming to implement Yosemite's VERP program. The plan developed by the VERP team had to be implemented by existing, already overworked, staff. In response to this directive, the original list of indicators was whittled down until it became almost meaningless, grossly inadequate for understanding, measuring, or limiting impacts on resources or the quality of the visitor experience.

In late winter of 2004, a new Chief of Resource Management entered on duty. At our first meeting, my new boss walked into my office, told me there was no more money available to support my position, and said I needed to move my stuff out soon because she was moving in.

I was stunned. She'd been on the job less than a month, yet she was laying me off. I believe she was concerned about her budget, but I also believe funding for my job "went away" because once again I was too outspoken in my defense of park resources. I had been a thorn in the side of park managers since I started work a little over a year earlier. My suspicions were confirmed as I watched numerous new positions open up in the Resource Management Division, including a position that focused on VERP.

The message was clear: This Lorax was not welcome in Yosemite.

CHAPTER 18
The Hidden Costs of Flushing

Journal

I met a friend for lunch today at Curry Village. After we parted, I took a cross-country route home, following the river where it fronted Lower Pines Campground. Many campsites near the river had been closed because of their susceptibility to flooding and to protect the riverbank, so there were few people around.

As I approached the river, my passage was blocked by a fresh streamer of yellow police tape cordoning off a section of the campground. The tape stated the area was closed. A sign tacked to a tree near the river's edge explained the closure:

CAUTION
THERE HAS BEEN A SEWAGE SPILL UPSTREAM FROM THIS SITE. SWIMMING OR OTHER WATER ACTIVITIES ARE PROHIBITED.

I saw four identical signs posted farther down river, all dated June 6, 2005—two days earlier. As I continued my walk downstream, a mother merganser and her eight downy chicks floated silently past me on a slow green current. A shame they couldn't read.

My liaison position was a "term" appointment, which meant Yosemite, or any other Park Service unit, could retain me for up to four years. Since Yosemite couldn't afford me, and I'd only worked a bit over one year, I sought and found continued employment outside of Yosemite. For the next two years, I worked on an Environmental Impact Statement for Point Reyes' *General Management Plan*, and wrote parts of a natural resource inventory and monitoring plan for four parks: Sequoia, Kings Canyon, Devil's Postpile, and Yosemite. I worked part-time from home, so my schedule left me plenty of time to watch the Park Service continue its destructive behavior: bulldozing meadows and forests, pouring new cement on old native soil, and fighting "radical environmentalists."

One chilly fall morning, I set out to investigate a friend's report of a construction snafu affecting the Merced River near the permanent tent camp called Housekeeping. As I walked through Yosemite Village, a young girl, maybe four or five years old, caught my attention. Long, shimmering blonde hair danced across the back of her powder blue down jacket as she ran in circles, chasing bright yellow big-leaf maple leaves drifting down from branches overhead. Shrieking with joy, she'd snatch a leaf from the air before it could touch the ground, then turn and dash off in a different direction to catch another slowly-spiraling golden star. I was deeply impressed by her complete focus on the moment, on the simple pleasure afforded by autumn.

I continued through the Village and the Camp 6 parking lot, then struck out for the river, traversing several low ridges and swales covered with sand and dotted with sedges and rushes. As my eyes swept across the river, the fall palette—gold, red, brown, and gray leaves on tawny sand, dark brown oak trunks and branches intermixed with deep green conifer foliage, and yellow-green sedge tufts—was interrupted by unnatural jolts of bright neon orange.

The disruption was a network of plastic construction fencing that surrounded a massive trench, several feet deep and one hundred feet or so wide. The hideous gouge began on the far side of the river and extended about halfway across the active channel. A front-end loader perched on a rise of sand in the middle of the river bed. I rock-hopped and waded across the languid river, and approached the loader. Beneath the belly of the beast, small pools of oily fluid congealed on the sand.

The trench was part of another of the Top 15+2 projects: the East Valley Utilities Improvement Project, a massive upgrade of the network of lines and pipes that conveyed utility services into, around, and out of, the Valley. The project's price tag: approximately $75 million.

Prior to the 1860s, Yosemite Valley didn't have, and didn't need, utilities. River, creeks, and springs provided water, wood provided heat. But Euro-American tourists and their keepers felt these basics were not enough, and they were driven to establish communication, power generation, and water conveyance systems. The first telephone lines in the Valley appeared in 1892, and a power plant began generating electricity at Happy Isles in 1902. These services were luxuries, not essential to a Valley visit. On the other hand, once the number of visitors started to climb, the dilemma of human waste disposal became extremely onerous and required resolution.

In 1901, a tent camp called Camp Lost Arrow was established near the base of Yosemite Falls. Yosemite Creek served as the camp's sewer system. When the creek dried up in summer, the camp closed. In 1905, when oversight of the Valley fell to the military, U.S. Army personnel were shocked by the lack of sanitary facilities. They closed several campgrounds and tried, without success, to close Camp Curry. In 1912, the Sentinel Hotel, located in the Old Village northeast of the chapel, had a sewer system, but it was inadequate and the river downstream was badly polluted. In 1914, eighty water closets served Valley campgrounds. When visitation swelled to over 25,000 people in 1917, the human waste issue could no longer be ignored. In response, in the early 1920s, the Park Service constructed a main trunk sewer and a treatment and disposal plant in the Valley. A new sewage treatment plant was built in El Portal in the mid- to late-1970s, and pipelines finally went in to convey untreated waste out of Yosemite Valley.

By the end of the twentieth century, the wastewater system carried up to 1 million gallons out of Yosemite Valley per day. The system needed frequent repairs. Corroded pipes surfaced in stream beds and leaked sewage when pipes failed. During the 1997 flood, approximately 2 million gallons of raw sewage spilled into the Merced River. Between April and October of 1999, when crews tried to fix the main sewer line and repair the flood-damaged El Portal Road, about 57,250 gallons of sewage entered the river in 9 separate incidents. Smaller spills occurred during flow tests of repaired line segments. During a July 2000 test, about 200,000 gallons of raw sewage mixed with fresh water flowed into the river. Seven additional spills, each from 200 to 7,000 gallons, occurred between April 1998 and June 2000 when grease and trash clogged sewer lines.

In August of 2000, Yosemite received a Cleanup and Abatement Order from the Water Quality Control Board listing numerous sewage discharge violations, many of which were deemed preventable. The Board threatened to levy significant fines for future spills caused by mismanagement, and for failure to submit timely reports and notification of tests.

To address the damaged and antiquated parts of the Valley's wastewater system, the Park Service decided to overhaul all Valley utilities—sewer, water, electricity, and communications—in one massive project. Plans called for consolidation of all utility lines into a series of large trenches running the length of the east Valley from above Happy Isles to Yosemite Lodge. I inferred from project maps that the new utility corridors would cover at least six miles. Numerous new sewage lift stations and electric transformers were required to keep the utilities operating.

The Park Service presented the massive project in a rosy light. The trenches housing the new utilities, they said, would be no more than twenty-six feet wide. But, a 100-foot wide corridor would be directly disturbed by construction, and the width of the disturbed area would increase to 150 feet at river and creek crossings. Planning documents stated over 90 percent of the corridors occurred along existing or proposed paved roads and trails or existing utility lines, leading readers to believe the impacts would be insignificant because most corridors were already disturbed and developed. Once again, though, there was a caveat; in many places, the Park Service claimed the project "could" result in some additional disturbance adjacent to the existing lines.

As part of the project, many old utility lines would be abandoned. Some of these crossed meadows, creeks, and the river. Some abandoned lines would be burst and left in place, and some would be removed. Reducing the threat of sewage spills and the need for line repair work in these sensitive habitats would benefit resources, but line removal also had substantial adverse effects.

Despite Park Service efforts to highlight the advantages of the project and downplay the impacts, portions of the new corridors would cross relatively undisturbed, high quality meadows, wetlands, and oak woodlands. Tremendous impacts on soils, water, air, wildlife, and cultural resources, as well as noise, road closures, and other disruptions were unavoidable.

Despite the project's massive scale and huge potential for causing adverse impacts, the Park Service prepared an Environmental Assessment, not an Environmental Impact Statement. Park managers received public comments encouraging them to prepare the latter, more detailed document, but the suggestions were ignored. True to form, the Park Service analyzed only two action alternatives in the Environmental Assessment, and the primary difference between the two was where the new corridor would cross the Merced River. Once again, it seemed as if Yosemite's managers cut corners to accelerate the planning process, to facilitate implementation of their favored alternative, and to avoid the complexity of a legitimate public involvement process.

When I reviewed the draft Environmental Assessment, one major issue jumped out: construction of the new corridor across the Merced River and Yosemite Creek. When flows were low, construction workers planned to divert the water, and carve out a 150-foot wide, 3-foot deep trench across bed and banks to emplace the pipelines. My experience with major interstate pipelines led me to believe there was a better way. As I understood it, the least environmentally damaging method for spanning a river or creek was a directional bore, not a trench. The bore drilled the corridor under the river bed, leaving the bed and banks relatively undisturbed.

I asked project managers if directional boring had been considered.

"We've looked into it. It's cost-prohibitive. And too difficult to do in this type of rocky substrate," they answered.

Yosemite had over $30 million to upgrade Yosemite Lodge, and almost $14 million for the Lower Yosemite Fall project. The utilities project budget was more than $75 million, which included the required sewage system repairs. But directional bores that would substantially reduce impacts to the Merced River and Yosemite Creek were considered too expensive.

I learned later that at the water crossings, the bundled utility lines would be buried about eight inches below the riverbed's surface, encased in a giant cement box extending from bank to bank; an effort to flood-proof the system. A directional bore wouldn't accommodate such a structure; the utilities required an open trench for their burial. I never saw reference to the cement containment structures in the Environmental Assessment, or any disclosure of their impacts.

The effects of the giant buried tombs will be significant and long-term because they form underground dams and alter subsurface flow. These hydrological changes will persist as long as the structures are in place.

The Environmental Assessment failed to accurately present project impacts on many natural and cultural resources. For example, the Park Service claimed the preferred alternative would result in "local, short to long-term, moderate to major adverse impacts on highly valued soils." Soils in and near meadows and riparian areas, in wetlands, and associated with glacial moraines are considered "highly valued" because they have potential to support important plant communities, are protected by federal law, or are otherwise sensitive. The description of impacts on these soils was accurate; but, later in the same paragraph, the assessment said these impacts would really only be short-term and minor, because they'd be mitigated by soil protection measures. Mitigation measures included promises to minimize chemical, fuel, or oils spills, soil compaction, and soil erosion; to salvage and replace disturbed soil; and to use trench plugs to minimize changes to subsurface flows.

What was lost in this discussion was the fact that mitigation would *not* protect soils. It was easy to say spills, compaction, and erosion would be minimized, but these impacts could not be avoided in this type of major construction project. This was clearly illustrated by the construction equipment that leaked fluids into both the Merced River and Yosemite Creek. In most construction situations, contractors place absorbent pads under equipment parked in sensitive areas to capture leakage; such pads were not used in Yosemite Valley. In addition, the negative effects of the project were worsened because construction of the Merced River crossing proved much more difficult than anticipated.

Heavy equipment sat in the riverbed for weeks while project engineers scratched their heads.

The Environmental Assessment went on to state soils would be salvaged, stored, and replaced. While these actions sound good, they don't protect soils. When soils are disturbed or removed from their place of origin, the soil profile—the naturally-occurring layers that form over time—is disrupted. The layers become mixed, and the integrity of the soil is destroyed. Many Valley soils have poorly developed profiles because they are young, repeatedly washed and re-washed by floodwaters, but they do have significant amounts of organic matter in their upper layers, which is a critical component of soil fertility. This organic matter comes from decomposing pine needles, oak leaves, grasses and other dead plant material. Minerals and nutrients released from the decomposing vegetation are carried down into the soil by rainwater, and become available to plant roots. When surface layers of soils are pulverized by vehicle traffic or removed to allow pipeline burial, the organic matter mixes with other soil layers, and the natural processes of decomposition and nutrient leaching are disrupted.

Impacts on soils affect more than just soils. The damage affects organisms living in the soil, plants growing on the soil, and wildlife that uses those plants for food or shelter. Damage to soils increases the likelihood that pollutants will enter the river and creeks. The utilities project, as planned, would adversely affect approximately 215 acres of Valley soils. Damage to soils is irreversible in our lifetimes, and many lifetimes to come.

The Environmental Assessment for the utilities project was 280 pages long, with another 165 pages of attached documents and appendices, plus an Executive Summary. The Park Service received only twenty-one comment letters in response to the draft assessment, which illustrated most people either did not know about the project or did not have time to review the document. One comment, however, submitted by "Tribal Organization, Mariposa, California" summed it up accurately and succinctly: "The Utility Improvement Plan will be the most destructive Project in Yosemite since the 1997 High Water Flood and it is the responsibility of all who love Yosemite to minimize the ground disturbance and rethink where the utilities should be placed without disturbing virgin soil and riparian zones."

To make matters even worse, the utilities project was overkill from the very beginning. The Park Service stated in the Environmental Assessment that most of the utilities in the Valley were "currently in adequate condition."

It was early morning. A strong, cool, west wind pulled oak and maple leaves from drying branches, then sent them spiraling high into the air against a backdrop of blue, white, and steel gray. Kaleidoscopic clouds drifted overhead, some dark and brooding, threatening showers, others light and wispy, hinting of clear skies to come.

The Soul of Yosemite

The few people out and about were bundled like fluffy caterpillars against the changing weather and enjoying the unusual peace and quiet. It was Saturday. For the most part, construction workers stayed home on weekends, and the tour buses stuffed with day users hadn't yet arrived.

I jogged across the Valley and behind the chapel, west to the base of the Four Mile Trail, and then back to the Swinging Bridge, which spanned the Merced River southwest of Yosemite Lodge. I crossed over a very slow, almost waterless river, and followed the paved bike path. Leaving pavement, a dirt foot trail carried me east in a contour around the meandering river toward the lodge. A light breeze sifted through ponderosa pine branches overhead, and a fat ground squirrel took a dirt bath behind the block of lodge rooms known as Hemlock. As I left the lodge and headed toward the almost dry Yosemite Falls, the peaceful morning was interrupted by a deep, surly whine.

I veered toward the noise and found the source: a generator parked right in the middle of Yosemite Creek. The creek was sluggish, poised between the dry of late summer and the wet of autumn, but water still flowed. The generator powered a large mobile pump, and these two pieces of equipment were parked within a 100-foot wide swath of destruction—a piece of the new utility corridor.

The pump pulled water from Yosemite Creek twenty-four hours a day, seven days a week, so contractors could dig the trench, build the cement box to house the lines, and then bury the tomb under the creek.

The mosaic of rock, cobble, and sand that once framed and anchored the creek bed sat in large piles, pushed off to the side to make way for the trench diggers. Fragments of grass and sedge, as well as roots, stems, and leaves of small trees formerly growing on the banks poked out of the piles at random angles, crushed and battered. The trench ran from bank to bank, a razor cut across a swollen vein in an unsuspecting wrist. The water was an inconvenience. It hindered construction, so they brought in a pump and removed it, draining Yosemite Creek's lifeblood.

I left Yosemite Creek with a heavy heart and followed the swath of destruction east. It cut like a highway through conifer and oak forest before hitting Cook's Meadow, where a 100-foot wide avenue of bare meadow soil sat exposed to the late morning sun, like skin cut and peeled back before surgery. The soil was dark brown, rich with organic matter. The meadow vegetation that formerly covered the ground, as well as the soil matrix, sat in piles at the edge of the cut. The construction equipment had blasted everything in its path.

Utilities maps reveal the stunning magnitude of the pipeline network hiding just beneath the Valley's surface. Every toilet, showerhead, and faucet must be connected to a sewage conveyance system, every light switch must be connected to an electrical grid, and every phone booth must be connected to a communication network. The lines look like a diagram of blood vessels in the human body, running almost everywhere. And every single one of those lines disrupts the Valley's natural environment.

The scale of the utility system required, however, is wholly dependent on the number of people in the Valley, their real or perceived needs, and the amount and distribution of Valley infrastructure. A re-examination and subsequent reduction in all three of these elements—numbers, needs, and infrastructure—would result in a reduction in the utility system and its impacts.

The horrific impacts associated with the Utilities Improvement Project were unique, different from those of the Curry dorms or the Lower Yosemite Fall project. Unlike a building or a road, the visual environmental effects of the utility lines will largely disappear from view in a few decades. Most people will never know that thousands of grasses, sedges, bracken ferns, and wild raspberries, as well as young black oaks, ponderosa pines, and incense-cedars, were uprooted and shoved aside so people could flush toilets, call home, turn on a light, microwave a cup of coffee, and wash their hands in warm water. In fact, as soon as workers pushed the rock and cobble back into streambeds, re-filled the trench with soil, and removed pumps and equipment, the project largely disappeared, and only a discerning eye could detect the changes: damage to creek bed and banks, disruption of soil, and a lack of shrubs or trees in the corridor over the buried lines. And no one will see the more insidious, long-term damage that continues as the underground flow of water through Yosemite Valley is altered by the new, invisible dams.

For the time being, utilities, at least those that carry sewage out of the Valley, are necessary. But it's important to understand and acknowledge the impacts of the utility system, even if those impacts are invisible, perhaps especially *because* they are invisible.

As we envision Yosemite Valley's future, let's consider the young blond girl I saw in Yosemite Village. Her joyous experience was not derived from infrastructure or utilities; it came solely from nature, from giant golden leaves, clean, cool air, and a forever blue sky.

Let's remember to keep our eyes on the prize.

CHAPTER 19
Troubled Waters

Journal

The spring flood is here! Flows may peak tonight. The bike path between the Lodge and Swinging Bridge is under several feet of water. The river ripples toward guest rooms in the Hemlock building. Like dark green swamp water in the South, it moves slowly, weaving itself around trunks of cottonwoods, willows, and alders.

Tom and I walk the bike path near dusk, when the water rises to its highest point in the daily cycle, wading barefoot and bare-legged through icy snowmelt, accompanied by the deep thunder of Yosemite Falls. Full to bursting, a celebration of sparkling white, the waterfalls seem joyous in their fullness, like carnival dancers, or wild animals at play.

The energy is palpable. The air pulses with the motion of water in freefall.

◆◆◆

Between early 2004 and late 2005, I explored the eastern part of Yosemite Valley from end to end, and came upon numerous hidden treasures: small rivulets running along cracks in vertical granite walls; dark, scat-filled bear dens in rock caves perched on steep slopes; and lichen-covered granite slabs tucked among groves of canyon live oak. I walked the Valley's trails and roads, as well as places without such easy access, and immersed myself in the day-to-day lives of the Valley's more-than-human inhabitants, both living and non-living.

When weather kept me inside, I visited the park's research library, and dug up information on past and present conditions in the Valley. The hours I spent poring over documents gave me a much deeper understanding of just how much the Valley had changed over time. The more I learned, the more I became convinced the Valley's ecological web had been seriously fragmented by human activities. I feared the changes were irreversible, and wondered if the Valley had reached an ecological tipping point. I investigated several components of Valley ecology, starting with the Valley's lifeblood: water.

In late March of 2003, I walked a section of the Valley Loop Trail between Lower Yosemite Fall bridge and Church Bowl, a picnic area north of Ahwahnee Meadow. The air was balmy. The trail wound through pine and oak forests and traversed old rock fall zones. Less than a mile past the Lower Fall, I crossed Indian Creek on a small foot bridge, and sat down on a large rock. The ground was covered with sharp-tipped live oak leaves, acorns minus their knobby caps, and small bits of gray granite. Oak seedlings struggled to gain a foothold in the thin soil. Delicate pink flowers that looked like pale up-side-down urns dangled from branches of Mariposa manzanita.

The creek bed was narrow, about fifteen feet wide, but the water flowed with sparkle and abandon, dashing around rocks and downed branches. Across the creek, a narrow waterfall dropped twenty feet straight down between two huge boulders; its voice drowned out all human sounds.

Indian Creek had started flowing just the day before. Two days earlier it was completely dry. The creek is a product of snowmelt; it only flows when a critical mass of icy water comes together and rushes down from the rocky gorge above. Its seasonal run starts at a slightly different time every year.

I left the creek and continued east, dropping into Church Bowl. My senses were assailed by sunlight reflecting off a piece of aluminum foil, the odor of three port-a-potties, parked and moving cars, a multitude of signs, a paved bike path, and a road that connected Yosemite Village and the Ahwahnee Hotel. Shallow sheets of flowing water covered the picnic area, bike path, and road.

This area floods almost every year, when rapidly melting high country snow sends huge volumes of water into the Valley. The flows fan out when they hit the Valley bottom, and the water slowly makes its way to the meadow to nurture deergrass, Queen Anne's lace, goldenrod, shooting stars, oak trees, coyotes, mule deer, and spiders, among others.

The bike path and road obstruct the water's flow. Oil, rubber particles, transmission fluid, coolant, and who knows what else, contaminate the water as it flows over the asphalt. Although the road separates Ahwahnee Meadow and Church Bowl, meadow grasses shoot up through the compacted soil of the picnic area, a telltale sign that the road and picnic area edge are not near the meadow—they are in it.

Water problems like those at Church Bowl occur throughout the Valley. The hydrologic systems, the natural flows of water into, through, and out of the Valley, have been abused almost non-stop since the mid-1850s.

In 1978, James F. Milestone, a Master of Arts student at San Francisco State University, authored a thesis titled *The Influence of Modern Man on the Stream System of Yosemite Valley*. Milestone presented early descriptions of Valley hydrology that paint a picture radically different from what exists today. In 1866, according to State Geologist J.D. Whitney, the Merced River made "many sharp and curiously angular bends, touching the talus first on one side then on the other." The river meandered back and forth across the entire Valley. More recent studies of abandoned river features such as oxbows and terraces indicate the system once was an interwoven series of braided channels. Except during floods, one channel now largely confines the river. Today's channel changes from year to year because of erosion and deposition of sediment and woody debris, but doesn't undergo major shifts in location.

Whitney also described a much wetter Yosemite Valley. Meadows were "swampy," with "deep peaty soil." "Sloughs and swamps" occurred where river banks were low. Milestone asserted the swampy conditions were related to physical barriers that impeded surface water drainage out of the Valley. Chief among these was an accessional moraine, a ridge of boulders and rocks left behind when glaciers retreated approximately 40,000 years ago. The moraine, together with rock and sediment that fell from Valley walls, dammed the waters just below El Capitan Meadow. A lake formed behind the dam when the glaciers retreated. Over time, river water filled the lake with sediments, leading to a relatively level, swampy valley floor.

Early accounts reported numerous logjams, which further affected river behavior and probably contributed to swampy conditions. Logjams start when fallen trees float downstream and run aground, or catch on a rock or protruding bank. Over time, particularly during floods, leaves, branches, sediment, rocks, and more logs pile up around the first log. The logjam serves as a natural dam, and water diverts around it, backing up and flowing into adjacent low-lying areas, or cutting into and eroding river banks.

The widely meandering river and swampy meadows created and supported the Valley's unique ecological conditions; but these natural features caused problems when construction of buildings and roads became a priority. According to Milestone, the Board of Commissioners appointed by the State of California to manage Yosemite Valley viewed the Merced and its tributaries as threats, with great potential to impair visitor access and facilities. Their views weren't surprising, since significant winter floods occurred in 1864, 1867, and 1871. Despite the Valley's propensity to flood, development continued, and the Commission tried hard to mitigate the threat posed by the river.

In 1879, Galen Clark, the Valley's state-appointed "guardian," wanted to improve livestock grazing, increase visitor access, and reduce mosquito numbers, so he blew up the El Capitan moraine and leveled the residual rock to increase water flow out of the Valley. This event reduced the moraine's height by four to nine feet. Recent studies indicated the demolition lowered water tables and accelerated riverbed erosion between El Capitan Meadow and Yosemite Lodge, which reduced water available for vegetation and wildlife, and ultimately changed the mosaic of plant communities across the Valley floor.

Starting in the early 1880s, park workers used additional methods to control water. They removed logjams; tried to stop bank erosion by placement of willow cuttings, heavy rocks, and dirt; and dammed and dredged Mirror Lake, increasing its size six-fold. In the late 1880s, the first rip rap revetment—large piles of boulders that armored against the action of river flows—was layered on the Merced's bank to protect a large sugar pine, deemed the "largest and handsomest tree in the valley." The tree still stands immediately downriver of the Sugar Pine Bridge on the northeast bank. Eventually, rip rap covered over 3.5 linear miles of the Valley's river banks. Milestone asserts if one stacked up all rip rap in the Valley, the column would be taller than the 14,495-foot Mt. Whitney.

In 1885, despite all these efforts to "manage" the Valley's water, the Commission stated, "[S]erious damage has befallen Yosemite Valley and more serious damage threatens if the watercourse remains ungoverned." The following year, the Commission declared Yosemite's streams had to be "attended to, cleared out, trained, and regulated."

The Commission's views created an interesting paradox. The river that was perceived as such a threat to the Valley was, in fact, the same river that created and sustained the natural masterpiece.

In 1890, the tone of the Commissioners' reports shifted, perhaps in response to the transfer of the Valley from the state back to the federal government. Future river work, the reports stated, should "molest nature as little as possible, but should protect her works against the too energetic exertion of her own forces."

By 1892, the Valley supported over twenty miles of roads, six bridges, twelve culverts, and twenty-four miles of equestrian trails. Each of these "molestations," as well as lodging facilities and rudimentary camping areas, altered the natural flow of Yosemite's water. In 1899, the Commissioners went so far as to suggest a dam be built on Yosemite Creek above Yosemite Falls to maintain flows all year. Thankfully, this never happened.

In 1916, the National Park Service was created to conserve park resources, but water management practices established by the Yosemite Commission set the stage in the Valley, and the Park Service stayed the course. Between 1928 and 1938, the Civilian Conservation Corps, created after the Depression, completed extensive stream control work, including bank revetment, channel clearing, dam building, pipe laying, and bridge construction. Logjams were removed, large reaches of undercut bank were re-sloped and re-vegetated, and river gravel was excavated to create reflecting pools. At the time, landscape architects were making decisions in the Valley, with a focus on creating an aesthetically appealing landscape, instead of allowing natural systems to operate.

In his thesis, Milestone documented thirty-eight bridges and fourteen dams in the Valley. Seven large stone bridges—Ahwahnee, Sugar Pine, Clark's, Tenaya Creek, Pohono, El Capitan, and Stoneman—were built in the late 1920s and early 1930s. Many of the bridges are too narrow for the amount of water that travels the channels they span, and they constrict river flow during high water. Water speeds up between the bridge footings and scours a deep pond just downstream of the bridge. When the water slows again, it drops sediment and forms a gravel bar a bit farther downstream.

The narrow bridges also create secondary channels when water flows around the footings. This increases the likelihood of logjams, which further alter flow patterns. Of the seven major bridges, Sugar Pine Bridge constricts flow the most, having a width of approximately 98 feet and a natural channel width of about 187 feet.

Numerous dams, created both intentionally and unintentionally, also significantly altered river and creek flows. Rock dams were built on Yosemite Creek to prevent damage to Yosemite Lodge and employee housing from flooding and frazil ice flows. Ten dams were created inadvertently with water pipelines. In places where six- to eight-inch diameter cast iron pipes emerged from a bank and spanned the river bottom, rocks were piled over the pipes to protect them. The effects of one of these "dams" can be seen just upriver from Superintendent's Bridge, where an old pipe creates a reservoir extending almost to Sentinel Bridge. This area supports a large reflecting pool that freezes in winter; neither the pool nor the freezing would occur without the pipe dam.

As Valley development continued, the Merced River and its tributaries provided a ready source of building material. Park records showed 7,388 cubic yards of sand and 12,769 cubic yards of gravel were removed from Valley waterways between 1877 and 1977. Additionally, 3,337 cubic yards of rock masonry and cement blocks were put into the river. These records are incomplete, and don't include gravel taken from the riverbed for concrete construction. Bridges, warehouses, and the Ahwahnee Hotel were constructed from river gravel, and miles of Valley roads were elevated with river gravel to reduce the chance of flood damage.

Application of rip rap, dam construction, and dredging continued into the mid-1960s. These efforts largely confined Yosemite Creek, Tenaya Creek, and the Merced River to single channels. This protected park infrastructure, some of the time. Simultaneously, these actions completely destroyed the elegant braided stream channel that watered the lush Valley for thousands of years prior to the arrival of Euro-Americans.

Unfortunately, mindless disruption of Valley hydrology continues. The 1997 flood destroyed Camp 6, an employee housing area near Yosemite Village. The site, a tired residential area of canvas cabins, was far from pristine before the flood. Native plants, soils, and overall ecological integrity were seriously degraded, but the area retained high ecological value. Nestled in a bend of the Merced River, it was surrounded on three sides by channels, oxbows, and wetlands that were inundated during periods of high flow. The 1997 flood gave the Park Service an opportunity to restore natural conditions in these critical riverine arteries. Instead of restoring the area, though, the

Park Service established a "temporary" dirt parking lot at Camp 6 to accommodate over 550 vehicles.

The 2000 *Yosemite Valley Plan Supplemental Environmental Impact Statement* proposed to upgrade the Camp 6 parking lot. The plan acknowledged the lot would flood, and that its presence could impede river migration, hinder development of natural channels, accelerate erosion when asphalt was washed downriver, and reduce riverbank stability. Then the document concluded the parking lot "could" result in localized, long-term, moderate, adverse impacts on hydrology and floodplain values. Despite the substantial impacts, and the ecological importance of the site, the Park Service decided to "formalize" the dirt parking lot. In other words, they paved it.

In addition to physical manipulation, Yosemite Valley's waters have been routinely polluted. In the early days of tourism, primary pollutants included raw sewage and waste water. More recently, lead, cadmium, and mercury have been detected in the Merced River at levels above drinking water and freshwater standards.

Rain, melting snow, and floodwater flowing over paved surfaces in the Valley pick up oil, grease, rubber particles, metals, litter, and other road detritus. A small portion of runoff from Valley parking lots is diverted into wastewater drains and then treated at the El Portal plant, but large volumes of runoff discharge directly into the river and creeks.

Water quality also is degraded and habitat is damaged by extensive, concentrated visitor use along the river and creeks. Visitors trample bank vegetation to dust, and the banks erode more rapidly without plants and roots to hold them together. Water cuts at the banks and channels widen. Adjacent wetlands, riparian areas, and meadows, all very important to wildlife, are reduced in size or lost. Water temperatures increase as shade-producing riparian vegetation disappears, and the amount of dissolved oxygen in the water, critical to aquatic life, declines because of a shallower river and warmer water.

One bright summer morning, I noticed park maintenance employees hard at work ripping up the southern part of Schoolyard

Meadow with a front end loader. They were creating a swale to capture wastewater.

The previous winter, heavy rain carried hundreds, perhaps thousands, of gallons of water mixed with oil, manure, plastic, and other human debris into the elementary school playground just east of the meadow. The toxic stew washed down from the nearby government maintenance yard, which also housed a fire station, gas station, search and rescue base, dog kennel, stables, and offices. The yard was used extensively for storage as well. While we were there, it sported giant garbage dumpsters overflowing with items like old cooking ranges and washing machines, an herbicide tank sprayer on a trailer, a front end loader, a large piece of equipment designed to lift giant logs, a broken helicopter cockpit, piles of pipes, stacks of split rails, a battered white dump truck, utility trucks, and impounded and crashed vehicles. The yard's nickname was the "boneyard."

Runoff from the yard ran into the playground because a culvert failed. To solve the problem, the Park Service buried a new culvert under the playground to carry the runoff away from the children. The swale under construction, an oval hole about 120 feet long, 10 feet wide, and 3 to 4 feet deep, was being excavated to receive the toxic brew at the culvert's terminus, where the liquid would flow out and soak into the soil. The west end of the swale was only about 100 feet from Yosemite Creek.

The Yosemite Valley Plan called for removal of the maintenance area, stables, gas pumps, and offices that were the source of the pollutants, but the Park Service had taken no action to accomplish the removal and clean-up. At a minimum, this toxic runoff should have been piped into the Valley's new sewage system and conveyed out of the Valley.

According to the *Yosemite Valley Plan Supplemental Environmental Impact Statement*, park managers consider meadows "highly valued resources." But Schoolyard Meadow was used as a toxic dump. During a subsequent visit to the Valley in 2008, I watched park workers erect a solid wood fence around the swale, most likely to keep children or wildlife from falling in.

In addition to diverting and polluting, humans also usurp a tremendous amount of the Valley's water for domestic purposes, including toilets, washing, cooking, laundry, cleaning, and lawn watering. Groundwater wells and a 2.5 million gallon water storage tank ensure an uninterrupted supply. The wells can provide about 1,400 gallons per minute, or over 2 million gallons per day. On busy days, up to 1 million gallons of water are extracted, used, and flushed into the wastewater system.

It's difficult to characterize or quantify the impacts of water extraction on Valley resources, but it's safe to assume other Valley water users, namely plants and animals, are adversely affected. It's also obvious the effects are more severe during dry seasons and periods of drought.

Like the underground utilities, just because we can't see or quantify precisely the impacts of water extraction doesn't mean they don't exist, or are inconsequential.

CHAPTER 20
Burned, Trampled, Grazed, Plowed, and Bulldozed

Journal

It's mid-morning. The sun warms my back as I bend over to grab another plant. A rosette of large, pale green, velvety leaves encircles the base of the thick, fleshy stem. A single, central stalk with scattered smaller leaves along its length emerges from the rosette, and reaches skyward to a height of about four feet. Tiny flower buds line the upper portion of the stalk. This is the perfect time to pull, before flowers and seeds mature. I reach for the base, as close as possible to the roots, and pull. The mullein doesn't come easily from the sandy loam soil. I pull again, harder, and the plant releases its hold.

A few dozen mullein plants grew here last year; slightly fewer appeared this year. If no one pulls them, the mullein, which was introduced to the Valley by humans, becomes more abundant and spreads. My morning routine includes pulling several each day until they're gone from the small meadow near Yosemite Creek, a few hundred yards from our house.

I straighten up to stretch my tired back and notice a mule deer standing about fifteen feet away, watching me. She doesn't run; instead she looks at me as if to say, "Are you going to eat those plants or just leave them lying around? I nod a greeting and continue pulling. She moves off to graze on more succulent-looking grass.

♦♦♦

Visitors rarely came to Schoolyard Meadow, which flanks Yosemite Creek. But I walked by or through it almost every day, witnessing its transformations. In response to the lengthening days of spring, sharp-pointed, neon green grass tips shot up through a tan mat of past year's growth. Summer brought waxy-looking, pink milkweed flowers adorned with small, black, green, and brown metallic beetles. Autumn's sharp chill turned giant swards of fine-leaved deergrass a glorious golden brown. And winter laid patchy, rumpled blankets of snow over everything.

The meadow exists by virtue of Yosemite Creek, which nurtures and sustains it year after year. It's a small meadow, a few acres at most, bounded by the creek to the west, mixed conifer and oak woodland to the south, and a neighborhood and school playground to the east and north. Deer, coyotes, voles, ravens, bears, and the occasional visitor forage, play, and bask in the meadow.

Schoolyard Meadow, like all of Yosemite Valley's meadows, supports a mix of native and non-native plant species. Of the latter, all the usual suspects are here—the invaders ubiquitous to the Valley—bull thistle, mullein, velvet grass, and a panoply of introduced forage grasses like *Poa pratensis*, also known as Kentucky bluegrass.

Most of the non-native species arrived with humans starting in the mid-1800s. Euro-American settlers brought numerous favored plants, including apples, blackberries, asparagus, and other foods; oats, bluegrass, and barley for livestock forage; and periwinkles, daffodils, and elms for their aesthetic value. Other species arrived when seeds hitchhiked in animal feed or manure, on socks, or mixed with mud encrusted on vehicle tires. Many of the non-natives survived and thrived. Hardy and adaptable, they out-competed the natives for growing space, sunlight, nutrients, and water. Over time, the new arrivals spread, with corresponding declines in native species.

The changes in plant communities engendered by the non-natives have a domino effect on other resources. As vegetation changes, the amount and distribution of sunlight on the Valley floor change, too, as do patterns of water movement and availability. Soil organisms, chemistry, and temperature regimes change. Wildlife species dependent on the displaced native plants for food, shelter, or nesting materials suffer. And, non-native plants in Yosemite Valley aren't limited to meadows; they grow in every plant community.

For three years, I pulled all the mullein and bull thistle I could find in Schoolyard Meadow. It took little effort, and by removing the few dozen plants, I prevented the species from spreading seed, multiplying, and setting off a chain of deleterious effects.

Vegetation in ecosystems is always in flux. Events like volcanic eruptions, fires, floods, glaciation, insect outbreaks, and shifts in wildlife populations change plant species composition, abundance, and distribution.

For most of Yosemite Valley's long history, vegetation changed when the natural environment changed. When Native Americans took up residence in the Valley approximately 4,000 to 6,000 years ago, their presence and activities changed vegetation in new ways. The native people pruned, weeded, and scattered seeds to foster growth and reproduction of favored plants. They ignited fires, sometimes annually, usually in late fall. Burning kept meadows open by killing young, encroaching trees, enhanced hunting by improving visibility and increasing forage for game, and helped desired plants establish and grow. In forests, fire consumed young trees and brush accumulations, which facilitated travel and reduced the likelihood of larger, more destructive fires. Burning conifers also favored black oak trees, thereby enhancing production of acorns, a critical staple.

For thousands of years, the mosaic of meadow, woodland, and forest in the Valley was a dynamic product of nature and culture. When Euro-Americans arrived in Yosemite Valley in the middle of the nineteenth century, their lifestyles and choices changed vegetation in still other ways—ways that are unraveling the finely woven ecological fabric of the Valley.

Many of the Euro-American's impacts were similar to those of the Native American's. Plants were removed, trampled, and used for construction, cooking, and keeping warm. Much of this damage could have been reversed, but the new settlers and early park managers did several things that irreversibly damaged the Valley's plant communities: They manipulated hydrology to dry out parts of the Valley and "control" the river and creeks; they brought in non-native plants and livestock; and they suppressed, rather than ignited, fires.

Of all the ways the Native Americans manipulated vegetation, burning had the most profound effects. The practice ceased, and naturally-ignited lightning fires were put out when the Euro-Americans took control. The effects of fire exclusion quickly became apparent. Galen Clark, the first manager of the Yosemite Grant, expressed concern in a letter to park commissioners in 1894. Clark claimed that when he'd first seen Yosemite Valley in 1855, about forty years earlier, young trees did not obstruct the views, and the meadows were four times more expansive. In the absence of fire, dense thickets of young trees, shrubs, and brush had grown up, reducing meadow size and obstructing views. At that time, Clark recognized that an accidental fire would be a "fearful menace" to people and scenery.

The National Park Service managed vegetation after assuming control of the Valley in 1916, but did so in erratic, inconsistent ways. Different superintendents had conflicting, often misguided views. Records show Ahwahnee Meadow was burned by park managers to eliminate encroaching vegetation in 1919, 1920, 1921, and 1930. The last dairy herd left the Valley in 1924, and most of the fences were removed. In 1930, both burning and grazing were banned in all meadows. Park Service activities to reduce numbers of deer, bear, rodents, and forest insects also affected vegetation.

Park managers could not have understood the far-reaching effects of their actions, but they did recognize the problems posed by non-native plants and the encroachment of trees on meadows. In 1930, managers ordered Valley residents to stop introducing non-native plants, and in 1934, thousands of small conifers and tens of thousands of non-native thistles were removed from meadows. At about the same time, though, the Civilian Conservation Corps conducted an extensive planting program around Yosemite Village. Many of the "native" plants used, such as red fir, redbud, spice bush, and wild grape, were not native to the Valley. The latter three species thrived and persisted.

The early threats to Yosemite Valley's native plants—non-natives, fire exclusion, changes in water flow and wildlife, trampling from pedestrians, destruction from livestock and automobiles, and development—continue to this day, and now these threats are further exacerbated by air pollution and climate change.

Some Valley plant communities have suffered more than others. The *Yosemite Valley Plan Supplemental Environmental Impact Statement* said 41 different vegetation types occurred in Yosemite Valley in 2000. The document identified meadow, California black oak, and riparian communities as "highly valued resources," indicating these communities would be subject to extra levels of protection. Sadly, this appellation was a euphemism for the fact that these ecologically critical plant communities were seriously imperiled, both inside and outside Yosemite Valley. The Park Service's approach to protecting these communities was inconsistent at best.

Meadows run in a discontinuous line on both sides of the Merced River in Yosemite Valley. In summer, viewed from above, they look like a necklace of large emeralds strung irregularly with beads of cottonwood, willow, and an occasional ponderosa pine. Flat and open, the meadows provide great places to take in Valley views. The meadows also are perfect for solo walks. They provide breathing room, giving one space to sort out and slow down the endless parade of thoughts marching through one's head.

I took such a walk one March morning. The sky defined blue that day, enriched by edges of silver-gray granite and the snow white plume of Yosemite Falls. I headed toward Cook's Meadow, east of the Lodge and west of Yosemite Village.

The Soul of Yosemite

Although I was solo, I wasn't alone. As I walked down Oak Lane, an acorn woodpecker's rattling call shot through the air like a bullet. A Steller's jay perched solidly on an oak branch looked at me with cocked head, leaned forward, and let out a raucous screech, followed by several short bursts of quieter chirps, as if he were speaking to me under his breath. On the far side of the road, a round-bellied robin splashed in a trailside puddle as rays of morning sun glanced off his bright yellow bill.

The perennial grasses that dominated Cook's Meadow formed a flat woven rug of tan, gold, and washed-out green. Small hummocks, swales, and four-foot tall skeletons of last year's Queen Anne's lace broke the monotony. A row of leafless cottonwoods stood at the edge between meadow and river. Evergreen Pacific mistletoe festooned the upper branches of black oaks, in bright relief against dark gray branches. Yosemite Falls roared. Unseasonable warmth had quickly melted the high country snow, and the giant white plume was as fat and full as I'd ever seen it. A raven called from a nearby pine branch, and a breeze blew hair across my eyes as I stood with face upturned to a late-winter sun. A jet droned overhead, depositing a jagged white contrail in the otherwise perfect blue sky.

I continued south, into shadows cast by a cluster of ponderosa pines that soared almost one hundred feet into the air. The breeze became wind, rattled a desiccated stalk of last summer's goldenrod, and made my eyes water. A single brown pine cone fell from high up in one of the pines, bounced off limbs as it journeyed earthward, and hit the needle-covered ground with a soft "whump." Patches of leftover snow in shade cast by the trees reminded me conditions were much different here just a few weeks ago. Change happened fast.

In May of 1949, park forester Emil Ernst published a piece in Yosemite Nature Notes called *Vanishing Meadows in Yosemite Valley*. Ernst stated that in 1866, 15 years after "the coming of the white man," meadows covered about 750 acres in Yosemite Valley. By 1927, meadows covered only 430 acres. By 1937, only 327 acres remained.

The Valley lost 56 percent of its lush, life-sustaining meadows in 71 years. In 1960, the number rose slightly to 349 because a few acres had been reclaimed. In 2000, the *Yosemite Valley Plan Supplemental Environmental Impact Statement* said the Valley had less than half of the meadow acres measured in 1866. Researchers believe the losses were, and still are, due primarily to large-scale, on-going manipulations of water linked to development, and lack of fire.

I reached the Sentinel Bridge parking area, and turned around to head back home through Cook's Meadow. The trail was paved for a short distance, and then it turned into a boardwalk made from recycled plastic. A few years earlier the Park Service "restored" Cook's Meadow. To help re-establish natural hydrology, workers removed an abandoned section of road that bisected the meadow, and filled in several old drainage ditches. A new boardwalk constructed across part of the meadow allowed hikers to traverse the seasonally wet swale without getting muddy. The boardwalk was elevated slightly to allow water to pass underneath. In 2005, the Park Service constructed another boardwalk in Cook's Meadow, where a paved bike path crossed a seasonally flooded area near the river. The "boardwalk" was about 200 feet long and was supported by steel I-beams and 7 large cement footings.

Contrary to their claims, the Park Service did not restore Cook's Meadow. They removed the asphalt of the abandoned road, which was beneficial, but instead of completely removing pavement from Cook's Meadow, a "highly valued resource," the Park Service left the paved trails and added even more artificial ingredients: steel and plastic boardwalks. Once again, development in the Valley increased under the banner of ecological restoration.

Paved trails and boardwalks in Yosemite's meadows present a conundrum. It's in the best interest of the meadow's ecological health to remove all trails. But, meadows are inviting and special places. Visitors should be able to enjoy them. Are paved trails and boardwalks the best option? Or should the Park Service remove all pavement from the meadows, and maintain only dirt trails? Such trails would have to be closed during wet periods, because people would leave the trails in search of drier footing. When repeated by multitudes of visitors, this action creates very wide, sometimes multiple, trails. Dirt trails would represent a tradeoff; visitors could only walk in meadows when trails were dry, and no bicycles would be allowed. Until the Park Service establishes meadow protection as a higher priority than meadow access (and reduces the number of visitors, which is the crux of all resource protection issues in the Valley), Yosemite Valley's signature meadows will continue to disappear and the land that does remain meadow by name will be damaged beyond repair—assuming it's not too late already.

California black oak trees grow in numerous places in Yosemite Valley, in stands mixed with ponderosa pine and incense-cedar, as well as in groves where the oaks predominate. In the late 1980s, the Park Service recognized that the latter areas, the oak woodlands, were in big trouble. Mature trees were dying, and very few oak seedlings had become established in more than one hundred years. Together, these factors spelled the eventual loss of the oak communities.

Yosemite Valley's black oaks are a critical wildlife support system. The foliage and acorns feed mule deer, black bears, raccoons, ground and gray squirrels, gophers, mice, blackbirds, chickadees, nuthatches, jays, band-tailed pigeons, and woodpeckers, among others. The oaks provide cover, as well as roosting, resting, and nesting places, for owls, hawks, and other species. Numerous invertebrates live in tree cavities that fill with rainwater and detritus.

Recent studies revealed fewer black oaks occur in the Valley now than in 1944, and today's trees are larger. The research indicated black oak seedlings and saplings either do not germinate or do not survive. Scientists have long suspected fire exclusion was one reason for black oak declines. The oak communities have co-existed with a regime of frequent, low-intensity fires, which killed competing conifers, opened up sunny seedbeds, and killed acorn and oak pathogens in the soil and litter. Trampling of soil in oak woodlands by humans also may adversely affect the oaks. Recently, a study conducted by scientists at Oregon State University shed new light on the problem, and Yosemite's mule deer were standing in the high beam.

According to the new study, the absence of predators that prey on deer, particularly mountain lions, may contribute to the oak decline. Early settlers and the Park Service essentially exterminated lions from the area by the 1920s. After that, hordes of visitors kept most lions that lived outside the Valley from coming in. With fewer lions, deer populations grew, and the deer weren't hunted by humans. Consequently, more deer ate more acorns, seedlings, and foliage as well as grasses and herbs under the oaks. The study also suggested Valley deer have become less afraid of predators over time, and consequently spend more time hanging out and eating in woodland and forest habitat, areas they would have moved through quickly if predators lurked in the dense growth.

In the late 1980s, park biologists launched a black oak woodland restoration effort that involved fencing people out of the woodlands, protecting oaks from herbivores, and propagating trees from locally-collected acorns. The work met with some success. On the flip side, when I worked as Resource Management Division Liaison, black oaks were cut down to make way for new utility lines and concession housing. Park managers did try to avoid removing oaks, but in any standoff between project and tree, the project usually won. The Park Service also cut down oak trees west of Yosemite Lodge, in preparation for the Lodge renovation project. Those trees were removed for a project that never happened.

Even worse, the Park Service approved removal of oaks at the site of the new Indian Cultural Center west of Camp 4. This project is the epitome of incongruity. California black oak acorns were a primary food source for Yosemite's Indians, and still provide for numerous wildlife species, but it was okay to cut the trees down to build an Indian Cultural Center. The Park Service frequently justifies cutting down oak trees in Yosemite Valley because some of the oaks harbor a fungus called *Armillaria*, and, they say, those trees would just fall over someday anyway.

Riparian plant communities, which occur along rivers and streams, grow in a patchy arrangement adjacent to the Merced and its tributaries. The Valley's most common riparian plants, white alder, black cottonwood, and various types of willow, shed their broad leaves in winter. The riverside communities thrive on seasonal floods. Disturbed routinely by soil removal and deposition, and by the action of flood waters, the riparian plants quickly re-colonize habitats at the river's edge.

A second variety of riparian forest characterized by big-leaf maple, white alder, white fir, and dogwood is less prone to flooding. These forests grow on moist, gravelly soils in sheltered areas near the bottom of the Valley walls, and on alluvial soils adjacent to streams.

Riparian vegetation is essential to the health of the Valley's river ecosystems. The trees and shrubs slow erosion of coarse, sandy riverine soils, and provide shade to keep water cool in summer. The riparian communities provide wildlife habitat and nutrients for meadow and river ecosystems. Leaves that drop into the river support a complex array of microorganisms and invertebrates involved in decomposition. Riparian plants influence the climate in and near rivers and creeks, affecting humidity, light, temperature, and shade.

According to the *Yosemite Valley Plan Supplemental Environmental Impact Statement*, riparian communities are among the most productive, sensitive, and biologically diverse communities in Yosemite Valley. They also are among the most degraded by humans, altered above and below ground by trampling and by the infrastructure, such as sewage lift stations, bridges, and underground sewer lines required to support large numbers of people.

Coincident with the loss and degradation of meadow, oak, and riparian habitats, the density and extent of conifer forests in the Valley have increased dramatically since the mid-1800s. Comparisons of historic and current photographs illustrate the changes clearly. While it's not possible to quantify the increase in trees precisely, it's safe to say the Park Service would need to remove tens of thousands of trees on the Valley floor to approximate conditions of the mid-1800s. The increased tree density has significantly affected all aspects of Valley ecology, including soil structure, nutrient content, and microorganisms; patterns and distributions of plants; wildlife species composition, food supply, and distribution; and the quantity, quality, and distribution of water.

Vegetation management problems in Yosemite Valley are not yet a thing of the past. All naturally-ignited fires in and near the Valley are suppressed because the risk of damage to lives and property is too great. Prescribed burns occur in the Valley, but they are generally small. Not all areas can be burned for fear of accidentally igniting structures, and excessively dense stands of trees and thick underbrush make burning difficult. To further complicate matters, when burns are conducted, visitors and Valley residents complain of smoke inhibiting views and exacerbating respiratory problems. To reduce accumulated fuel, the Park Service cuts and burns brush and small trees in late fall after rain has fallen. Although the Park Service recognizes the crucial role of fire in maintaining Valley ecosystems, prescribed fire as it is currently applied will never duplicate effects of natural fire or Native American burning regimes.

Non-native plants continue to spread throughout the Valley, and new species of invaders crop up continually. The park never has had enough employees dedicated to seeking out and removing the non-natives to slow the spread. Some resource managers believe it's already too late, that we will never be able to control non-native plants in the Valley. It's only too late, though, if we don't start now.

CHAPTER 21
Killing Them Softly

Journal

Raven chatter filled the air as I passed the chapel and approached the Valley's southern wall. I swung right on the Valley Loop Trail and spotted the source: four big, shiny, black birds perched side-by-side on a ponderosa pine branch, about fifty feet up. The birds regaled one another with stories of plunder they'd found that morning at the Swinging Bridge picnic area.

"I got half a ham sandwich, with Swiss. It was slathered with greasy mayonnaise, and had a lot of sand mixed in," crowed the first bird.

"I got an empty Krispy Kreme box, with loads of gooey sugar congealed on the sides and bottom," said the second.

"Yeah, well, I got an almost full bag of marshmallows," the third bird groaned. "I think I'm gonna be sick."

Yosemite Valley's waterfalls, granite walls, forests, creeks, and river are awe-inspiring and deeply appreciated by visitors and residents alike, but I suspect the Valley's best-loved, most sought after attractions are the animals. Valley visitors routinely see jays and woodpeckers, as well as gray and ground squirrels. Lucky people may chance upon a coyote trotting down the trail, encounter a solo buck or a herd of does with fawns munching acorns, or glimpse a bobcat before it disappears behind a boulder. And almost everyone longs to see a bear.

Unfortunately, despite all the love, the Valley's wild residents have been under assault by humans, in ways both intended and accidental, for a long, long time. As with other resources, most of the damage was inflicted after the mid-nineteenth century. Although the Native American residents hunted, it's unlikely their actions drove species completely out of the Valley, or resulted in much unintentional death.

The same cannot be said of the actions of Euro-American settlers or park managers. Alfred Runte, in *Yosemite: The Embattled Wilderness*, quoted a 1906 Report of Yosemite's Acting Superintendent: "The Yosemite Valley itself had, during recent years, been a death trap to all game that was unfortunate enough to enter it. Practically every person living in the Valley kept a rifle, shotgun, and revolver, and any animal or bird...was immediately pursued by the entire contingent, and either captured or killed." Unfortunately, the situation did not improve after the National Park Service took the reins in 1916.

Relationships between humans and wildlife in national parks always have been awkward and one-sided. As with water, fire, and vegetation, managers thought they knew what was best for wild animals and sought to control them. Protecting wildlife was a primary purpose of national parks, but if animals were "detrimental to the use" of the parks, the Organic Act allowed managers to kill them. In the early days, "good" animals like deer were protected, while "bad" animals—usually predators—were hunted without mercy. The list of undesirables included mountain lion, coyote, wolf, lynx, bobcat, fox, badger, mink, weasel, fisher, otter, and marten.

Bounty hunters and rangers did most of the killing. According to Richard West Sellars in *Preserving Nature in the National Parks: A History*, some rangers sold hides and pelts to augment their salaries. During the 1920s, rangers in Yellowstone even destroyed pelican eggs; they believed fewer pelicans would mean more trout and better sport fishing. Campaigns also were mounted against forest insects and diseases, even though the pathogens were natural.

For the most part, bears escaped persecution because visitors adored them. The Park Service allowed roadside bear feeding, and presented "bear shows" at garbage dumps and formal viewing areas. But the bears were the recipients of mixed messages; rangers shot and killed those who became overly comfortable with their human guests.

In response to increased knowledge of wildlife and ecology, as well as demands from outside the Service to put a higher priority on wildlife protection, park managers gradually worked to improve wildlife-human relationships starting in the 1930s. The Park Service curtailed hunting in most parks, stopped wiping out predators *en masse*, and prohibited the introduction of non-native species. Despite the advances, though, wildlife in national parks is still far from fully protected.

Yosemite's animals were not exempt from misguided management. Sellars cited a 1919 Superintendent's report that said California's "official cougar killer," Jay Bruce, killed more than fifty of the large cats in or near the park over a three to four year period. Open pit dumps overflowing with food scraps and garbage provided bears with gold mines of rich gleanings. Visitors fed bears by hand at the dumps, and the Park Service condoned this behavior.

In 1924, the Yosemite National Park Company constructed bear feeding platforms a mile west of the Old Village in Yosemite Valley. Company employees conditioned bears to come for food at the same time every evening. The Company then conveyed visitors, for a fee, to the platforms to watch the bears eat. The Park Service eventually recognized feeding bears was unnatural and potentially dangerous, and discontinued the practice in 1940.

The good news is the Park Service no longer shoots predators or feeds bears to entertain visitors; the bad news is a staggering number of Yosemite's beloved animals still are maimed or killed in the park every year. Most of the carnage is unintentionally caused by humans, and much of it goes unnoticed. But the Park Service still sanctions the killing of "problem" animals, targeting individuals who adapt too well to living in close proximity to humans. In most cases, the animal identified as a problem is a bear.

To try to reduce the number of disruptive encounters between humans and bears, Yosemite initiated a formal black bear management program in 1975. The "program" consisted of one employee tasked with managing the ursine park residents. The program's name, the Human/Bear Management Program, indicates accurately the problems are not the fault of the bears. In almost all "incidents" involving the two species, the bears are simply foraging for food; it just happens to be food belonging to humans. Frequently, the targeted food is stored or disposed of improperly. Sometimes the food is put out intentionally (and illegally) to entice bears to come closer. The outcome is always the same: The bears lose.

Every year, bear managers document the number of reported bear encounters (the number of additional, unreported encounters is anyone's guess), property damage and injuries caused by bears, and the number of bears "destroyed" or euthanized in the "interest of public safety."

For decades, the number of incidents and the amount of property damage that occurred from human-bear interactions increased almost every year. The numbers peaked in 1998, with 1,584 reported incidents, and almost $660,000 in damage to property, primarily cars. Most incidents occurred in Yosemite Valley during summer. Although bears occasionally injure people in the park, injuries are almost always minor and none have been fatal. Generally, people are injured when they catch a bear by surprise, or confront one over food. In most cases, the bear reaches out, swats the person, and then runs away, leaving minor scratches and pounding hearts.

Between 1960 and 2004, the Park Service killed 446 "problem" bears in Yosemite. Forty-eight were killed in 1971 alone. Since the Human/Bear Management Program began in 1975, the numbers have come down, but the Park Service still kills bears almost every year. Since 1960, there have been only three years in which no bears were euthanized.

Yosemite has more problems with bears than other national parks. In the mid-1990s Yosemite had twice as many incidents every year as did neighboring Sequoia and Kings Canyon National Parks, and seventy times more than Yellowstone, Grand Teton, Glacier, or Shenandoah. This may be because Yosemite has numerous developed areas located in good bear habitat, and an over-abundance of people. In addition, Yosemite bears descended from a long line of bears who like human food and know how to get it. Once a bear learns how to open up a car or cabin with sharp, strong claws and teeth, the bear will, in the words of a Yosemite wildlife biologist, "corrupt" other bears. Mothers teach babies, and "naïve" bears see other bears getting food and mimic the behavior. Yosemite also may have more incidents because Yosemite's rangers generally do not cite visitors who fail to store food properly. During my tenure in Sequoia and Kings Canyon National Parks, rangers cited visitors regularly for such violations. Proper food storage was, and still is, the law. Visitors responded by being much more diligent in managing food and garbage.

Yosemite personnel routinely catch and sedate "problem" bears. Data like age, weight, and coat condition are recorded, and some bears get distinctive ear tags or collars with radio transmitters to facilitate ease of identification and tracking. Repeat offenders, captured bears with a history of run-ins with humans or their property, sometimes are translocated away from developed areas.

In 1995, an average year, biologists completed thirty-five captures involving twenty-five different bears (several bears were captured more than once). The Park Service euthanized three bears that year after repeated translocations failed and the bears continued to be aggressive or destructive. A fourth bear died of undetermined causes while being sedated. That same year, motor vehicles killed at least seven bears; a bear tagged inside the park was shot legally outside of the park; a young adult bear was killed by a mountain lion in El Capitan Meadow; and a bear was found dead of unknown causes. An additional twelve bears were hit by drivers and their fates were not determined. Altogether, fourteen park bears died and twelve more were injured in 1995, not including other bears that died in the wild for various reasons. Twelve of the deaths and all of the injuries were caused by park visitors, residents, or employees.

In December of 1998, after park biologists spent years publicizing the magnitude of human/bear problems in Yosemite, Congress passed a bill providing $500,000 per year to address the situation. The park hired additional staff to roam campgrounds, parking lots, and cabin areas to remedy food storage problems, educate people on coexisting with bears, and chase bears away from developed areas. Immediately, the number of incidents dropped more than 50 percent—from 1,584 in 1998 to 768 in 1999—and continued to decline over time. Between 2000 and 2004, the number of incidents ranged from 80 to 306.

The story of Bear #2247, described in Yosemite's 1995 *Black Bear Management and Incident Summary Report,* is a good example of how a wild bear becomes a "problem bear." Bear #2247 was first captured on June 12, after stealing food from campsites during the day in Upper Pines Campground. Visitors either backed away and the bear helped itself, or the bear-proof food storage lockers had been left open. The bear was tranquilized, ear tagged, and moved to Hetch Hetchy. Bear #2247's fate was sealed. There would be no going back to wildness.

Two weeks later, the bear was back, raiding overflowing garbage cans and ripping into Curry Village tent cabins, primarily those of concession employees, to get food. Although food was not allowed in employee tent cabins, this prohibition was violated frequently. The bear also tore the screen from an open window of a residence. These incidents often occurred during the day, while people watched or tried to chase the bear away. On August 19, biologists captured Bear #2247 for the second time, after it tore off another window screen and entered a cabin. The bear got a radio collar and was moved to the Merced Grove.

Two weeks later, the bear was back and broke into more tents and cabins. As before, much of the problem resulted from food in concession employee tents, and it appeared that concession employees had left food out purposely to attract bears.

On September 1, Bear #2247 tore the screen on a house near the medical clinic. Employees tried to chase it away, but the bear bluff-charged them—a behavior that involves a bear running a short distance toward a person, sometimes grunting or woofing, to scare the person away. It usually works.

The bear then tried to pry windows off a neighboring house while people were inside. Someone called park wildlife staff. By the time help arrived, Bear #2247 was trying to re-enter the first house. Based on its boldness, and the frequency and severity of incidents, park managers and biologists decided to "destroy" the bear. Bear #2247 received a lethal injection later that day.

October of 2003 was bright and beautiful. Dogwood leaves blushed to a deep red under the frosty glances of old man winter, the river slowed to a green and brown crawl, and bucks young and old sparred among belly-deep, amber meadow grasses. In addition to the usual colors, reports trickled in from Curry Village about a pair of visitors who added an unusually rich golden tone to the autumn palette: visitors of the large feline variety.

The reports cast me back to a cool June morning in 1998. I was driving a little-used road in the Trinity Alps in Northern California, en route to a wedding. The early morning sun warmed my left shoulder. As I rounded a gentle curve, a huge, tawny body with a long, heavy tail bounded down the slope from the right, hit the pavement with four giant cat feet, and then disappeared down the hill below in two great leaps. The animal was there and gone in the blink of an eye.

I stopped the truck and turned to look at my traveling companion. We stared at each other in silence.

"Oh, my God," she said at last.

I was thirty-eight. She was a few years older. We were both biologists and had spent much of our lives outside in mountain lion country. Neither of us had seen one in the wild. Such sightings are few and precious.

Five years later I was living in Yosemite Valley, a place once occupied by lions. The big cats had, for the most part, moved out of the

Valley after being targeted for extermination, and then crowded out by too many tourists. Lions did pass through the Valley occasionally, sometimes lingering for short periods, but they rarely stayed long. In hopes of seeing the Curry visitors, Tom and I walked the area at dusk on several consecutive evenings. Wandering among boulders at the base of the walls that tower over the Curry Village cabins, I wished fervently for a glimpse of the elusive cats. No such luck.

In addition to our feline guests, unusually large numbers of raccoons were busy in the Valley that fall, drawn in by human food, garbage, and not infrequent hand-outs offered by uneducated or scofflaw visitors. Park biologists concluded the lions were attracted by the raccoons, a favored prey species.

Several weeks passed, and people continued to see the lions. Usually the presence of lions in the Valley is not problematic. For example, during the summer of 2001, an adult female and two sub-adults lived in the Valley on and off for several weeks. This happened a few times over a few successive years. In 2001, more than 60 percent of reported sightings involved a lion chasing, killing, or eating a raccoon. The lions all eventually moved on. For some reason, though, the lions of 2003 were different. Or were they?

Park managers became uncomfortable with the length of time the lions stayed in the Valley, and with the fact that they seemed unafraid of people. Biologists tried to chase the cats away by shooting them with rubber bullets, and firing off cracker rounds—noise-makers shot from a starter's pistol.

Then a park employee claimed to see the lions exhibiting "stalking behavior" toward humans.

A few days later, a Park Service news release announced that park biologists had euthanized two mountain lions. The lions, the release claimed, displayed threatening behavior and were routinely sighted by visitors and employees. The adult female and what was likely her cub were trapped and killed.

I was shocked, disappointed, and very angry. When I queried park biologists, they said the cats had been seen watching children playing, and managers were concerned the cats viewed the children as potential prey. The Park Service has a range of options for managing "problem" wildlife. In this case, park employees tried to chase the lions away, but failed. The Park Service did not try translocation, perhaps because the technique can be problematic. Translocated animals often are challenged, and sometimes killed, by members of their species already established in the new locale; and some animals return to where they were captured.

There was a third option I suspect the Park Service didn't consider seriously, if at all: closing Curry Village until the cats moved on. It was late October, which was not a busy season. The children who were gazed upon by the lions were part of an organized outdoor education group, and they could have been moved to another area. It was not necessary to kill the cats. It was simply the most expedient way to ensure the Park Service did not get in trouble if the lions decided to test the human-as-prey theory.

A three-year study of Yosemite's mountain lions initiated in 1996 led me to further question the decision to kill the lions. During the study, the National Park Service and U.S. Geological Survey, in cooperation with the California Department of Fish and Game and the U.S. Fish and Wildlife Service, captured, radio-collared, and tracked seven lions—six females and one male. The researchers also tried to track non-collared lions, and evaluated records of past lion sightings in the park.

None of the past sighting reports mentioned any sign of lions exhibiting aggressive behavior towards humans. Most reports implied the cats were oblivious to people despite their proximity, often only meters away. On three occasions, researchers used radio telemetry to follow and observe lions at close range. The cats were aware of the researchers, but didn't show any reaction to their presence. In another case, an un-collared lion located by calls and tracks also seemed indifferent to the researchers.

Based on this information, the research team concluded mountain lions don't perceive humans as potential prey. This suggests lions in developed areas are not a threat to human safety. The researchers acknowledged, though, that the risk of a problem always exists, and is likely to increase as the frequency of encounters between lions and humans increases. California Department of Fish and Game data support the researchers' conclusions. In the 117-year period between 1890 and 2007, the Department documented only 16 cases where mountain lions attacked people in the state. Six of the sixteen were fatal attacks, but two of the six fatalities were linked to rabies. Mountain lion attacks are not common, but they get extensive publicity when they occur.

In December 1998, during Yosemite's lion study, a female mountain lion collided with a snow plow as she crossed a road with her two yearling cubs. The impact broke one of her front legs. Researchers tracked the lion for the remainder of the winter. She was often seen scavenging road kills the following spring. In June, after her cubs left, she began searching for food in the developed area of Wawona. Researchers monitored her for several weeks, and then she died. A necropsy revealed she starved to death.

Although mountain lions usually don't linger in developed areas, the injured mama cat's story indicated nutritional stress may attract lions to developed areas, especially when reliable food sources are available. Human food and garbage, as well as wildlife feeding, draws bears, raccoons, coyotes, and mule deer into Yosemite's developed areas. The researchers concluded some female lions, faced with the nutritional demands of feeding offspring, take advantage of this concentration of prey. They also speculated that coyotes and raccoons may be ideal prey for young mountain lions learning to hunt.

On Christmas Day, 2003, two months after the mountain lions were killed, a rockfall occurred at Curry Village very close to the site where the lions met their sad fate. On October 8, 2008, five years after the lions were killed a massive rockslide at Curry Village prompted the Park Service to permanently close 233 cabins. At least some parts of Yosemite's wild nature remain unmanageable.

Walking home from the Village Store one summer morning, a glint of something shiny on the road shoulder caught my eye. As I leaned over to identify the object that was lit by the slant of sun, I saw it was the body of a metallic, chocolate-brown beetle. As long as a dragonfly and as wide as a tablespoon, the beetle was dressed in a fine suit of armor. Its dark wings maintained their impressive width out to the very tips. I squatted down to pay my respects and felt my stomach clench when I realized half of the big beetle's body was crushed, mangled by a windshield, tire, or shoe.

In 2006, a man named Moose Mutlow conducted an informal survey in Yosemite. He drove thirty miles of park roads twice a day for 290 days. As he drove, he completed an unorthodox wildlife inventory: His focus was road kill. Although the survey began as a joke of sorts, Mutlow discovered the number of animals killed by automobiles in the park was staggering. He found 250 dead animals, including squirrels, opossums, skunks, coyotes, deer, and bear. And he couldn't count everything. The bodies of beetles, butterflies, dragonflies, lizards, and other small creatures don't lend themselves to such a survey, and cars obliterate millions of these smaller park residents every year.

Common species aren't the only victims of automobiles. Great gray owls, which are endangered in California, nest and hunt in and around the park's open meadows. The largest North American owls, with wingspans up to five feet, great gray owls sometimes cross paths with drivers as the owls pursue prey. At least sixteen great grey owls have been killed by cars in Yosemite since 1966. In 2008, biologists estimated the entire state of California supported only one hundred great gray owls. We can't afford to lose any more.

Between 2002 and 2007, sixty-eight collisions between bears and cars were reported in Yosemite, and fifteen dead bears were found along road sides. No one knows how many collisions with bears go unreported. In 2008, a park employee found a young bear with two fractured legs by the side of the road. It was euthanized. No one had reported it. Most bears that are hit are females, or young bears forced out of prime habitat by older males. Usually only a small percentage of hit bears are killed outright; most limp off into the woods to uncertain fates, according to a Yosemite wildlife biologist. Based on the damage to the cars, however, most of those left limping probably wandered off to die elsewhere.

Gray squirrels may be the hardest hit by the direct impact of cars in Yosemite. Spring and early summer are the worst because the squirrels are preoccupied with finding a mate, seeking out nesting materials, and gathering food. They dart across roads without looking both ways. They don't understand the need to cross carefully and quickly, the need to be decisive and run in one direction if they see a car bearing down on them. Often they are caught in the midst of crossing, when a large metal beast suddenly roars around a curve at 40 miles per hour. "Oh no! Which way do I run? This way, maybe, no, that way, no…" Too late; that moment of confusion is fatal.

In spring and summer, I saw at least three or four dead squirrels on the roads every time I drove. It's safe to say hundreds of gray squirrels are run over every year in the Valley alone. My heart hurts when I see their mangled bodies.

Roadkill in Yosemite is a solvable problem. It could be reduced substantially if drivers would slow way down and pay attention. I suggested to a friend that the Park Service should stop maintaining park roads, should simply let them deteriorate. Potholes and irregularities would slow drivers down. She wasn't sure if I was serious or not. I was. I am. Sadly, on a recent trip to the Valley, I saw the main roads had been upgraded with brand new, slick, smooth surfaces. Most drivers were exceeding the speed limit.

The stories I've told of Yosemite's bears, mountain lions, squirrels, and beetles illustrate the impacts of humans on, and the demise of, individuals. In professional wildlife management circles the long-term health and viability of wildlife populations is viewed as very important, while the fate of any one individual often is discounted and deemed inconsequential. While I agree that protecting populations is very important, I disagree with the idea that the loss of individuals is not important. Individuals make up populations, and the loss of any of them as a result of human carelessness or ignorance *is* consequential. By disregarding individuals, we give ourselves permission to not care, we sanction harming or killing animals in the interest of research, we accept accidental deaths of bears during captures, and we allow mountain lions to be euthanized for looking at children. This is wrong.

It's also ironic, because I believe the people who are present when these animals die—those who see the bear die in the trap, or watch the lion starve to death, or inject the lion with drugs to end its life—grieve for those animals. I know they care. As professionals, though, they are expected to keep a stiff upper lip and pretend they don't care, because the loss of individuals doesn't matter in the long run.

But they do care, and it does matter. Our very survival, human survival as well as survival of our fellow species on Earth, depend on people caring. We must allow ourselves to care, and to care deeply. We need to care about every bear, every lion, every coyote, every gray squirrel, every beetle, every butterfly, every clam, and every coot. We need to slow down and give our fellow creatures all the respect and attention they so richly deserve—in Yosemite, and all across the planet.

We must learn to care again.

CHAPTER 22
And the Damage Done

Journal

The invitation read as follows:

Monday, April 18, 2005
Eleven O'Clock in the Morning
The Magic Circle, at the Base of Yosemite Falls

  Yosemite Falls, the highest waterfall in North America, is one of the nation's greatest natural icons. Plunging 2,425 feet from the rim into Yosemite Valley, it represents the very essence of Yosemite, the perfect embodiment of the eternal interplay of water, granite, sunlight and air.
  On April 18, 2005, The Yosemite Fund and the National Park Service will celebrate the completion of a ten-year, $13.5 million restoration of the lower Yosemite Fall area. The Park's 3.5 million annual visitors now approach Yosemite Falls in a revitalized setting that showcases the Falls' natural beauty with improved vistas, visitor amenities and access for the disabled.

❖❖❖

  As luck would have it, the great falls were at their finest on April 18, 2005. Energized by snowmelt, icy torrents cascaded, tumbled, dropped in free-fall, rebounded off rock, reflected rainbows, hit bottom, and finally flowed south to nourish greening meadows, stately oaks, thirsty coyotes, industrious squirrels, and human hearts and minds.

West of Yosemite Creek, at a slight remove, a bevy of cars, buses, and bicycles materialized as a growing swell of humans gathered for the late morning celebration. The breeze held traces of a cool winter past as it pushed pine needles, oak leaves, and a candy wrapper across the sidewalk. A man in the grey and green National Park Service uniform trotted after the wrapper. This was an important event; there must be no litter.

Heavy equipment clanged and droned as park staff scurried to sweep the streets and make nice for the long list of attendees, which included the National Park Service Director. It seemed the park didn't need to be clean and in good repair for visitors, only for the Director. This situation was sadly symbolic of the times in Yosemite Valley; the focus was on politics, money, and those who were steeped in both, instead of on preservation, native species, and those who seek to protect and be inspired by nature.

By 11AM several hundred people were milling around the so-called "Magic Circle," a human contrivance at the head of the Lower Fall trail sporting benches, curved rock walls, a mosaic stone floor, and strategically placed boulders. The celebration marking the completion of the new and improved, "restored" Lower Yosemite Fall was a big media event. Cameras and microphones of all shapes and sizes were angled to catch and transmit the roar of Yosemite Falls to audiences across the planet.

The Director told the assembled crowd that national parks were "America's gift to the world"—taking credit, as if somehow we humans had fabricated all this incredible beauty. Next, the project designer directed placement of the last boulder for the newly designed setting, the finishing touch. Rocks with just the right aesthetic qualities had been collected from all over the park and brought here. Apparently the native boulders that landed here millions of years ago were not good enough. Of the last boulder, the designer stated it was "a boulder that looked natural and had a sense of purpose for that particular spot." Say what?

During the self-congratulatory speeches, one person noted with a chuckle that the project designer "turned more water on to the falls, just for the day." I wasn't sure if the statement was funny, or the epitome of arrogance.

Somewhere along the way, I thought, we humans got it all very, very wrong. Yosemite Valley itself is the great entity here; we humans and all of our contrivances pale in comparison, and always will. It's the Valley in all its natural glory we should be celebrating, not the things humans build in the Valley, which only serve to mar and scar. The Lower Fall project was lauded as laying "gently on the land." I couldn't understand how tons of steel and asphalt could lie gently.

The part of the ceremony that made me the saddest was when the Yosemite Elementary School children sang *America the Beautiful*. Destruction of one of the nation's most precious natural treasures was made to seem patriotic. The April 18 event was really a double "Sell-ebration." It was a means by which to sell the Lower Yosemite Fall Project to the general public, and a reminder that the Park Service sold out when they allowed the project to unfold as it did. The agency turned responsibility for project design and implementation over to the project's major benefactor, The Yosemite Conservancy. The Conservancy wanted a glorious, showy project, which would attract more donations to their organization than would a subtle, simple project. And the Park Service let the Yosemite Conservancy run the show.

Some Park Service employees, as well as the Yosemite Conservancy and other project supporters, believed the Lower Fall Project was good for Yosemite. But only one aspect of the project was good: removal of the old parking lot. Any reduction in pavement in Yosemite Valley is beneficial. The project made it easier for some visitors to maneuver wheelchairs to the base of the Lower Fall, but this could have been accomplished by a much less ecologically destructive alternative. The wait to use the restroom on busy summer days was shortened. But do these reasons justify further degradation of nature in Yosemite Valley? The damage to hydrology, vegetation, wildlife habitat, and the aesthetics of the wild far outweighed any reputed benefits.

I walked the newly paved Lower Yosemite Fall trail the morning after the ceremony. The project transformed the environment near the iconic waterfalls from semi-wild to distinctly urban, replete with bomb-proof bridges, five-foot-wide paved trails, rock walls, benches, stout wooden fences, a plethora of signs, bike racks, garbage and recycling cans, a pay phone, a shuttle bus shelter befitting a Montana dude ranch, and a restroom large enough to accommodate elephants and giraffes. The shiny new pavement was already collecting cigarette butts, used Kleenex, and gum wrappers. The message was clear: When the Park Service urbanizes part of Yosemite Valley, people will treat that part like an urban environment. The unique, special nature of the place is disregarded, no longer respected.

After the "restoration," solitude, peace, and native wildlife were replaced by noise, litter, and dogs. The opportunity to touch and be touched by nature was gone. The spirit of the place had fled. The project drove another large nail in the coffin of Yosemite Valley's wild nature. It was not cause for celebration; it was cause for deep mourning.

Ultimately, it doesn't matter if one likes or dislikes the changes wrought by the Lower Yosemite Fall Project. The damage was done. Much more ominous was the Park Service's failure to effectively plan or manage the project. Park managers didn't disclose project details to the public, so people didn't have a chance to provide input. Planners failed to present or analyze a range of alternatives or disclose fully the effects of the project on natural and cultural resources. Let's hope this type of planning charade does not happen again.

In late summer, 2005, a few months after the celebration, Tom accepted a job at the National Interagency Fire Center in Boise, Idaho.

I was sad, but relieved. It hurt to watch the Park Service wreak havoc in the Valley, and I was ready for a break from the pain. But Yosemite Valley was my heartland. I hated to leave again.

The autumn before we moved, I wandered the Valley and said my goodbyes. One Saturday in September, light rain drizzled from a weighty gray sky as I crossed the river and angled up behind the chapel. Glancing across the southern piece of Sentinel Meadow, I saw two large, fuzzy ears and the crest of a soft brown head jutting above a horizon of meadow plants, like a small boat becalmed on a sea of autumn. The doe's body was hidden among dense layers of fall color: the farewell green of wet meadow sedge, the bright yellow of dying milkweed, and the withered gray of goldenrod. I said goodbye to the doe and to the vibrant, juicy life of summer. I said goodbye to my Yosemite dreams.

We left in December, and moved into a big house in a Boise foothill suburb too new to have trees. A foot of crusty snow covered the ground, and temperatures were in the teens. Before we moved, I'd chosen a paint color called "malted milk" for the dining room, which originally was a dark olive green. When we arrived, the dining room was pink. I wanted nothing more than to run away screaming.

I missed the Valley with an ache that bordered on despair. I missed seeing Yosemite Falls every morning, and being kept awake by rattling windowpanes when the Falls boomed in late spring. I missed the Merced River and its ever-changing moods—the joyous rage of spring, the smooth run of summer, the meandering, green-gold lethargy of autumn, and the frigid black edge of winter. I missed the chatter of gray squirrels chasing each another at top speed up and over the picnic table in the front yard. I missed the solemn, liquid gaze of the old mule deer who grazed near the house and drank from the birdbath.

I missed the sounds and smells of the Valley that got under my skin and became forever a part of me: the call of white-breasted nuthatch announcing a late spring arrival, the rant of Steller's jay digging for grubs outside the kitchen window, and the rolling *quork* of raven perched in the oak above the picnic table. I missed the sharp tang of drifting campfire smoke, the sweetness of pine resin, and the spicy aroma of cottonwood buds at river's edge.

I did not miss flotillas of rafts conveying hordes of visitors downriver on hot summer days, or traffic gridlock on holiday weekends. And, I did not miss watching the ongoing destruction of Yosemite Valley.

I knew too much. It hurt to know so much.

In February of 2007, a bit more than a year after we moved, Tom and I returned to the Valley for a visit. Snow fell every afternoon and night. Masses of big, wet flakes drifted down and settled gently on every exposed surface. White silence blanketed the meadows. Large mocha colored leaves held tight to black oak limbs. We walked along the river and reminisced, accompanied by the trills of American dippers.

On the second day, we walked east to Curry Village to see the new dorms. As we walked past Ahwahnee Meadow, a flash of gray and russet caught my eye. Two coyotes stood knee-deep in snow near the meadow's north edge, where grasses give way to bracken fern and black oak. As still as granite, not a muscle moved until an oblivious vole tunneled a bit too close to the snow's surface. A quick skyward leap was followed by a pounce straight down, and a pointed snout cleaved the snow: coyote breakfast.

Tom and I had last seen the Curry dorm site on a rainy winter day in 2005, just before we moved. At that time, the construction area had been an absolute mess. Our access had been blocked by an 8-foot tall chain link fence, but we could see the formerly undeveloped forest was a sea of mud dotted with rectangular cement islands, the foundations for buildings to come. It had rained that day, and the water washed newly exposed soil away from the site to the river. Port-a-potties, dump trucks, a backhoe, a generator, piles of black pipe, construction cones, and bright orange plastic fencing littered the area. Signs were everywhere: Do Not Enter. Wrong Way. Road Closed. Construction Traffic Only. No Trespassing. Keep Out. Construction Zone. Authorized

Personnel Only—Violators Will Be Prosecuted. Danger. Keep Out. Rewards Up To $1000 For Construction Theft/Vandalism Tips. Keep Out.

My worst fears about the dorm project were confirmed during our 2007 visit. Rows of identical, drab-brown, two-story buildings stretched out over the once-natural landscape. The former network of swales lined with granite gravel and edged with native gooseberry, currant, and raspberry, and the forest of black oak, incense-cedar and ponderosa pine that towered over all had been replaced with roads, parking lots, cars, trucks, fire hose boxes, fences, signs, streetlights, and a few randomly-placed, blue port-a-potties. Piles of dirty snow under a leaden gray sky made the already bleak scene even more depressing.

We explored Yosemite Lodge on the third day of our visit and found it blessedly unchanged, except for the lack of the numerous large trees that were cut down for the Lodge renovation and road re-route, neither of which ever happened.

Litigation over planning for the Merced River and the Valley stopped some development, at least temporarily. The parties involved in the lawsuits reached a settlement in 2009, and the Park Service immediately began developing another new and improved Merced Wild and Scenic River Plan. These renewed planning efforts will prove critical to Yosemite Valley's future. The new river plan must put resource protection and preservation first, and it's up to members of the public who care about Yosemite to make it so. Otherwise, the new plan will be another iteration of past plans, written in the interest of those who benefit from a developed Valley. And the Park Service will pick up where it left off prior to the litigation, dashing headlong down a path of construction madness.

Fortunately, the litigation stalled two major, environmentally horrific projects: the Yosemite Lodge Area Redevelopment Project and the Curry Village and East Valley Campground Improvement Project. The Lodge project included several independent actions in addition to lodge renovation. Northside Drive was to be re-routed where it passes the Lodge. Sunnyside Campground, also known as Camp 4—the climber's campground—would gain an interpretive display building, food storage lockers, group fire rings, and a cooking pavilion. And the new Indian Cultural Center was planned for a site west of Camp 4.

These three components of the project would have caused significant environmental impacts. The re-routed Northside Drive, slated to run next to an active side channel of the Merced River, would directly impact critical wetland habitat. The road would flood frequently, and runoff and floodwater would carry contaminants into river and wetlands. The cooking pavilion and group campfire areas proposed for Camp 4 would be bear magnets. Late night clean-up of food and garbage is apt to be spotty at best. Improper food storage in the Valley already is problematic; too many bears get killed because of it. It makes no sense to create another problem area.

The proposed Indian Cultural Center was to occupy a former Native American village site. The area had recovered since the old village was razed, however, and the land supported a mixed, open stand of pine, incense-cedar, and black oak. During the project's early planning stages, I expressed the opinion that the Park Service should not build an Indian Cultural Center, or any new structure, in Yosemite Valley. When it appeared the Center was another "done deal," I suggested at least they could site the Center on presently developed land, not in the middle of healthy woodland habitat.

The second impending project, the Curry Village and East Valley Campground Improvement Project, involved a massive re-design of the East Valley. Thirty extra-large sites for super-sized recreational vehicles and four new restrooms were to be built in Upper Pines Campground. The area immediately north of Upper Pines, between the campground road and the river, would get fifty-nine new walk-in campsites, with parking for sixty-four cars. In addition, an entirely new campground with ten group and sixteen individual sites, parking for forty-six cars, and three restrooms was slated to be built on undeveloped land east of Curry Village, south of the Happy Isles access road.

At Curry Village, the store was to be expanded and two new buildings constructed: a 2,000 to 2,400 square-foot check-in station and a centralized shower and restroom facility for campers. The part of Southside Drive that crosses Stoneman Meadow would be removed. Eastbound traffic would be routed through Curry Village, and only visitors staying in campgrounds could drive beyond the check-in station.

The Park Service also planned a new amphitheater at the site of the concession horse stables, if the stables were removed. The Yosemite Valley Plan called for removal of the stables—an ecological bonus—but the Park Service backtracked on the removal, in theory because the stables may be a "contributing element" to the Yosemite Valley Historic District. In reality, it's likely because the concession operator opposes the loss of revenue generated from guided rides.

Tom and I returned to Yosemite again in mid-November of 2007 to celebrate my mom's seventy-ninth birthday and my parent's fifty-fifth anniversary. Tom, my brother Marc, and I set off one morning to hike up the first part of the John Muir Trail to the Vernal Fall Bridge; the site where, as a teen, I first connected to the Earth.

The day was sunny, clear, and cool. We disembarked from the shuttle bus at Happy Isles, walked across Clark's Bridge, and turned down a dirt path to catch the trail. As we approached the trailhead my stomach flip-flopped. I thought I was hallucinating. The trail appeared very dark, almost black, and smooth. When we arrived at the trailhead sign I realized with sinking heart that I was seeing correctly. The first mile of the John Muir Trail, the famous route that leaves Yosemite Valley to traverse the High Sierra to Mt. Whitney, the highest point in the lower forty-eight states, had been paved.

I fumed all the way to the bridge, my feet, heart, and mind repulsed by the four- to six-foot wide black highway. Small chunks of fresh asphalt lined the trail, waiting for the next big rain to carry them into the river. This segment of trail was first paved in the 1930s by the Civilian Conservation Corps. Over time, weather, erosion, and millions of feet wore away at the old asphalt. Prior to the most recent "rehabilitation," the trail consisted of segments of dirt interspersed with patches of old, pot-holed asphalt.

The Park Service had several options for managing this famous route. They could have removed the remaining asphalt and left behind a real trail, a dirt trail. Based on the intensity of use the trail receives, though, and the steep slopes it climbs in several areas, a dirt trail would be subject to heavy erosion and washouts. The Park Service could have engaged Yosemite's world-class trail construction crews to craft a carefully-placed rock route in the steep, erosion-prone areas, while leaving a dirt trail in more stable areas. The latter would have been more expensive than the option chosen by the Park Service, which involved slapping down three inches of asphalt. But, of all the trails in the United States, it surely seems the John Muir Trail should be a natural trail.

Before we left Yosemite in 2005, I'd heard rumors that the Park Superintendent also wanted to re-pave the Valley Loop Trail, which runs up one side of the Valley and down the other, hugging the Valley walls in most places. The Valley Loop Trail, also known as the valley bridle path, was designed in the late 1920s. In 1928, thirteen miles of the trail and fourteen associated foot bridges were built. Like the lower segment of the John Muir Trail, the Valley Loop Trail still shows signs of past paving, but the residual asphalt is patchy and broken as the trail slowly restores itself to a more natural condition. After seeing the depressing transformation of the Muir trail, I became firmly convinced re-paving the Valley Loop Trail would be a travesty.

The Valley Loop Trail travels through some of the last quiet and wild parts of Yosemite Valley, and provides critical access for wildlife traveling through the East Valley. Its presence creates corridors where animals can escape or avoid the endless noise of roads, buildings, people, bikes, and dogs that occupy the bulk of the East Valley. Additionally, the trail is the only good route for runners because much of it is unpaved.

Jogging along one summer morning between the chapel and the head of the Four Mile Trail, which ascends to Glacier Point, I was startled by a loud rustle of leaves and a deep grunt. After my eyes adjusted to the dim light filtering through a dense tree canopy, I saw a large dark mass moving near a fallen log about fifty feet away. I stopped. As soon as the bear realized I'd seen him, he stood up on his hind legs and stretched tall to see me better, then hurtled his dark, shaggy body around, leaped over the log, and ran in the opposite direction—the very best thing for a wild bear to do.

If the Valley Loop Trail is paved as proposed, and opened to bicycle use, we can say goodbye to more of Yosemite's wildness, and, most likely, its wildlife.

I returned to the Valley again in November of 2009, for the annual anniversary and birthday gathering. After hearing rumors that the Park Service was working on the Indian Cultural Center project, I paid a visit to the site. As I left the Lodge parking area, a soft breeze pushed the last remaining leaves from the black oaks. As usual, I discovered my suggestion of four years earlier to preserve the ecological integrity of this site had been a complete waste of breath.

The formerly undeveloped woodland was marred by piles of freshly cut logs, including black oaks, aggregations of cut log rounds, large piles of soil pushed away to permit construction, a round excavation about fifty feet in diameter with sloping sides lined with granite boulders (the future roundhouse), partially-carved totems, and signs and yellow flagging tape reading "Do Not Enter" and "Tribal Parking Only." A large, new sign posted at the site entrance proudly proclaimed the Indian Cultural Center project was funded, at least in part, by The Yosemite Conservancy. It turned out, as part of the lawsuit settlement, all parties agreed that work on the Indian Cultural Center could proceed. The construction was separated from the larger Lodge area project, and no environmental compliance was completed. The project was pushed through under the radar. And one more wild piece of Yosemite Valley was destroyed.

When considering ways to fix the broken planning process in Yosemite, it must be mentioned that the park's 1980 *General Management Plan* is long overdue for revision. Such plans are assumed to have a fifteen to twenty year lifespan. Preparation of the new *General Management Plan* would reasonably precede and form the foundation for all other park planning efforts. Ideally, the new plan would be based on the goals of the 1980 plan, be fully exposed to the light of day with extensive public involvement, be completely free of the influence of politics and economics, and would reflect the critical need to protect wildness and wild land. Surprisingly, there has been no indication that the Park Service is even considering development of a new *General Management Plan*, although the agency is in the throes of writing management plans for both the Tuolumne and Merced rivers.

Several short legal documents were released by the National Park Service after the lawsuit over Merced River planning was settled. The National Environmental Policy Act, or NEPA, requires preparation of a Finding of No Significant Impact, or FONSI, document after an Environmental Assessment is finalized, and a Record of Decision, or ROD, after an Environmental Impact Statement is completed. In 2010, after the settlement was reached, the National Park Service issued two Revised FONSIs, one for the Curry Village and East Valley project and one for the Yosemite Lodge project.

In the revised documents, the Curry Village and East Valley project was reduced to two actions: reducing the number of tent cabins at Curry Village (which already was done in response to rockfall hazards), and tree removal at the proposed site of new campsites and parking areas at Upper Pines Campgrounds, which also had already happened. The rest of this horrific project was stopped.

The Lodge project was reduced to tree removal for parking lot expansion near Camp 4, removal of an electrical substation near Camp 4, and the Indian Cultural Center—all three of these project components also were well underway or completed before the Revised FONSI was prepared.

Although not well known, at the eleventh hour, just before the seven-year statute of limitations was about to expire late in 2007, the plaintiffs in the Merced River litigation also sued the Park Service over the Yosemite Valley Plan. The suit focused on the fact that the Yosemite Valley Plan tiered off of the Merced River plan, so if the former was not adequate, neither was the latter. The government and the plaintiffs agreed on a settlement with respect to litigation over both the Merced River Plan and the Yosemite Valley Plan late in 2009. In 2010, a Revised Record of Decision was prepared that rescinded all actions contained in the Yosemite Valley Plan that had not already been completed. The only ongoing work involves the utilities project.

New construction and re-construction in Yosemite Valley, have, at least for this bright and shining moment, stopped.

PART THREE

ROOTS OF PROBLEMS, SEEDS OF SOLUTIONS

*And don't be unwilling
to make yourself a little unpopular
by trying to protect something
that people want to unprotect.*
-David R. Brower
Let the Mountains Talk, Let the Rivers Run

*You may say
that I'm a dreamer.
But I'm not the only one.*
-John Lennon

CHAPTER 23
A Murder, a Curse, a Riot, Some Restoration, and a Few Revelations

Journal

A small, dark cloud passed over a group of women and children bent to the task of collecting acorns. The cloud's shadow ran quick and sure across everything in its path: gnarled black oaks; a slowly meandering river; and open meadows charred by recent fire. The shadow whispered of white people and dark times coming. A young boy shivered. The cloud passed and the sun returned. The people didn't notice.

The group resided in a valley of abundance and beauty, embraced by vertical granite walls and surrounded by cool forests, lush meadows, and sparkling white waterfalls. Waterways and cold clean springs and a rich array of plants and animals nourished their bodies. The grace of warm sun, the sweet smell of pine, the songs of canyon wren and coyote, and night skies cradling moon and stars nurtured their spirits.

The group gathered the fruit of the oak not knowing one day they would be forced to leave, not knowing one day their home would become one of the most popular places on Earth, not knowing the meaning of the message carried in the cloud shadow's whisper.

♦♦♦

The truth is obscured and many have argued the details, but it's now believed Yosemite Valley provided a home for humans for 4,000 to

6,000 years before European-Americans arrived. In the early 1800s, Native Americans living in the Valley called their home *Awooni* or *Owwoni*, which translates as "big mouth" or "gaping mouth." Lafayette Bunnell, the first white person to write the name after hearing it spoken, spelled it *Ahwahne*, and later *Ahwahnee*. The Valley occupants called themselves the *Ah-wah-nee-chee* or "people of *Ahwahnee*."

The Ahwahneechee initially were oblivious to the migration of Spanish soldiers and missionaries into California, but eventually these changes shattered the lives of the native people. Within a few decades of the Europeans' arrival, new diseases swept up and down California. When epidemics hit Yosemite Valley, the survivors left to live among neighboring bands of Paiute and Mono.

Around 1821, a small band led by Chief Tenaya returned to Yosemite Valley to live. The name of this group is elusive, but it's believed the aforementioned Mr. Bunnell named the spectacular valley *Yosemity*, later spelled *Yosemite*, after the group. "Yosemite" may be a corruption of the word *usumati*, which has been interpreted to mean "those who kill," "the killers," and "grizzly bear." Neighboring tribes apparently feared the Yosemites—the fierce renegades.

The 1848 discovery of gold at Sutter's mill near Sacramento, and the resulting flood of Euro-Americans into the Sierra Nevada, served as the final death knell for the Yosemite people's way of life. In keeping with conditions across the nation, hostilities erupted as the newcomers encroached on land used and occupied by the native people.

On January 24, 1851, the Mariposa Battalion, comprised of over 200 mounted volunteers led by James D. Savage, mustered in with a mission to "make peace" with the Yosemites and remove them to reservations. Historians believe the Valley was occupied at that time by a mixture of Southern Sierra Miwok, Mono Lake Paiute, Central Sierra Miwok, and former Mission Indians from Yokuts, Plains Miwok, and Ohlonean groups.

During the Battalion's second raid on the Valley, one of Chief Tenaya's sons was captured and killed. Lafayette Bunnell, a battalion member, translated the chief's impassioned declaration upon hearing of his son's death.

"Kill me, sir captain. Yes, kill me, as you killed my son; as you would kill my people if they were to come to you! You would kill all my race if you had the power. Yes sir, American, you can now tell your warriors to kill the old chief; you have made me sorrowful, my life dark; you killed the child of my heart, why not kill the father? But wait a little; when I am dead I will call to my people to come to you, I will call louder than you have had me call; that they shall hear me in their sleep, and come to avenge the death of their chief and his son. Yes, sir, American, my spirit will make trouble for you and your people, as you have caused trouble to me and my people. With the wizards, I will follow the white men and make them fear me.

"You may kill me, sir captain, but you shall not live in peace. I will follow in your footsteps, I will not leave my home, but be with the spirits among the rocks, the water-falls, in the rivers and in the winds; wheresoever you go I will be with you. You will not see me, but you will fear the spirit of the old chief, and grow cold. The great spirits have spoken! I am done."

A few of the gold-seeking immigrants found the precious metal, but most failed to secure their fortunes. Upon seeing Yosemite Valley, though, some within the latter group recognized a different kind of mother lode; they knew people would covet the Valley's incredible beauty. In 1855, only four years after the Mariposa Battalion's initial foray into the Valley, James Mason Hutchings brought the first tourists to see the wonders for themselves. Uncontrolled commercial development in Yosemite Valley was off and running.

The relationship between Euro-Americans and the Valley was conceived in anger, born in murder, and baptized in greed—not the most promising start. Since the initial taking of the Valley, it's been subject to alternating moods: at one moment sublime, peaceful, and beautiful, and the next caught up in cataclysmic natural events and endless bitter controversy. Yosemite is well known as one of the National Park System's most difficult children, one of the hardest to manage. And it's not the hundreds of thousands of backcountry wilderness acres that are hard to manage; it's the few thousand acres of Yosemite Valley itself.

On June 8, 2005, my forty-fifth birthday, I met a good friend for lunch at the east end of Stoneman Bridge. We walked to the Camp Curry Mexican food window, ordered tacos and coffee, and then set off in search of a quiet place to eat.

We wandered through large crowds of visitors of all shapes and sizes, and past cars, trucks, bikes, buses, and fences before selecting a premier spot: the middle of Stoneman Meadow boardwalk, where a blanket of grass and sedge was transitioning from glossy spring green to a darker summer tone, tipped with the barest hint of autumn gold. We sat facing down-valley. A solid wall of majestic ponderosa pine and incense-cedar rose in the foreground, at meadow's edge. The sylvan screen was backed by a wall of grey, black, and white granite, which in turn was crowned by the Valley's jagged rim.

Stoneman Meadow was quiet that afternoon, unlike another fateful day in 1970, when cultural angst fueled by war and disillusionment erupted in Yosemite Valley. On Saturday of the July 4th weekend, a confrontation broke out in the meadow between visitors and the Park Service.

According to former National Park Service employee Charles R. "Butch" Farabee, Jr. in *National Park Ranger: An American Icon*, the scene was filled with rock music, fireworks, loud vehicle mufflers, alcohol, and drugs, all combining to create an "almost primitive, jungle-like atmosphere" as obscenities were traded between "tribal enclaves." Farabee stated visitors assaulted rangers with rocks and words.

Late that afternoon, the ranger staff heard about a protest to be held at Stoneman Meadow. They alerted neighboring law enforcement officials of impending "major problems." By dusk, roughly 400 to 500 people had gathered at the meadow. Farabee reported, "Psychedelic peace symbols, love beads, and long hair predominated." Rangers on foot and sixteen employees on horses tried to disperse the crowd. Rangers tried to "lasso the hippies." Rocks flew. Bottles were broken over horses' faces. According to Farabee, the mob "quickly became vicious," and "park employees had to flee for their lives."

By dawn, about 150 federal, state, and county law enforcement officers responded to the park's call for help. Before it was over, two police cars were destroyed, two deputies had discharged firearms and required medical attention, and there were numerous "bloodied hippies." Officers arrested about 150 people. The "Yosemite Riot" at Stoneman Meadow was a major turning point that affected the entire National Park Service. The Service's law enforcement program turned professional. Rangers became police officers.

Less than twenty years later, Stoneman Meadow was the site of another major turning point when the Park Service constructed the first modern boardwalk and fencing in Yosemite Valley with the intent to restore and protect the meadow. Before construction began, park biologists had to work very hard to convince managers that keeping people from trampling the meadow was important enough to warrant such actions. Managers feared visitors would react badly to the visual intrusion of fences around meadows and would be upset by the control imposed by fences, boardwalks, and signs. Once construction was finished, though, the public raved about the changes and wondered why the Park Service had waited so long to make them.

In an ironic twist, critics of the Park Service believe the 1970 riot could have been averted, and tensions diffused, if rangers had tried harder to educate the crowd, if they had told them to disperse in order to protect the meadow.

As I munched tacos and my friend sipped coffee, we caught up on one another's lives, and then our conversation moved to a topic that frequently dominated our exchanges: our shared dismay at the amount of construction occurring in the Valley. That day the list included road construction, the utility system upgrade, and the Curry dorms.

The Soul of Yosemite

On any given day in the Valley construction projects assaulted one's senses. Fences of orange plastic and chain link, backhoes, front-end loaders, tractor-trailer rigs hauling materials into the Valley, stakes, signs, flagging, and piles of sand and soil severely marred scenery, changing the sublime to the sullied, the breathtaking to the battered. The incessant *beep, beep, beep* of trucks backing up, pounding jackhammers, and droning diesel trucks set one's teeth on edge, over-riding the wind in the trees, the canyon wren's trill, and even the roar of Yosemite Falls. The construction also violated the delectable odors of the Valley. Foul smelling, dark grey exhaust belched out of heavy equipment and fresh layers of road oil emanated a leaden stench, drowning out the collective aromas of sun-baked cottonwood, incense-cedar, and azalea.

Our conversation eventually shifted, as it usually did, to an examination of ways to stop the damage. I told him I'd always believed the most effective way to save the Earth and its wild places would be to start a new religion, an Earth-centered religion. I volunteered to be the next Billy Graham, but vowed to expound on a message based on reverence for land and wildness.

As I rambled on, my companion admired the granite walls rising up all around us. Meadow grasses waved and bowed to an intermittent breeze, and brooding dark clouds migrated slowly overhead, occasionally blessing us with a light baptismal shower. My friend turned to look me in the eye, and said, "You know, this place didn't happen by accident."

We had never talked about our religious beliefs. I didn't know if he was Christian, Buddhist, Pagan, or something else entirely. But it didn't matter, because I knew exactly what he meant; that the place of infinite beauty we call Yosemite Valley had to be the inspiration and the creation of some entity much larger than all of us, much larger than a random biogeochemical coming together of elements, much larger than anything we humans can begin to comprehend. It had to be the creation of God, or whatever name one chooses to give this exalted power.

I was silent for a moment, considering my own beliefs. I think anything is possible, and much is likely, and there is an infinite range of right answers when it comes to explaining how our world came to be. A few minutes later he said something to the effect of, "Okay, even if I admit for a moment that it did come about due to some random collection of geological, biological, and chemical events, something has been instilled in us as humans to feel that this place is sacred, a cathedral, and this something causes us to feel a profound and inexplicable sense of reverence, or holiness if you will, when we are here. So, tell me, why are we allowing this temple to be desecrated?"

I had no answer for him. But my conviction that the events occurring in Yosemite Valley—the development, the impacts, and the complete disregard for the environment—were wrong and unacceptable grew stronger as I pondered the question. As Stoneman Meadow worked its alchemical magic beneath me, I realized complaining about the situation was of limited value. I realized Yosemite Valley needed a new blueprint, a new vision for a future with less development and less commercialization; a vision to break the cycle of abuse fueled by greed that has characterized the Euro-American relationship with the Valley since the Mariposa Battalion first rode in. I realized the new vision had to be based in love and respect, had to honor and cherish the Valley, its wild nature, and all of its more-than-human inhabitants, both sentient and not—a vision aligned with the views of Frederick Law Olmsted. I realized someone had to begin the process of crafting that new vision.

And I realized, with a sigh, that someone was going to be me.

CHAPTER 24
Essential Wildness

Journal

I miss being close to places where I can't see, hear, or smell anything made by humans. Places where I see only granite walls with lower slopes of rock and scree, flowing water, pine and oak, and meadow grasses swaying in an up-canyon afternoon breeze. Places where I hear only a solo raven passing overhead with a soft whoosh of ebony wing beat, the splash and roar of water making its way, or the wet snort of a mule deer leaping up from a grassy nest. Places where I smell only cool, damp humus and standing water in the shallow depression at the meadow's center, mingling with the sharp scent of pine needles and bark drenched in sunlight.

I miss silent winter nights, just after a heavy snow, when the full moon illuminates every rocky crack and crevice, when every tree and shrub wears a snow cape, and every surface is coated in white chiffon—an angel's landscape of shining night, where all really is calm and bright, silent, and holy. Nights when anything can happen, when the land's white hot energy runs full tilt, and magic dances at the edge of awareness. Nights when I imagine for a moment that all is right with the world, or could be if only we made the effort.

I miss the endless reach of stars on moonless nights, and coyote's howl as he chats with the light those stars pour down onto his perfect, furry little head. I miss the wild.

◆◆◆

When Tom's new job pulled us out of Yosemite and planted us in Boise, I left my wild roots behind in the Valley's rich loamy soil and decomposed granite. I felt adrift. I rose to anger quickly, paced around a too large house on a too small lot, overate, and under-exercised. Surrounded by retail establishments, I shopped. My head ached from endless tail-spinning thoughts. I'd left the home of my heart to live in a big city. I was bereft, homesick for nature, for wildness.

We struggled to find a place to live that was reasonably close to Tom's new office. Our realtor, who had the patience of Job, showed us home after home. Many of the houses were fine, but their locations made me claustrophobic—small lots, close neighbors, nothing of the natural environment remaining. We decided our best option was the foothills north of town. Even there, though, the land seemed the antithesis of wildness. The hills presented a tired and worn profile, beaten nearly senseless by the generations of hungry cattle and sheep that preceded the suburban sprawl. But it was quiet, and I could see stars at night.

Winter turned to spring, the snow melted, the slick clay dried, and I ventured out to explore the slope behind our house. My spirits soared, way out of proportion to the event, when I spotted purple blossoms of *Astragalus*, a native member of the Pea family, hidden among dense swaths of non-native medusahead. Remnant pockets of sagebrush and rabbitbrush, also native, made me smile as they greened up in advance of the equinox. Sparkling white chunks of quartz emerged from a heavy clay matrix. Flocks of Canada geese called as they passed overhead, and red-tailed hawks, Cooper's hawks, and kestrels pursued mice and voles. On very rare occasions, I heard the unmistakable cackle of sandhill cranes, and, early one morning while Tom and I sipped tea in the breakfast nook, a badger strolled across the back lawn.

Different flavors of wildness penetrated the subdivision under cover of night to avoid cars, trucks, bikes, skateboards, scooters, leaf-blowers, dogs, cats, and children. Coyotes howled as the moon waxed, ghost deer pruned the roses we so carefully planted and tended, and a pair of great horned owls danced their intentions on our next door neighbor's roof. One winter morning, I discovered a large pair of talons with lower legs attached, and a few widely scattered tan and white feathers on the strip of lawn north of our house. A barn owl had been ambushed and dismembered just below my bedroom window.

One at a time, assorted remnants of the wild nature of the Boise foothills revealed themselves to me. I realized even though the obviously wild no longer surrounded me, wildness still was present. I became more comfortable in my new home once I began to connect to the essential wildness of the place.

Compared to Boise, Yosemite Valley supports a wealth of wildness. For many visitors, it's the wildest place they've ever experienced. Others believe humans chased the wild out of the Valley a long time ago. Clearly, wildness means different things to different people, and individual meanings tend to be derived from past experience.

In February of 2009, I attended a workshop in Joseph, Oregon that focused on "Re-imagining the Wild," sponsored by a literary organization called Fishtrap. Despite differences in age, background, and lifestyle, the workshop attendees held several things in common: we valued wildness and wild nature, we wanted to ensure these entities survived in our increasingly tame world, we knew people protect what they need and love, and we sought ways to share the magic and blessings of the wild with the uninitiated—to spread the gospel of wildness.

During the first session, Roderick Frazier Nash, author of *Wilderness and the American Mind*, told us defining wilderness was like "nailing Jell-O to the wall." The term is slippery and elusive. The Oxford English Dictionary defines "wild" as: not domesticated, cultivated, civilized, controlled, or restrained. "The wilds" denotes a remote, uninhabited, or sparsely inhabited area. An animal, plant, or person can "run wild"—grow or develop without restraint or discipline—and "wilderness" is an uncultivated, uninhabited, and inhospitable region.

According to Nash, the root of "wild" can be traced through early Teutonic and Norse languages to "will," meaning self-willed, willful, or uncontrollable. From "willed" came the adjective "wild." The Old English "deor," meaning animal, was linked to "wild" to describe creatures not controlled by humans. "Wild-deor-ness," then wilderness, likely emerged when "wildeor" was contracted to wilder, or wildern. "Wild-deor-ness" then translates to "the place of wild beasts."

"Wilderness" has another, legal definition in the United States. In 1964, Congress passed the Wilderness Act and created a Wilderness Preservation System. Over time, about 107 million acres in 704 different areas became designated federal wilderness "where the earth and its community of life are untrammeled by man, where man himself is a visitor who does not remain." A federal wilderness retains its "primeval character and influence, without permanent improvements or human habitation." Wilderness areas appear to be "primarily affected by the forces of nature," and provide outstanding opportunities for solitude or "primitive and unconfined" recreation. Less than 5 percent of land in the United States is federally-designated wilderness. If Alaska lands are excluded, that number drops to about 2.5 percent.

Despite the name, designated wilderness areas are not necessarily wild; visitors can hike or ride horses on improved trails, raft and ski, and in some cases, hunt or fish. In Alaska, motorized vehicles are allowed in some areas, as is construction of cabins and aquaculture systems. Over 700 miles of trails run through the 704,000-acre Yosemite Wilderness in Yosemite National Park.

As Nash pointed out, although not completely wild, wilderness areas represent an unprecedented effort to share the planet with other species, and to exercise restraint in our endeavors instead of allowing human development to occupy every place on Earth. Although wilderness doesn't always equal wildness, designated wilderness areas often provide our last best chance to know wildness in its purest sense.

While the Fishtrappers sat in the rustic great room in the Wallowa Lake Lodge, wildness pursued its own agenda outside. Blankets of snow insulated the forest floor around the frozen, glacial lake. When we took a break, I spotted a bald eagle soaring over the icy expanse.

"Civilization created wilderness," Nash informed us. Before humans became "civilized," taking up agriculture and creating towns and cities, there was no wilderness. Early societies of hunters and gatherers had no concept of wilderness; it was simply the land, the matrix within which they lived. Gary Snyder stated this well in *The Practice of the Wild*, when he said nature is not a place to visit, it is home.

In *Wilderness and the American Mind*, Nash chronicled the evolution of Euro-American attitudes toward wilderness. Early white immigrants to the New World were steeped in Western thought and Judeo-Christian beliefs. As a result, most viewed wild, unsettled country—wilderness—as dangerous, filled with wild people and predators. Challenging, unpredictable, and undesirable, it was to be loathed, feared, avoided, or conquered. It was the antithesis of paradise. The latter, in contrast, was hospitable, comfortable, provided abundant water and food, and allowed people to believe they were safe and in control—the Garden of Eden.

Throughout America's early settlement period, a few individuals did appreciate and extol the virtues of wilderness, but they were exceptions to the rule. Historians believe a more widespread shift in attitudes began around 1890, when the U.S. Census announced the "frontier" no longer existed. As Nash put it, "Civilization had largely subdued the continent." From that time forward, appreciation of wild country grew into a network of wilderness areas. For some, this appreciation grew even further, into a belief that wild land was critically important to humans and all other species.

As we waded deeper into our exploration of wildness, writer and mountain guide Jack Turner said wild systems are self-organizing and autonomous. Kathleen Dean Moore, environmental writer and Distinguished Professor of Philosophy at Oregon State University, told us wilderness has both intrinsic and instrumental value; wilderness is good in and of itself, in addition to its usefulness to humans. Then Moore meandered into more personal and contemplative waters. She said humans yearn for, yet are afraid of, wilderness; that it's both extraordinary and mysterious. Turner, in *The Abstract Wild*, includes wildness with qualities of spirit, enchantment, the sacred, holiness, magic, and soul; terms that are hard to define because they refer to the "human experience of the material world rather than the material world itself."

All three speakers touched on the fact that wilderness is outside of human control, and Turner emphasized the difference between "control" and "influence." Scientists acknowledge few, if any, places on Earth are not influenced in some way by humans. But, Turner said, "Influence alone does not destroy autonomy." The question is: How much influence is too much? At what point does a place lose its wildness, its sense of self, its ability to self-organize, to be self-willed? And when does influence become an attempt to control? As Turner spoke, I gazed up at the moose head with the empty, glassy-eyed stare that was mounted on the Lodge wall. He reminded me how easily autonomy can be stolen, how quickly the wild can disappear.

Henry David Thoreau told us, "In wildness is the preservation of the world." No one, except Thoreau himself, knows exactly what he meant by this, but his words resonate with many people, and set their imaginations flying. I translate Thoreau's words in simple terms: We all need wildness.

For me, this need is crystal clear. Wildness and wildlands are as essential to me as clean air and water, good food and love. Many others have shared my sentiments. David Brower, in *Let the Mountains Talk, Let the Rivers Run*, said: "When you lose contact with wildness, you've lost an important part of yourself." He thought such losses made people sad, "without their even knowing why, deep down." In the words of Jay Griffiths in *Wild: An Elemental Journey*, "to be most alive is to be most free is to be most wild." The sage Wallace Stegner believed, "Something will have gone out of us as a people if we ever let the remaining wilderness be destroyed." Brower echoed Stegner when he wrote "Killing trees, habitat, and animals and separating ourselves from nature is making us all a bit crazy. We need to restore the Earth because we need to save the wild. We need to save the wild in order to save ourselves."

We need wildness, a wild Earth, for an eternity of reasons, all of which are grounded in connection and relationship. We know the wild Earth provides our fellow species with habitat: places to live, eat, shelter, and procreate. But we've lost sight of similar connections of our own, the essential relationships between humans and the wild Earth. We've separated ourselves from the ground we once walked, sat, and slept on, and the food and water we once procured directly from the land. Wildness reminds us we are but a strand in the intricate web of life, and helps us rediscover our inescapable, infinitely rich connection, which is as critical to our survival as an umbilical cord is to a fetus.

Wildness reminds us we are never alone. In 1996, I moved from Santa Cruz to Nevada City, where I knew no one. My friend Rod was dying of cancer and I spent much of my time with him in Sacramento; but often I found myself alone, as lonely and sad as I have ever been, in a small house on nine acres near the banks of Deer Creek.

When I pulled my head out of my solitary gloom enough to look around, I began to notice the other residents of the place: the pair of geese who came to the pond at the same time every evening, the large doe who nested below the deck out back, the wood ducks who swam in and out of view in the cattail patch, and the rowdy gang of wild turkeys who passed through several times a week, kicking and scratching to dig up grubs. The deep familiarity of these animals with their habitats reminded me once again that we humans are part of something much larger, connected by our breath and our energy to everything else, to the flow of life. My loneliness abated when I watched my wild new friends immersed in their lives. They were separate from mine, but we were inextricably linked.

Wildness reminds us of our mortality and our vulnerability. If we're willing to experience wild areas on their own terms, in all their glorious spontaneity and unpredictability, they will present us with real risks (no cell phones allowed). Accepting and melting into the wild requires us to accept the risks inherent in being alive, to let go of fear, transcend limits, join the living dance.

Wildness reminds us to pay attention. The wild *is* the present moment, the now, not past, not future, just now. When we pay attention to the wild moment, our future fears are laid to rest; all the "what if" questions, which reside in tomorrow, become irrelevant. Wildness reminds us to rest in, to savor, this moment.

Wildness reminds us to dream, and to imagine. Albert Einstein told us imagination is more important than knowledge. Imagination—the new, the creative, the thought, the idea, the vision—can't live in the past and can't be found in the future; it arises only in the present moment, only in direct experience.

Wildness reminds us we are much more than our thoughts. It pulls us out of our heads, brings us back to our bodies, to our hearts, lungs, arms, legs, feet, noses, tongues, ears; it brings us back to our senses. Fourteen years after the event, my tongue remembers foraging near Gustavus, Alaska; remembers yearning for the tiny, bright red, wild strawberry attached to its thin runner, sprawled over sand warmed by the summer sun; remembers biting into the tender flesh; remembers the explosion of sharp sweetness; remembers the berry's essential wildness bursting through, shaming its dull, mass-produced brethren. The perfect berries displayed on sloping racks in Safeway only dream of possessing such power.

Wildness reminds us we are complete and perfect. It fills up our spirits, and in so doing, quells our burning desires to acquire things, to own, to shop, to buy, to try desperately to fill our empty inner spaces with stuff. Wildness quiets the pervasive inner voice, the one that says, "My life will be complete, I will be forever happy, I will fit in and belong if only I own that book, necklace, fetish, pair of shoes, shirt, dress, pretty wooden box."

Wildness reminds us other beings reside above us on the food chain. I still feel the chills that ran down my spine as the lion roared just outside our thin-walled canvas tent in the middle of a moonless Serengeti night. Wide awake, I had to pee, and that meant going out there. I didn't get more than two feet past the tent entrance before I stopped to squat in the grass. This was pure, raw, essential wildness. The lioness told me in no uncertain terms I was starving to death on an American diet of calm, placid and safe. She reminded me of how desperately I want to connect to the Earth in a way that is integral and primal. She reminded me I was alive, but won't be forever.

Nash is correct. Defining wild, wildness, and wilderness is difficult. Each person's definition is unique, colored by their own experiences, by the places they go, the people they go with, the weather, the number and type of insects they encounter, their health, the fit of their boots, how well their stoves work, or whether their freeze-dried chicken cacciatore is tasty or is stolen by a bear. In the end, each of us will come to our own conclusions; will have our own definitions of what is wild.

Personally, wildness helps me understand my place in the world, and who and what I am in relationship to. It helps me feel connected to the Earth and to the great Other. I think we all need to feel that connection, to be able to build a personal, inner foundation anchored in the land, in a place that feels like home, regardless of how many times we've changed our physical address. This is especially important in our insanely mobile society, where perpetual motion in residences, jobs, and relationships too often takes the place of true connection.

Wildness has blessed my life beyond measure. When I reflect on my turbulent years as a teenager trying to make sense of life in Southern California, I realize two things kept me from spiraling deeper into a vortex of self-destruction: horses and Yosemite Valley. The young woman who leaned over the bridge railing below Vernal Fall lacked a firm foundation, lacked connection. She found both in wild swirling water, in the steady gaze of granite faces, in the peace radiating from the eye of a deer, all within a place steeped in mystery and wonder of the highest order. Yosemite Valley's wild nature may have saved her life, *my* life.

To this day, Yosemite Valley retains some of its original wild nature, but much was lost soon after Euro-Americans arrived. The losses compounded over time as human influence increased and spread. The remnants of the Valley's native wildness that do persist are under assault, at risk of extinction. It can be argued that Yosemite's losses are but a faint echo of the destruction of wildness occurring daily across the planet, and are inconsequential compared to losses of wild rainforest in South America or Borneo, or loss of wild Arctic lands, sacrificed to appease our gluttony for energy. I disagree; the losses of wildness in Yosemite Valley are extremely consequential.

Wildness is the Valley's most important, most essential attribute. Wild lands and wildness are critical to all life on Earth, and offer human beings their best, and perhaps last, chance to learn to live with humility, respect, and grace in their relationships with one another and with the more-than-human world. I believe our fate as a species depends on our ability to learn this lesson quickly and to learn it well. Wildness in Yosemite Valley is particularly important because of the place it holds in so many human hearts. What better place to begin our lessons, to re-learn how to live in connection, to re-learn how to live?

CHAPTER 25
Yosemite *Is* Different

Journal

I believe in magic, the everyday kind as well as the extraordinary, and I most appreciate those experiences that are a rich and subtle blend of the two. Yosemite Valley is a stage set and ready for magic, which readily spins off into contemplation, transformation, and, ultimately, connection with the land.

Last week Tom and I walked to the Ahwahnee Hotel for a light dinner at the lounge. We crossed the parking lot, and as we walked past a large, red Cadillac Escalade, a small, red damselfly zipped past my left ear. I raised my right hand high in the air, index finger aimed straight for the sky. The damselfly, a bit smaller than most dragonflies, circled once, and then came in for a direct landing on the tip of my extended finger—an invited guest, unafraid, making connection.

A shiver ran through me. I thanked the damselfly for honoring me with this visit. A moment or two later, she lifted off into the gentle warm breeze and circled Tom's head. I suggested he put his finger in the air. He did, and the damselfly landed on his finger, working her magic a second time.

I've experienced this magic with dragonflies on a few precious and rare occasions, and once, with a butterfly. These connections with the small, wild, winged creatures have only happened to me in Yosemite Valley.

♦♦♦

Crowds of people milled around the patio in front of Degnan's Deli, in search of coffee, newspapers, and ice cream cones. As I bit into my turkey sandwich, my Park Service lunch buddy looked at me and said, "You know, it makes me sad to say this, but I've come to view Yosemite Valley as a sacrifice area."

I heard this sentiment repeatedly in Yosemite, whenever conversations with seasoned employees steered toward the urbanization and exploitation of the Valley. My associates disliked the excessive development and overuse, some of them intensely, but they accepted it. They viewed it as a tradeoff: If the Park Service condoned commercialization of the Valley, those who sought to exploit Yosemite would keep their focus on the Valley and leave the rest of the park alone.

Over time, I learned that many employees who were resigned to conditions in the Valley already had tried their best to change the situation. Without support from upper level managers, they failed. Ongoing destruction of resources and diminishment of the park experience seemed unstoppable. After much head-banging, these fellow advocates of the wild gave up the fight out of self-preservation, or left to work for other parks or agencies. Those who stayed turned their efforts toward protecting areas outside of the Valley.

My initial responses to this capitulation included sadness, disbelief, and outrage. This was not the National Park Service I knew and loved. In other parks I'd worked in, it seemed managers honestly tried to protect park resources. I wanted to believe the same was, or could be, true of Yosemite. I wanted to believe if Yosemite's managers really understood the importance of the Valley, they would come to their senses and bend over backwards to reduce development and increase protection.

In 1990, when I first stepped up to advocate for nature in Yosemite, the Chief of Resources fired me for being too preservation-oriented, which, he told me, may have been okay in Sequoia, but, Yosemite was different. Despite the trauma of losing my job, I still refused to believe Yosemite was different. In 2002, when I tried again to protect

Yosemite's resources and met with similar dismal results, I finally understood the frustration of others who had tried and failed.

But I refuse to capitulate. Yosemite Valley is far too special and important to be sacrificed any longer to feed insatiable human appetites for economic gain, entertainment, and ego fulfillment.

As I watched the events of 2003 through 2005 unfold in Yosemite Valley—giant trees replaced by restrooms, oil floating down Yosemite Creek, fragile meadow plants bulldozed, the Yosemite Creek drainage filled with cement—I traveled an emotional rollercoaster of grief similar to that described by Elizabeth Kubler-Ross in her book, *On Death and Dying*. At first I was in denial. I couldn't believe the Park Service could allow, much less promote, such destruction. Then I hit the second stage and got really, really angry. I'm not sure whether I went through the third stage, bargaining, or just dropped immediately into the fourth stage, depression. I became physically ill. A persistent pain in my upper left ribcage defied diagnosis by my doctors.

I still haven't entered the final stage of grieving, acceptance, but I did shift from a position of blind rage to one of conviction and analysis. Convinced the situation in the Valley must change, I began to develop a set of specific actions to help the Valley and its visitors far into the future. Once I set my anger aside, and separated my personal feelings about the Valley from the events I witnessed, I could see the situation in a larger context. In doing so, I realized the Chief of Resources was absolutely right, although not in the way he meant. Yosemite *is* different.

Kubler-Ross' cycle of grieving was presented as the response of people who learn they have a terminal illness, or who have lost a loved one. Fortunately, in the case of Yosemite Valley, the patient is not dead—yet. But parts of the ecological web, including great gray owls, spotted owls, willow flycatchers, foothill yellow-legged frogs, and California red-legged frogs, are scarce or completely absent, and many other parts are deteriorating. The integrity of the Valley has been compromised, and sacrificed, for over 150 years. It is time for this sacrilege to end.

Yosemite Valley's "difference" was clear to the Native Americans who called it home. The Valley's special and unique qualities also were obvious to the Valley's earliest white visitors. In 1886, James M. Hutchings provided numerous quotes from early writers in his book, *In the Heart of the Sierras: Yo Semite and the Big Tree Groves*, including the following:

> "The isolation of the Yo Semite, the absolute wilderness of its sylvan solitudes, many miles from human settlement or cultivation, its cascade 2,000 feet high, though the stream which makes this leap has worn a channel in the hard bedrock to a depth of 1,000 feet, renders it the grandest marvel that ever met my gaze."
> -Horace Greeley, *N.Y. Independent of March 1860*

> "I think I shall see nothing else so sublime and beautiful, till, happily, I stand within the gates of the Heavenly City."
> -Sidney Andrews' *Letter to the Boston Advertiser*

> "Even the most frivolous spirits among us were struck with sudden calm, as if they stood at the portals of some divine mystery..."
> -Mary E. Blake's *On the Wing*

> "The only spot that I have ever found that came up to the brag."
> -Ralph Waldo Emerson

John Muir, in his book, *The Yosemite*, described in detail the glories of the deep, grassy Valley:

> "Every rock in its walls seems to glow with life. Some lean back in majestic repose; others, absolutely sheer or nearly so

for thousands of feet, advance beyond their companions in thoughtful attitudes, giving welcome to storms and calms alike, seemingly aware, yet heedless, of everything going on about them. Awful in stern, immovable majesty, how softly these rocks are adorned, and how fine and reassuring the company they keep: their feet among beautiful groves and meadows, their brows in the sky, a thousand flowers leaning confidingly against their feet, bathed in floods of water, floods of light, while the snow and the waterfalls, the winds and avalanches and clouds shine and sing and wreathe about them as the years go by, and myriads of small winged creatures—birds, bees, butterflies—give glad animation and help to make all the air into music."

According to Muir, it was: "…as if into this one mountain mansion Nature had gathered her choicest treasures, to draw her lovers into close and confiding communion with her."

Yosemite Valley's "difference" prompted national leaders to create what is now one of America's oldest, best known, and most frequently visited national parks. Yosemite Valley, despite its small size, about seven miles long, less than a mile wide, and approximately 4,500 acres, is Yosemite National Park's crème de la crème. The remainder of the park, approximately 740,000 acres of mostly federal wilderness, wraps itself around the Valley like a protective cocoon. This vast wilderness is spectacular, but the Valley is unquestionably the heart of the region, the exceptional, precious, one-of-a-kind shining star. Approximately 80 to 90 percent of park visitors aim for the Valley. For many, if not most, "Yosemite" is the Valley.

While it has accrued tremendous social significance as a result of stunning beauty and extensive and continuous media coverage, the Valley's importance, its difference, extends far beyond its value as a showpiece of scenic beauty or a travel destination. Cradled within the embrace of towering granite walls, the Valley safeguards a treasure-trove of stories of the past, both before and during the time of humans, and is of vital importance to the lives of its many more-than-human occupants.

Stories of the past make the Valley different. A living textbook of Earth's evolution, the Valley's structure illustrates changes wrought by earthquakes, glaciers, rivers, fires, rockslides, floods, and climatic variability over a multi-million year lifespan. Beginning 4,000 to 6,000 years ago, the human stories began to unfold; physical evidence of the lives of the early inhabitants gives us pieces of those stories. The Valley is considered an archeological district, is on the National Register of Historic Places, is home to three National Historic Landmarks, the Ahwahnee Hotel, the Rangers' Club, and LeConte Memorial Lodge, and protects more than one hundred sites with evidence of human occupation and use. The Valley continues to be extremely important to Native Americans with ancestral ties to this most sacred place.

Plant diversity makes the Valley different. For its size, the Valley is home to an unusually rich collection of native plants. This richness is linked to a broad array of habitat types resulting from multiple variations in basic ecological themes: slope, aspect, soil, moisture, temperature, and solar exposure. A short, wall-to-wall trek across the Valley beginning at the base of the boulder-strewn southern wall just behind the Yosemite Chapel illustrates this variability. Behind the chapel, we enter a dark, cool, and moist environment, because the towering south wall blocks the sun until very late morning, and the sun disappears again by early-afternoon. During contracted winter days, much of the land tucked up close to the south wall remains shaded all day. The relatively cool, damp conditions favor growth of bigleaf maple, and intermittent Douglas-fir, white fir, incense-cedar, and ponderosa pine. Scattered dogwood and California laurel grow beneath the upper canopy.

The sun meets us as we move north to enter an expansive network of meadows that fringe the winding river corridor. The lowest, wettest meadow areas are covered almost completely with sedges, while drier portions support more grasses. Sadly, the two grasses now dominating Valley meadows, Kentucky bluegrass and Idaho redtop, are non-native invaders. The rich soils underlying the green carpets are saturated with river and runoff through much of the growing season. Occasionally, isolated patches of land within or adjacent to the meadows support dense patches of less abundant native species, including needlegrass, deergrass, penstemon, and dogbane. Patchy stands of black cottonwood and white alder, as well as several willow species, shade the banks at river's edge.

North of the river, the meadows give way to black oak woodlands, often underlain by patchy quilts of bracken fern, dragon sagewort, and herbs like yarrow, milkweed, buckwheat, and goldenrod. Farther north, the oaks thin out and are joined by ponderosa pine and incense-cedar.

The vegetation changes again as we approach the north Valley wall. The added warmth and dryness foster woodlands with ancient canyon live oak, scattered incense-cedar and Douglas-fir, and an understory of Mariposa manzanita, California laurel, and even the occasional sagebrush.

Our mid-Valley transect includes many, but not all, Valley plant communities. Numerous expressions of mixed conifer forest, composed largely of differing proportions of ponderosa pine, incense-cedar, white fir, Douglas-fir, and sometimes black oak, occur throughout the Valley. If we travel east toward Happy Isles, our feet will get soaked in a marshy fen, a rare habitat dominated by horsetails, grasses, and rushes, accompanied by cow parsnip, white alder, dogwood, and raspberry. In addition, lawns, orchards, dumps, playgrounds, and tennis courts, areas devoid of native plant communities, cover large patches of land.

The Valley's diverse mix of plant species and habitats, coupled with a relatively mild, Mediterranean-type climate of hot summers and cool, moist winters, meet the needs of an equally diverse assemblage of wildlife species. The *Yosemite Valley Plan Supplemental Environmental Impact Statement* states that 150 bird species regularly occur in Yosemite National Park. Of these, at least 84 species, more than half of those found in the entire park, nest in the Valley. Numerous bat species also live in the Valley, including the spotted bat, one of North America's rarest, which nests high up on the Valley's walls. Simply put, the Valley is a great place to live.

The Merced River makes the Valley different. As Yosemite Valley is the heart of Yosemite National Park, the Merced River is the heart of Yosemite Valley. Although the iconic, cover-girl features, Yosemite Falls, Half Dome, and El Capitan, garner the most attention from the media and travel marketers, visitors who return to the Valley time after time know the river is equally, if not more important than the images gracing the magazine covers. The rocks and waterfalls create the dramatic setting, but the river sustains life.

The Merced River's earthly origins, its headwaters, coalesce many miles east of the Valley, in the far reaches of the park near Mt. Lyell and the peaks called Triple, Merced, and Red. The river gains volume and velocity as it sings its way west. Much of the flow travels to and through Yosemite Valley via the river's main stem, but a distinct part of the river, the South Fork, takes a different route, through Wawona. The reunion of the two waterways occurs near Savage's Trading Post, outside park boundaries.

On November 2, 1987, Congress recognized the superlative qualities of the Merced, and granted Wild and Scenic River status to 122 miles of the river. This designation directed federal agencies to preserve the river's free-flowing condition, and to protect the river and its immediate environment for the benefit and enjoyment of present and future generations forever. Yosemite National Park embraces 81 of those 122 miles.

Compared to its flat countenance in Yosemite Valley, most of the Merced River's course is steep, narrow, and rocky. The Valley is the largest U-shaped, glacier-carved valley occurring on the western slope of the Sierra Nevada, and is one of only two areas where the Merced River flows through a relatively broad, flat piece of land, a floodplain. As the water enters the Valley and spreads out, it slows down and deposits layer upon layer of sediment, creating a rich substrate for plants. The river and the gorge it has carved, in both frozen and liquid form, also provide a corridor critical for the movement of wildlife traveling to or from the high country.

Location makes the Valley different. Ecologists working to save endangered and imperiled species and their habitats, and to protect the land base that supports us all, recognize we must preserve large tracts of relatively undisturbed land. In this light, preserving Yosemite Valley's ecosystems is extremely important, as the Valley is completely surrounded on all sides by wild land. The combination of exceptionally high biological diversity, its function as a wildlife corridor, and its location in the middle of hundreds of thousands of acres of wilderness make Yosemite Valley highly significant, locally, regionally, and globally.

And, finally, human longing makes the Valley different. People fall in love with the Valley quickly and easily; frequently it's love at first sight, because the Valley embodies our collective visions of both wilderness and paradise. Yosemite Valley looks, feels, and even smells like the Garden before The Fall. It appears bountiful, able to provide us with everything we need without our having to toil or trouble. The Valley feels safe. Even without all the human contrivances, it would still feel safe. It's flat, and has a moderate climate and plenty of water. Even though the perception of safety is an illusion—flooding, rockslides, and fires are frequent, and wildlife can injure humans—the Valley feels benign and friendly. Because it feels so safe and welcoming, it's the perfect place for people who are unfamiliar with or afraid of nature to meet the wild on its own terms. Yosemite Valley is the perfect teacher, the best possible emissary of wild nature.

The Chief who fired me was right. Yosemite *is* different. It's different in terms of its beauty, its wealth of natural and cultural resources, the sacred place it holds in the hearts of millions of people, and its potential to teach us how to live well on the planet. But these attributes are not what the Chief meant when he fired me. He was referring to something very ugly: the exceptionally strong and pervasive political and economic forces at work in Yosemite Valley, and the influence those forces have on how the Park Service manages the park. As a GS-7 temporary employee, I was largely unaware of the ugliness; but after my stint as liaison, I began to understand the Chief's definition of "different."

Dysfunctional management makes the Valley different. During my tenure, the numerous park Divisions—Administration Management, Business and Revenue Management, Facilities Management, Interpretation, Planning, Project Management, Resources Management and Science, and Visitor Protection—resembled an octopus with nine arms and no head. It seemed no one in the management circle had any clear sense of what was happening in the park as a whole at any given time. The number of employees working for the Park Service, for concessionaires, and for other entities was too large, and the complexity of park operations was too great. The system was out of control.

I wondered if this situation was a by-product of the age of the park. Each successive superintendent and all the division chiefs and program managers working in Yosemite through the years, as well as each concessionaire, each interested Congressional representative, and each administration had their own pet projects and priorities they would initiate during their time of influence. It seemed park priorities weren't revised and refined over time; rather, all new ideas and new priorities were implemented *in addition to* all the ideas and priorities that had come before. As a result, new employees had to be hired constantly, and everyone was continually overworked despite an ever-expanding staff. To further complicate matters, the park was not managed as a unified entity; managers provided most employees with only enough information to do their jobs, and often not even that much. As a result, job satisfaction and employee morale were extremely low. People stayed in their jobs either because they loved Yosemite too much to leave, or because other aspects of their lives, such as children in school or proximity to family, kept them in place.

Yosemite's reputation as a difficult place to work is well known throughout the National Park Service. Many employees won't even apply for Yosemite jobs. One former employee, who now works in a different park, said no one should work in Yosemite for more than four years because the working environment is so toxic.

During my tenure, the toxicity was exacerbated by the presence of a well-defined "good ol' boy" network composed of managers at or near the top level. If an employee was not part of the network, he or she was often marginalized. Many members of the "the club" moved on to other pursuits subsequent to my departure from Yosemite. Bon voyage.

The relationship between Yosemite's managers and citizens interested in protecting the park makes the Valley different. During my tenure, managers frequently ignored the views of members of environmental groups trying to participate in park planning. In some cases, managers refused to even speak to concerned individuals. Some Park Service employees resorted to public name-calling when they repeatedly lost in court over the inadequacy of the Merced Wild and Scenic River Comprehensive Management Plan. One employee told the media the plaintiffs were just a "fringe group of radicals." The truth is that the plaintiffs cared deeply about the Valley and wanted the opportunity to voice their ideas and opinions about the Valley's future. At the very least, they wanted the Park Service to comply with environmental laws.

Politics make the Valley different. Based on personal observations and research, there never has been any strong political will to maintain the ecological or the spiritual integrity of Yosemite Valley, or to restore what's been lost. As soon as some of the earliest Euro-American visitors cast their greedy eyes on the Valley, dollar signs began to obscure the view of its profound beauty. And, because the Valley provides huge revenues to concession operators and local economies, the Park Service succumbs to the political pressure, and doesn't embrace resource protection and preservation as the highest priorities for Yosemite Valley. Even worse, we, the people of the United States, have accepted this sellout. We've allowed managers to avoid taking the high road and protecting the Valley by buying into, and selling, the idea that Yosemite is different and therefore must be managed differently.

In National Park Service circles, two parks stand out in terms of their management complexity: Yosemite and Yellowstone. Known informally as the "Y" parks, these two national wonders are among the oldest, largest, most beautiful, and most economically profitable of the national parks in the United States. It's no surprise they are also the most heavily influenced by politics, and are managed accordingly.

Ultimately, though, these parks should not be managed any differently than any other national park. If anything, we should honor their age, their historic significance, and their incomparable beauty by being even more protective of their natural and cultural values.

Managers in non-Y parks seem, for the most part, to elevate resource protection to a high level and act accordingly, and not be quite so obsequious in their relationships with concession operators, gateway businesses, the recreation industry, and others who seek to expand commercialization at the expense of park resources. Yosemite managers may have a longer history of playing to commercial interests and politicians, but it's time to learn from past mistakes instead of perpetuating this disgraceful behavior.

It's also time to change the nature of the sacrifice. Instead of sacrificing Yosemite Valley, let *us* begin to make the sacrifice, to forego, for once, our human desires, in the interest of protecting our incomparable Valley.

CHAPTER 26
First, Do No More Harm

Journal

The mingled roar of dump trucks, loaders, and cranes assails my ears. Chainsaws manned by workers removing allegedly dangerous tree branches scream in accompaniment. Half a dozen barking dogs, a school bus, an army of trucks—garbage, recycling, UPS, FedEx— and the penetrating click, click, click of a nail gun replacing a roof add to the auditory assault. Back-up warning signals on the trucks provide a counterpoint. The noise has been non-stop for two days. I'm ready to add my screams of irritation and frustration to the mix.

My teeth clench, my jaw tightens, and my shoulders creep up toward my ears. I am blessed to be able to live in a national park. And not just any national park, but one of the crown jewels, one of the most beloved. But, this neighborhood is far noisier than most urban neighborhoods. It is, by far, the noisiest place I've ever lived.

The noise is avoidable and unnecessary. The school doesn't belong here, nor does the housing area. Remove all the houses, or leave a few for emergency rangers and fire staff, and the amount of garbage and recycling decreases. Fewer houses mean fewer new roofs, fewer dogs, fewer delivery trucks, less vehicle exhaust. As much as I love living here, the benefits of downsizing Yosemite Valley are too numerous to count.

◆◆◆

Big, white, puffy clouds trailed across the sky. A chilly late winter breeze cooled my face and slipped under the collar of my jacket as I walked across Cook's Meadow to the river's edge. My tenure as liaison was over, and I'd started work on Yosemite's visitor carrying capacity program. In response to litigation, our small working group had been directed to focus our efforts on the river corridor where the Merced ran through the Valley.

I sat down under a tall pine, armed with pen and notebook, to prepare for an upcoming workshop. The task ahead involved identifying "indicators," things to measure that would help quantify visitor impacts on resources. To start, I listed all the ways I knew human actions in the Valley affected resources. It was a long list.

The impacts, some intense and some slight, begin as soon as visitors arrive, when their car, truck, or bus emits exhaust. Every item purchased by visitors after they arrive, things like stove fuel, matches, guidebooks, moleskin, Pepto-Bismol, postcards, newspapers, key chains, ball caps, travel mugs, and t-shirts, as well as every bite of food and each swallow of drink, has to be trucked in, adding noise and air pollutants. Each tap turn and toilet flush uses Valley water, and a complex utility system is required to remove used water and waste. All park and concession employees who provide information, guide tours, write speeding tickets, clean guest rooms, flip pancakes, and serve drinks bring their own load of impacts related to transportation, consumption, and elimination. Every impact I observed as liaison, from large trees falling to the chainsaw's blade and oil and hydraulic fluid polluting water to pavement appearing in formerly unpaved areas, was directly linked to human use of the Valley.

As I generated the list, I found it difficult to single out any one impact for scrutiny, because each one bled into several others, and all were linked in a huge web with countless connections. Many of the links between impacts were obvious, like foot traffic damaging vegetation, but others were indirect, unexpected, and unseen by almost everyone, like the link between horseback riding and declines in native songbird populations, or the one between hazard tree removal and bear mortality.

The *2000 Yosemite Valley Plan Supplemental Environmental Impact Statement* indicated about 14,000 visitors take guided horseback rides in the Valley every year. Additionally, the Park Service keeps horses and mules in the Valley for summer ranger patrols and packing. Horses aren't native to the Valley, and they're hard on the mountain environment. They pulverize soil, snatch at trailside plants, and leave urine and manure behind. Flies lay eggs in the manure, and fly numbers increase at an unnatural rate. The manure can harbor bacteria, worms, viable seeds of non-native plants, or traces of antibiotics or pesticides used to de-worm the horses.

Afternoon thunderstorms commonly develop over the Sierra Nevada crest in summer, and rain washes manure into waterways. The manure fertilizes the water, adding large concentrations of nitrogen, potassium, and phosphorus. Aquatic plants, insects, fish, or birds may take up or ingest decaying manure or its by-products or contaminants. A doe and fawn coming to the river to drink swallow more than clean water.

Non-native brown-headed cowbirds congregate at the stables, picking through manure and eating stray feed. Cowbirds present a dire threat to native songbirds; they are nest parasites who lay their eggs in native birds' nests. The alien eggs tend to hatch before those of their hosts, and the larger babies benefit from the surrogate parent's care and feeding. The cowbird hatchlings then out-compete the rightful chicks for food, or push the native birds right out of the nest.

Prior to the recent spate of construction, the Park Service hired contractors to identify and map Valley wetlands. Workers used sixteen-inch long wire pin flags to mark wetland boundaries. They left the flags behind when the project was finished.

I tired of seeing the flags, so one afternoon Tom and I set out to remove them. As we approached Upper River Campground, which was abandoned after the 1997 flood, we saw numerous freshly cut stumps where giant pines once stood. The reason for the cutting was unclear, but the stumps indicated the trees were dead before they were cut. Standing dead trees, or snags, provide valuable habitat for wildlife, including bats and owls. But the Park Service often deems such trees a hazard (branches, or the trees themselves, could fall on someone), so the trees are cut down. Following a lawsuit over this issue, Yosemite's "hazard tree program" grew exponentially; now thousands of trees are removed every year. Several smaller black oak trees nearby were smashed as well, their trunks and limbs damaged by the falling pines; an unfortunate, but common consequence of hazard tree removal.

We resumed our walk, and I noticed a bright orange, half-full bottle of Gatorade at the edge of the disturbed site, possibly left behind by the tree crew. From an ecological perspective, the loss of the snags was bad, but the forgotten Gatorade may have been the worst aspect of the tree cutting operation. If a wild bear was attracted to the bottle's bright color or sweet odor, the bear would quickly discover the nectar inside. After this single experience, the bear would forever be on the lookout for more treats. In the future, if the bear saw a similar bottle, or caught the same smell emanating from a car or tent cabin, he or she could break in to retrieve the prize. If the animal acquired a taste for human food, as most do after just one experience, and became a nuisance or a perceived threat to people, it would be killed.

If the thousands of connections between human actions and natural resources in Yosemite Valley were sketched out on paper, the diagram would resemble a huge spider web with all parts connected. And like a web, if even a small part is disturbed, the disturbance reverberates through each and every strand of the web. The impacts of humans on the Valley are constant, and the cumulative effects worsen with each passing day.

It's clear that visitors, and actions in support of visitor use like building visitor centers or employee dormitories, adversely affect resources. It's also clear the Park Service is responsible for protecting those resources. The 1916 Organic Act directed the agency to promote and regulate park use in ways that conserve scenery, natural and historic objects, and wildlife; and to provide opportunities for people to enjoy parks, but only in ways that leave the parks unimpaired for the enjoyment of future generations.

Although charged with preventing "impairment" for over ninety years, the Park Service has never clearly defined the term, or developed useful standards to help managers determine if a certain use or management action could impair resources. Admittedly, defining impairment is difficult. It can't be done at the national level because a unified set of definitions wouldn't address resource variability among parks. For example, impairment definitions appropriate for Gettysburg National Military Park would be useless for Yosemite. In response to this complexity, instead of developing park-specific standards, the Park Service has chosen to remain vague.

The current version of the "how-to" guide for park managers, *Management Policies 2006: The Guide to Managing the National Park System*, states managers must "always seek ways to avoid, or to minimize to the greatest extent practicable, adverse impacts on park resources and values." But the Service has "management discretion" to allow impacts when necessary and appropriate to fulfill the purposes of a park, as long as resources and values are not impaired. Impacts are okay, but impairment is not. In most cases, park superintendents have the final say about whether or not an impact constitutes impairment. In rare instances, their decisions are challenged in court.

In *Southern Utah Wilderness Alliance v. Dabney, et al.*, plaintiffs challenged part of Canyonlands National Park's proposed Backcountry Management Plan. Among other things, the plan addressed resource damage inflicted by off-road vehicles. Park Service managers inherited the off-road problem when the responsibility for Canyonlands was transferred from the Bureau of Land Management.

The Preferred Alternative in the draft Environmental Assessment for the Backcountry Management Plan, released in December of 1993, included prohibiting vehicles along a ten-mile segment of the Salt Creek Road. Salt Creek was the only perennial freshwater stream in the park, and off-road vehicle use was damaging important resources. Off-road vehicle advocates opposed the closure. The Park Service modified the final plan to allow continued, but limited, vehicle use.

The Park Service was sued over several issues associated with the plan. Relative to Salt Creek, the District Judge decided in favor of the plaintiffs, stating vehicle use would cause "permanent impairment of unique park resources," which was a violation of the Organic Act. The motorized vehicle contingency and Southern Utah Wilderness Alliance both appealed the decision for different reasons. Despite their "win" over Salt Creek, the latter did not get everything they wanted.

The 10th Circuit Court of Appeals stated the Park Service, under the Organic Act, was responsible for striking a balance between resource conservation and visitor enjoyment, and said, "The test for whether the NPS has performed its balancing properly is whether the resulting action leaves the resources 'unimpaired' for the enjoyment of future generations."

The court remanded the case back to the Park Service with a directive to reconsider its compliance with policies and laws. In response, the Park Service clarified its interpretation of "impairment." As a result, twenty-first century versions of *Management Policies* say more about impairment than previous versions. The new guidance states: "Congress, recognizing that the enjoyment by future generations of the national parks can be ensured only if the superb quality of park resources and values is left unimpaired, has provided that when there is a conflict between conserving resources and values and providing for enjoyment of them, conservation is to be predominant."

This elevation of conservation over use didn't happen because the Park Service experienced an epiphany and realized park resources and values had to come first; it happened because a concerned group of citizens filed a lawsuit.

It could be argued that the Park Service's failure to define impairment is intentional because they want to retain maximum flexibility in decision-making. In 2003, draft guidelines for assessing impacts and impairment to natural resources were circulated among a few Park Service employees, including me, but the draft was not finalized. If the concept of impairment is vague, if the filter remains coarse, most projects will slip through without friction. The only projects likely to be caught in the filter, and therefore not implemented, are those that grossly and overtly disregard park resources or values, like building a Wal-Mart in Yosemite Valley.

As long as determinations of impairment are "based on the professional judgment of the responsible NPS manager," in other words, are subjective, very few, if any, proposed projects will be found to impair resources. For example, if a superintendent wants to build a new visitor center, it's highly unlikely he or she will claim their pet project would cause impairment, even if it would.

The fox is guarding the henhouse. In too many cases, park managers will do what they want to do—until or unless they are challenged in court.

The Park Service's website dedicated to the impairment issue strengthens the argument that the agency does not really want to define impairment. A document on the site, *The Impairment Issue: Questions and Answers*, discussed the two key environmental laws that constrain actions in national parks: the National Historic Preservation Act of 1966 (specifically Section 106), and the National Environmental Policy Act of 1969. The document stated, "...Section 106 and NEPA require merely that we fully analyze and disclose the adverse consequences of our proposed actions. As long as we take all the steps required under those laws, and do the best we can to mitigate or avoid adverse impacts, they allow us to pretty much do whatever we want."

When I worked as a consultant in the 1990s, I realized even the strongest environmental laws in effect in the United States do not protect resources. When I returned to work for the Park Service, I assumed my favorite agency held itself to higher standards than the private sector. In many, if not most, parks, it does. But, once again, Yosemite is different. Like the National Historic Preservation Act and the National Environmental Policy Act, the National Park Service Organic Act provides only a basic framework for protecting parks. Preservation of resources and values depends on the integrity and "professional judgment" of park managers. As long as this holds true, the parks are at risk. It's up to vigilant and caring individuals and groups to ensure managers use good judgment and err always on the side of resource protection, and to hold them accountable if they do not.

As a result of Southern Utah Wilderness Alliance's lawsuit over Salt Creek, park superintendents must declare in environmental documents that proposed projects and actions either will, or will not, impair park resources. I reviewed dozens of these documents for Yosemite Valley projects, and never saw a statement that admitted impairment would, or even could, occur. In the view of managers, none of the egregious impacts I witnessed constituted impairment. Based on the standards Yosemite managers appeared to be using, it seemed nothing short of a new Wal-Mart would have caused impairment. As long as these inadequate standards hold sway, Yosemite Valley will continue to be degraded, its resources forever impaired.

As my list of visitor use impacts grew, I realized, in some cases, the affected resources can be identified and probable causes for the impact can be assigned. For example, the lack of California black oak reproduction in Yosemite Valley is probably linked, at least in part, to human trampling, deer browsing on seedlings, and lack of fire. But for each impact that can be identified and linked to a causative agent, dozens more occur that no one has ever even considered. Results of a study conducted in Yosemite in 2008 provide an example of this problem.

The massive rock walls that embrace Yosemite Valley are not simply broad expanses of solid gray granite. Like stripes on a zebra's belly, the walls exhibit myriad vertical stripes in a range of colors and widths. Scientists once believed the lines were oxidized minerals deposited over the centuries by falling water. Recently, though, they've discovered some of the stripes are alive, made up of lichens, symbiotic associations of fungi and certain types of algae or cyanobacteria (also called blue-green algae).

Lacking roots, lichens absorb water and nutrients directly from air. They also absorb air pollutants and are exceptional indicators of air quality. Based in part on its proximity to large metropolitan areas, including Los Angeles, San Francisco, and Central Valley cities like Fresno, the southern Sierra Nevada is prone to bad air quality. Despite their great potential to help monitor this problem, little was known about Yosemite's lichens until recently.

In 2008, lichen surveys began in Yosemite, with financial assistance from The Yosemite Conservancy. More than 100 new species were identified in the first year, and lichenologists predicted there could be as many as 500 species in the park. This yawning gap in knowledge is not limited to lichens. Just within the last few years, a previously unidentified orchid and three new types of bee were discovered in Yosemite. The Park Service knows these information gaps are untenable. Largely in response to publication of Richard West Sellars' book, *Preserving Nature in the National Parks* (1997), which pointed out the importance of science-based park management, the Park Service began developing a program to comprehensively inventory and monitor natural resources. This is a great program, but the work is very costly and funding for the program has not been adequate.

It's likely some species that occurred in Yosemite Valley when Euro-Americans first arrived disappeared before anyone ever knew they were there. Such losses do not constitute good stewardship. Logically, resources must be identified before they can be protected, with certain exceptions. Some resources will fall under the umbrella of protection provided to other resources. For example, if the Park Service took all possible actions to protect bat species known to occur in the Valley, other bats that occur, but haven't yet been identified, may also be protected. In a larger sense, when the Park Service finally takes *all possible actions* to truly protect *every* natural resource known to occur in Yosemite Valley, many unknown entities will benefit in concert with the known. Comprehensive surveys to document resources, their condition, and ways they change over time are absolutely essential for long-term resource protection. If managers don't know what resources are present, they can't understand, assess, or minimize the impact of visitors on resources, nor can they claim resources are not being impaired.

Science-based management of national parks started late and is still in its formative stages. The complexity of ecosystems ensures we will never know or understand them completely. As a result, park managers have to make decisions based on the limited information that is available to them. Compared to many parks, Yosemite, especially the Valley, has been well-studied. I suspect, though, that a great deal of salient information never reaches the decision-makers. The wealth of knowledge available for Yosemite must be accessible and understandable to be fully incorporated into decision-making. To further this objective, I propose the Park Service complete several basic tasks to support informed decision-making and the long-term welfare of park resources.

The first task involves consolidating all existing resource information pertaining to the Valley in one place. At present, information is spread out among many park divisions, libraries, program and project offices, and various nooks and crannies within and outside of the park. In the interest of accessibility and efficiency, a separate building, or set of rooms located outside of the Valley, could be dedicated to house the information. The Yosemite Valley Resource Information Center would contain everything known about Valley resources, from black bear behavior and the effects of non-native bullfrogs to water quality data and rockslides, as well as all resource-oriented maps and reports.

Next, I suggest the Park Service catalogue each information source into a computer database with appropriate metadata. Then, compile a 3-volume *"Atlas of Yosemite Valley." Volume One: Natural Resources* would include copies of all resource maps, past and present, narrative descriptions of resources, and what is known about their historic and current conditions, summaries of all studies and research, and information about disturbance agents such as fires, floods, rock fall, and diseases. *Volume Two: Infrastructure* would contain maps and descriptions of all existing human-built elements in the Valley—roads, bridges, buildings, parking areas, utilities, trails, campgrounds, lodging facilities, stables—as well as discussions of the environmental impacts caused by each infrastructure element.

Then, in *Volume Three: Alteration and Restoration*, the information generated in the first two volumes could be used to chronicle how the Valley has been disturbed or altered by humans. The Park Service could begin by collecting and summarizing all records of prehistoric and historic alterations; documenting the current status of altered areas using maps and narrative descriptions of disturbance type, magnitude, and timing, and discussing and documenting through photographs all physical evidence of resource alteration linked to human activity, like river diversions, pipe dams, rip rap, and areas where soil has been displaced or fill added. Then, each disturbed site could be ranked according to the significance of the disturbance or how severely it affects natural ecological structure and functions. Finally, for each site, ascertain whether or not site rehabilitation is possible (e.g., the activity field behind the Yosemite School has been completely converted to non-native plants, the soils are compacted, the drainage is impaired by culverts and drains, but, once the school is removed, the site could be restored to more native habitat).

This information would form a solid foundation to help establish priorities and sequencing for a comprehensive ecological restoration program for the Valley. Detailed discussions of the known and potential visitor impacts on all resources and all known threats to resources that come from outside park boundaries like regional air pollution or climate changes, also can be included in Volume III. This information can be applied to long-term monitoring of visitor use impacts on Valley resources.

As these volumes are compiled, other information suitable for inclusion will surface, and a more effective structure or organization may arise. The objectives are to get the information together, and to make it easy for present and future managers to find and work with it. Once the Atlas is completed for Yosemite Valley, I suggest the idea be expanded to other areas of the park.

The second task involves evaluating existing resource information and preparing a report on current resource conditions: a report on the *"State of Yosemite Valley."* The Park Service would be wise to organize a series of workshops to pool the knowledge and expertise of resource managers, and others well-versed on Valley resources to describe and assess current resource conditions. The ultimate objective of this task is to determine how healthy, or how ill, the Valley is from an ecological perspective, with respect to soils, hydrology, vegetation, wildlife, air, natural sounds, and natural rhythms of dark and light, or, in Park Service lingo, dark night skies.

The value of compiling the atlas and assessing the current state of Valley resources is immesurable. The information would apprise managers of the precise status of Valley resources, and would serve as a point of reference for documenting future changes. When ecologists set out to restore a forested area, they'd know where to find information on site history, soil type, species currently on the site, tree density, and age and size classes. As funding became available for restoration, managers would know which high-priority areas to tackle first. Once the number of employees living in the Valley is reduced, and day use limits are imposed, managers would be able to evaluate subsequent reductions in the amount of solid waste removed from the Valley. Biologists could track changes in numbers or locations of non-native bullfrogs, acres of wetland, or miles of severely eroded riverbank.

A great deal of the information described above already exists in park databases from past and present programs, including preparation of the 2000 Yosemite Valley and Merced River plans, myriad Environmental Impact Statements and Assessments, initial work on the Visitor Experience and Resource Protection program, the natural resource inventory and monitoring program, various ecological restoration efforts, and numerous other projects and scientific studies. Information generated for and from those efforts can provide a solid base for the data collection efforts.

Assessments of the status and condition of park infrastructure tend to be done routinely, usually to ensure visitor safety, but a similar undertaking has never been done for the Valley's natural resources. The time has come to complete this assessment to ensure the safety of the resources.

Documenting resources, assessing human-related disturbance, and identifying obvious impacts are only the first steps. Intelligent, effective management over time will require increased knowledge and understanding of impacts and their implications for resources. The Park Service has only begun to perceive the multiple strands in the intricate spider web of resource impacts, the numerous links between cause and effect. I suspect what we don't know is greater by far than what we do know. How do contaminants in road runoff affect aquatic organisms? How do humans affect the spread of non-native plants? How do non-native plants affect native plants and wildlife? How does withdrawing water from the river for domestic use affect caddis flies, coyotes, and canyon wrens? Intensive efforts to better understand human impacts on resources can occur in tandem with identification of the resources themselves.

In recognition of the fact that we know very little about the consequences of human use or actions on park resources, conservative decision-making is the only approach that makes sense, erring *always* on the side of resource protection and preservation. To this end, I propose a change in course for Yosemite's managers. I propose a total moratorium on any and all projects in Yosemite Valley that have a physical footprint, except projects designed to truly restore natural processes and structure, not just reconfigure or rebuild infrastructure. The moratorium will remain in effect until the Park Service gains a much better understanding of Valley resources and their condition, as well as resources that have been lost or damaged, and the reasons behind the changes.

Additionally, I strongly encourage the Park Service to identify all ways visitor use affects the Valley, and clearly define, with extensive public input, how much, if any, resource degradation is acceptable. Clear definitions of impairment are long overdue, as are thresholds that will determine when resources are, or have been, impaired.

Completion of these tasks is crucial to ensure long-term preservation of the Valley's ecological integrity. It's also important to realize the Valley's cultural resources, its archeological sites, historic features, cultural landscape, and value and significance to Native American Indians, are inextricably linked to the Valley's ecological integrity. Cultural resources will lose their context, and much of their meaning, if their natural setting is destroyed. Fully manifesting a new vision in Yosemite Valley will take time. In the meantime, immediate steps are required to stop the ongoing degradation of resources.

Initially, I was outraged when Yosemite's managers, ignoring the professional opinions of resource specialists, doggedly pursued projects that damaged resources. One dark, dreary day, as I watched rain wash dark red-brown soil off the Curry dorm project site and into the river, it occurred to me the National Park Service was slowly killing Yosemite Valley, one acre at a time. Each part of each project represented another nail in the coffin. My anger transmuted to deep concern when I realized that every day more people come to the Valley and inflict more damage.

As time passed, my concern increased in direct proportion to my knowledge and understanding of the human impacts and the Valley's ecological processes. I feared the place I loved most in the world—Yosemite Valley—was gasping its last wild breath.

In 1983, I completed coursework to become certified as an Emergency Medical Technician. The instructors hammered home the concept of *Primum non nocere*. Latin for "First, do no harm," this basic tenet of concern and humility recognizes human actions, even those with the best intentions, can have unexpected, even destructive consequences. I suggest we adopt this tenet in all of our interactions with Yosemite Valley. A modification of the phrase may be in order, though; perhaps it should be: "First, do no *more* harm."

CHAPTER 27
Embrace Transparency and Humility

Journal

A small conference room in the southeast corner of park headquarters in Yosemite Valley bears witness to weekly meetings of the Superintendent and his division chiefs. These gatherings are called "Squad meetings," or sometimes just "Squad," as in, "Hey, you going to Squad today?" Other committees and groups also meet in the conference room. Major decisions about Yosemite's future are set in motion in this room.

A set of doors exits the room to the east, providing access to Yosemite Village. A sign mounted over the doors continuously poses a question to meeting participants: "Is it in the best interest of the park?"

The intent of the sign is brilliant and inspired, but the words are far too vague. "The park" can be interpreted in too many different ways. I propose the sign be modified to read: "Is it in the best interest of the park's wildness, and natural and cultural heritage?" The sign is large, but bland; I doubt most people even see it after their first or second meeting. The new version of the sign should be conspicuous, perhaps with flashing neon, so it can't be missed, so its meaning can't be mistaken.

❖❖❖

By the time Tom and I left Yosemite to move to Boise, I had lost all confidence that the Park Service could or would protect resources in Yosemite Valley. In theory, parks are well protected. A plethora of regulations constrain Park Service actions, including the National Environmental Policy Act, the National Historic Preservation Act, the Antiquities Act, the Endangered Species Act, the Clean Air Act, the Clean Water Act, the Wild and Scenic Rivers Act, the Wilderness Act, and numerous Executive Orders, Director's Orders, and management guidelines.

After working only a few weeks in Yosemite, though, I harkened back to a lesson learned during my days as a consultant: planning is only as good as the planners. Even the best laws and regulations won't work unless those who apply them are rigorous and sincere in their intent. My experiences in other parks had led me to believe Park Service employees exercised very high levels of rigor and sincerity. But, as I continued to learn the hard way, Yosemite was different.

Many of Yosemite's planning problems arose because managers and planners often operated under a deeply flawed set of assumptions and beliefs. They assumed they knew what was best for Yosemite, regardless of how long they'd worked there or how well they knew the park. They assumed anyone with ideas at odds with theirs was wrong and could be ignored. They believed getting projects done quickly was the highest priority, and they didn't hesitate to keep secrets or cut corners to expedite projects. And, they believed that visitors always came first.

Because of these skewed perceptions, Yosemite's planners planned backwards. Instead of identifying a park need, considering all possible ways to meet that need, analyzing pros and cons of all alternative approaches, and selecting an approach that met the need while minimizing environmental impacts, managers first decided what they wanted to do and then crafted a pseudo-planning strategy to support their decision.

This planning approach is not limited to Yosemite or to the Park Service. It evolved in part from bureaucratic systems that value and reward conformity and thrift. Compliance with environmental laws is viewed as a necessary evil; any person or thing that complicates the process is an inconvenience, an impediment. Creative thinking is discouraged and filtered out of the work force.

But breakdowns in Yosemite's planning efforts can't be blamed entirely on the bureaucracy. The individuals involved in the process also play a significant role.

On Summer Solstice, 2005, the Valley awakened to a bold blue sky with a few wispy cirrus clouds, and a river overflowing with the effects of sun on snow. The big falls appeared smooth and soft from a distance, but proved vital and arousing up close, showering their devoted masses in cool, wet passion. The park was thick with tourists. School was out and the media had swollen the ranks with accounts of the sublime riches of paradise drenched in warm sun and water.

My Solstice run took me across Superintendent's Bridge. Earlier in the season, flood waters had carved away chunks of asphalt from the bike path on both ends of the bridge, and ferried away large granite boulders that supported the path where it rose to meet the bridge steps. Park Service workers tasked with repairing the damage had the day off, but evidence of their presence remained. Numerous black spots littered the bike path; the work truck leaked oil. The next rain would wash the oil into the meadow or the river. In the interim, a passing coyote or raccoon could step in a slick, and then ingest the toxins when he licked his paws clean.

These small oil spots seemed relatively insignificant, but when added to all the oil that leaks daily from vehicles and equipment in the Valley, the spots became part of a much bigger issue. But the oil, as well as all other environmental impacts of the bike path repair, would never be analyzed or acknowledged because of a loophole in the National Environmental Policy Act called the Categorical Exclusion.

Under the Act, minor actions like routine maintenance don't require in-depth analysis if the actions won't have an impact on the environment. Instead, a short checklist and a brief project description are signed by the park superintendent and filed. Boilerplate language on the exclusions states: "Your proposed project is an action that has been determined to result in no measurable environmental effects. It is therefore categorically excluded from further National Environmental Policy Act analysis." This process takes hours, as opposed to the months, or even years required to complete Environmental Assessments or Impact Statements. Yosemite's managers hide thousands of adverse environmental impacts behind hundreds of Categorical Exclusions; most cover benign activities like painting, but a few give a silent green light to actions with significant impacts.

Two of the most egregious "excluded" activities are the commercial use of pack stock and commercial tour bus operations. The generic category used for these exclusions applies to "Incidental business permits involving no construction or potential for new environmental impact." On the surface, this use of exclusions seems acceptable because the commercial use permits carry over from year to year, usually with little or no change; "new" impacts, therefore, are unlikely. The problem is that the impacts of stock use and commercial tour buses have never been assessed. Stock use affects water, soils, vegetation, and wildlife, as well as park visitors when they hike on dusty, deeply rutted, manure-filled trails teeming with flies. Commercial tour buses bring noise, exhaust, and lots of people; and the buses leave behind oil, transmission fluids, and human detritus. But park files contained no detailed environmental compliance documents for these activities; the Park Service claims they have no measurable effects.

Another Categorical Exclusion covered the park's Forestry Work Plan, which primarily involved removal of hazard trees and limbs. Soils, water, vegetation, wildlife, and visitors are adversely affected by these activities, not to mention the target trees themselves. The text of the Categorical Exclusion for the work plan reveals the program's magnitude: "Timber sales in recent years removed an average of 2,275 tons of logs from roadsides which were sawn into boards, and 200 tons of logs were transported to park firewood yards." Once again, the program had no measurable impacts in the eyes of the Park Service.

The lack of impact documentation for stock use, tour buses, and hazard tree removal was irresponsible and inexcusable; but the Park Service chose to bury these activities in Categorical Exclusions.

Preparing Environmental Assessments or Impact Statements would take substantial time and money. Additionally, once the impacts of these activities were exposed, Yosemite's managers would have to limit or curtail them, or figure out how to justify the status quo. The controversy and political fallout generated by such exposure likely would annihilate even the toughest manager. At best, such integrity would be rewarded with a career change or early retirement. Most managers won't engage in such efforts, regardless of the effects on resources or visitors.

Sadly, even if managers did prepare comprehensive compliance documents for these activities, any resulting changes likely would be minor. Some areas might be closed to stock use, the number of tour buses might be slightly reduced, or the cutting and selling of fewer hazard trees might be authorized, but the activities would continue. Commercial use of pack stock and tour buses would continue because these activities are money-makers for permit holders. The hazard tree program would continue because it makes money for contractors; and, theoretically, reduces the likelihood of trees or limbs falling on visitors.

Ironically, if minor changes were made that did not affect anyone's bottom line, the responsible managers would be publicly lauded for making ecologically meaningless adjustments to the programs; they'd get cash awards for being environmentally-friendly. Nevertheless, the Park Service is required to analyze commercial stock use and tour bus permits, as well as Yosemite's forestry program, in Environmental Assessments or Impact Statements with full public input to disclose all impacts of the programs, and to minimize impacts to the greatest extent possible. The National Environmental Policy Act review process is far from perfect, but it's the best we've got at the moment.

During my time as liaison, when Yosemite managers did complete environmental compliance processes, the result often was overwhelming: massive, multi-volume documents that obscured, confused, and confounded. The length of the documents, and the mind-numbing redundancy, discouraged even the most committed park advocates. Additionally, the documents made it look as if the park's preferred alternative was not pre-selected, but was chosen after careful assessment of all alternatives. The impacts of the preferred approach were played down to make it look like the pre-selected approach was the most environmentally-friendly. And the plans made it seem like every project they chose to do, even major development, would benefit resources.

A good example of the Park Service acting independently and doing what it wanted to do involves the Indian Cultural Center. Yosemite's 1980 *General Management Plan* called for construction of the Center in a presently undeveloped area west of Camp 4 (Sunnyside Campground). The site, which happens to be the location of the last occupied historic Indian village in the Valley, supports open woodland habitat and slopes gently up to meet granite boulders and the north Valley wall. The Center was to be constructed and operated by the American Indian Council of Mariposa County under terms of a cooperative agreement and a special use permit.

The *Draft Yosemite Valley Plan Supplemental Environmental Impact Statement* included construction of the Cultural Center as a proposed action; but the action was dropped from the *Final Yosemite Valley Plan Supplemental Environmental Impact Statement*. The final document stated the reason for the deletion: "...the cultural center would be established with or without a Yosemite Valley Plan." It was a done deal; it would be built, regardless of its environmental effects.

The Park Service planned to include environmental impact review for the Cultural Center in the Yosemite Lodge renovation project assessment, even though the two projects were completely unrelated. But the Lodge project was put on hold as a result of the Merced River litigation. When a settlement resolved the litigation, the plaintiffs backed off and gave the Park Service the green light on the Cultural Center. Thus, environmental compliance was never completed for the project, despite the fact that it altered an undeveloped area in the Valley, necessitated removal of mature black oak trees, and further impeded natural drainage patterns between the Valley's north wall and the river.

The words that come to mind are those of a co-worker from my consulting days. When editing an especially rough portion of a report, he would write in the margin: "No, no, all wrong."

I left the oil spots behind and continued jogging north. Before I reached Northside Drive, I encountered signs and barricades marking the freshly excavated utilities trench. The long, gaping wound cut through an area formerly occupied by incense-cedar, ponderosa pine, and black oak, and then cut across a corner of Cook's Meadow. Park managers claimed they were committed to avoiding any and all impacts to Valley meadows because they are "Highly Valued Resources," as well as "Outstandingly Remarkable Values" of the Merced River. Nonetheless, the utility line ran right through the meadow edge.

While I apologized to the meadow and its denizens for pain and suffering inflicted by relentless human folly, a large dump truck rumbled by on a new dirt spur road established during the project. The tapestry of forest soils and their nurturing mulch of pine needles, oak leaves, and dead ferns and grasses were reduced to a naked strip of pulverized dirt. The weather was warm, the soil dry. A large dust cloud billowed up in the truck's wake, coating everything within 100 feet, including me, in a thin layer of meadow remains.

The Park Service had three strikes against it just within this short segment of the utilities project: the line should have avoided the meadow completely; the spur road, although short, should not have been created; and dust abatement measures were not in place. The first violation was a planning failure. The second and third occurred because the Park Service didn't follow through on promises they'd made to mitigate utility project impacts. The latter failures highlight a key problem with development in national parks: the Park Service is responsible for monitoring itself and its contractors. There is no watchdog on duty.

All Yosemite's plans include multiple pages of mitigation measures intended to reduce impact significance. In reality, many mitigation actions are little more than balms used to salve guilt. Park planners imply that mitigation nullifies adverse impacts, but the only way to nullify an impact is to completely avoid it, and sometimes even avoidance isn't fail-safe. The utility line in the meadow is a good example. To offset the impact of the trench on vegetation, the line was routed to avoid large oak trees. This mitigation could spare individual oaks, but if the trench was close enough to the trees to sever primary roots, or if the trench changed water distribution patterns, the trees would still die. It would just happen more slowly.

Planners compiled eight pages of text describing eighty-eight different mitigation measures for the utilities project. Each "measure" included from one to several activities, and redundancy was rampant; at least ten measures addressed erecting fences to mark construction area boundaries and resources to ensure the two did not collide. The planners simply cut and pasted text from other plans into the utilities document. Additionally, many measures contained language that committed the Park Service to doing absolutely nothing; "could" and "should" appeared frequently, as did "to the extent possible," "as much as possible," "where possible," "whenever possible," "if at all feasible," and "where practicable."

Mitigation also fails because park managers aren't vigilant after construction begins. Contractors often lack experience in parks, are unaware of or don't understand the mitigation measures, and sometimes cut corners when no one is looking. When construction began on the Lower Yosemite Fall project, I was shocked to learn there was no plan for monitoring mitigation measures, nor was there money allocated to develop such a plan or to conduct the monitoring. Making promises to mitigate impacts was easy and greased the skids to get projects approved. After projects were underway, however, the promises were forgotten as everyone got sucked into the next project in the queue.

There is one notable exception to the Park Service's failure to mitigate impacts. Laws protecting cultural resources in national parks seem to be clear-cut and stringent, and Native Americans and others concerned with our nation's history and prehistory help to make sure those laws are adhered to. When projects in Yosemite Valley entail ground disturbance, Native American monitors are on site to watch for inadvertent excavation of artifacts or human remains. I only wish the laws designed to protect natural resources could be so clear-cut, and the Park Service's commitment to protect them so rigorous.

    The sign at the head of the walkway west of the Valley Visitor Center read "Open House." I proceeded up the walkway into a small plaza behind the Visitor Center and entered the door to the east auditorium. The Park Service hosted Open Houses about once a month to meet their legal requirements for public outreach on park projects. Park planners and contractors set up displays, gave PowerPoint presentations, and answered questions. Occasionally, the Park Service held Open Houses outside of the park, usually in neighboring communities, but most occurred in the Valley.

    The process was a sham. The Open Houses seemed like nothing more than smoke screens. Attendance often was paltry, the numbers countable on two hands. This makes sense. Who wants to spend precious vacation time at an Open House? The events seemed designed to tell people what was going to happen or what already was happening, to sell projects to the public, as opposed to honest attempts to engage visitors in planning. But the Open Houses allowed the Park Service to claim citizens were fully informed and "involved" in project planning, with the silent rejoinder that the public, therefore, supported and approved of the projects.

    The national parks are public lands. The public should be able to participate in planning and voice their opinions on decisions affecting parks. If Yosemite's managers were serious about reaching out and listening to the public, there would be more Open Houses outside the park and on weekends. In a perfect world, the Park Service would come together with everyone interested in Yosemite Valley and arrive at consensus on how the Valley should be managed. For many reasons, this situation will never happen. The number of opinions on what the

Valley should look like and what the park experience should be run rapidly toward infinity; they are as varied as snowflakes. Some people view the Valley as a playground put on Earth only to be of service to humans; others believe the Valley is here for its own sake, and should be left completely undeveloped. Most opinions fall somewhere between these two extremes. In lieu of consensus, the Park Service does what it wants to do; it finds the path of least resistance and bends over backwards to avoid controversy.

While I was working as Liaison, park planners did solicit feedback on proposed projects from people interested in Yosemite's future, but they then made it very difficult for people to provide meaningful input by writing obtuse documents, failing to provide adequate details on proposed projects, and providing too little time for readers to submit comments. Without easy access to accurate information and enough time to formulate their thoughts and ideas, it was impossible for the public to respond intelligently. And once the comments were in, the Park Service rarely made substantive changes in projects, unless the person or group behind the comments had strong political connections.

Baffled and blindsided, the average Yosemite lover wound up lost on the environmental compliance trail, once again up to their knees in flies and manure. Bogged down and discouraged, they stopped trying to participate in the process.

It would be easy to blame Yosemite's planning debacles on too many different projects with short timelines occurring simultaneously, government disincentives for creative problem-solving, the complexity of park resources, and a broad spectrum of advocates with different ideas about how the Valley should be managed, including the "fringe group of radicals" bent on derailing the process. These conditions do create planning headaches, but I think the most significant barriers to effective planning for the Valley's long-term ecological health and viability are money and its evil stepchildren: greed and fear.

The frantic pace of Yosemite planning I witnessed was driven by greed. Park managers asked for loads of money after the 1997 flood to implement massive changes, primarily for facility repair and development in the Valley, and they got it. Greed dissolved into fear when they realized if the money was not spent quickly, it could disappear. Additionally, if concession operators or other economic or political forces were unhappy with the slow pace of redevelopment after the flood, heads could roll. The speed led to planning shortcuts, which in turn led to lawsuits. Plans for post-flood projects were put on a back burner while planners scrambled to complete comprehensive plans for the Valley and the Merced River. The delays and costs of these efforts compounded the pressure on Yosemite's managers. In response, managers made independent decisions to streamline the planning process, fearful of the political repercussions of moving too slowly, losing money, or angering constituents. Many of these decisions led to significant resource damage.

Future planning for Yosemite Valley should aim to protect the long-term integrity of natural resources before we run out of time and the exquisite natural fabric of the Valley unravels completely. The court's decree to start over with Merced River planning provides the Park Service with a great opportunity to manifest the dream of a wild future for the Valley. It's a chance to slow down and finally get it right, to finally embrace the paradox presented by the Organic Act, to finally balance the elements of preservation and use, to finally pay attention to Frederick Law Olmsted and the framers of the goals of the 1980 *General Management Plan*, and to finally put the needs of Yosemite Valley instead of human desires in the forefront.

As new plans take shape, though, it's important for concerned citizens to be extremely diligent to ensure the interests of the Valley and its resources prevail over economic and other special interests. Public input is essential to ensure Park Service managers adopt resource protection as their highest calling. If the past is any indication, they won't, or can't, do it on their own.

Back in 1998, as I drove to work on my first day as Point Reyes' Plant Ecologist, I took a good long look at the land with its steep slopes covered with Douglas-fir and Bishop pine forests, tawny grasslands dotted with seasonal ponds, brackish marshes graced with great blue herons and great egrets, and riparian willow thickets. A soft wave of dizzy nausea rolled through me when I thought about my new job. I was somehow responsible for "managing" all the plants that grew within the boundaries of the Seashore's 90,000 plus acres. I realized immediately how ridiculous that thought was; no person, group, or committee of any size or configuration can possibly take on such a responsibility. In my role as plant ecologist, I did the best I could to keep those plants healthy, and tried to ensure the actions of park visitors and the Park Service did not cause them further harm.

Park Service managers often mistakenly believe they can control complex natural systems. Since day one, Euro-Americans have tried to control Yosemite Valley's wildness to meet their needs and desires—control the river, control the rockslides, control the plants, control the animals. They couldn't. We can't.

It's time to stop our futile attempts to control that which is outside of ourselves, and adopt a large measure of humility. It's time to take full responsibility for our actions and impacts. It's time to control ourselves. Adopting a more humble approach to our relationship with Yosemite Valley will allow us to make intelligent choices for the good of the Valley and all of its inhabitants for all time. It's not all about us; it's all about the place.

Humans are not the most important things in the world. We are transient. We are visitors. We will come and go; the Valley will remain. It's time to stop approaching parks, and all land, with a view to control and to use, and step into more responsible roles as gentle, compassionate tenants, as temporary passengers on Mother Earth's amazing ship.

CHAPTER 28
Establish Limits

Journal

    Not a cloud in the sky. Car horns toot and engines idle. Waterfalls roar and trees filter wind with a sigh. The river rises. I sit on a blanket of pine needles west of Sentinel Bridge, south of the river. Swirling water licks the top of the bank. Willows and cottonwoods stand in deep water, bending and flexing with the surging current. Most years, the river peaks sometime in the first half of June. It's only the third week of May.

    Downriver, the water is smooth. Shimmering reflections of trees and rock walls color its surface in greens and grays. Will the big incense-cedar I've watched for so many years, the one that leans out over the river at a precarious angle, surrender its hold this spring?

    Ants fall from pine branches overhead. I shake my head and shiver. A fat-bellied robin lands atop a stunted cottonwood about fifteen feet away, surveys the scene, and then drops to the ground. She cocks her head to listen, then grabs a not-so-well hidden bug. Pine needles fly.

    A motorcycle engine rumbles. The up-canyon breeze picks up and amplifies the sylvan wind song. A red-winged blackbird glides over the river, lands, and walks up to me as if I'm invisible. He circles around me, methodically turning leaves over in search of bugs, chirping once with each leaf turned. He completes his circle and flies away.

The Soul of Yosemite

A small pine cone drifts slowly up river, against the flow, caught in an eddy triggered by an upstream cottonwood. I often feel like that cone, caught in circumstances way beyond my control. Next weekend is Memorial Day weekend, when Yosemite's crowds reach peak flow.

◆◆◆

As early as the 1950s, headlines proclaimed America's national parks were being loved to death and the issue of overcrowding in Yosemite Valley dominated the discourse. According to the National Park Service Public Use Statistics Office, over 4 million people visited Yosemite in 1996, the largest number in park history.

The first tourists arrived in the Valley in 1855. A total of 653 visitors were recorded over the next 8 years. Difficult access kept visitation low until about 1914, when the estimate was just over 15,000. In 1915, that number doubled, and visitation continued to rise quickly. The All-Year Highway to the park opened in 1927, causing a jump from roughly 274,000 to 490,000 visitors in one year. World War II caused a lull, but numbers rebounded to 640,000 in 1946. Over 1 million people came in 1954, almost 100 years after the first tourists cooled their toes in the Merced. Over 2 million came in 1967, over 3 million in 1987, and more than 4 million in 1996.

Despite obvious overcrowding in Yosemite Valley, and directives outlined in the 1980 *General Management Plan*, the Park Service took no serious action to control visitor numbers. In 1997, nature forced the issue by ushering in the New Year with an industrious, wet housecleaning.

After the flood, the media message flip-flopped: "Yosemite's visitation is down! Americans must be losing interest in their national parks! Gateway businesses are losing money!" As presented, the situation was dismal. In reality, Yosemite experienced only a 9 percent drop in visitation between 1996 and 1997. Declines did continue until 2006, when the number of visitors was 20 percent below 1996 figures. But in 2010 the Park Service once again reported over 4 million visitors; equal to, or possibly greater than, the 1996 record. The decline in visitation after the flood was a temporary aberration. The overcrowding issue did not disappear.

Statistics on Yosemite's visitors are taken very seriously, especially by those who equate visitors with dollars. Park officials and the media report visitor numbers as if they were accurate, but they're not. They are gross estimates. Individual park visitors are not counted. Electronic devices count vehicles as they roll into the park. The totals are adjusted down to account for residents, commuters, contractors, and deliveries, and then multiplied by an average number of people per car. Bus riders are counted separately.

During my time in the Valley, I learned the counting system was riddled with problems. Traffic counters frequently malfunctioned and were not fixed. For example, in 2006, employees reported numerous issues. On April 1, the Arch Rock (Highway 140) counter was broken. On July 1, Arch Rock and Big Trees counters were "out all month," and South Entrance and Badger Pass were out some of the month. On August 1, counters at Arch Rock, South Entrance, and Big Trees appeared to be "out of order." On September 1, three counters were still having problems. In 2008, one report said the Big Oak Flat counter now "uses correct inbound figures." It had been counting cars in a secondary lane, and the inbound and outbound counters were reversed.

Yosemite's numbers game is confounded further by the people-per-car multiplier. The Statistics Office states the multiplier is 2.9. On July 14, 2005, the Fresno Bee reported the multiplier was 2.8. A former Yosemite employee told me the multiplier was 2.3. The multiplier changed over time, supposedly to reflect changes in average group size, but I was unable to determine when the changes occurred.

In June of 2005, the Valley's waterfalls put on an extraordinary show, and multitudes came to bask in the energy of falling water. Local business owners described June as "phenomenal" and "huge."

Initially, Park Service visitor counts for June of that year nearly broke all previous records for that month. Upon review of the numbers, though, someone caught an error. The Tioga Pass traffic counter had tallied about 92,000 people in June, but the Tioga entrance was closed most of June due to snow. The numbers were adjusted, and on July 14, 2005, the Fresno Bee reported that Yosemite had recorded an 8 percent loss in visitor totals, despite it being one of the "busiest Junes in memory." Clearly, at least one other counter must have malfunctioned. The same Fresno Bee article later stated, "Nobody is quite sure what the estimate really is."

That same June, I overheard a woman talking to a group of people near Sentinel Bridge. She stood next to a commercial mini-bus, and wore an official looking name tag. When she mentioned the Park Service, I slowed my pace to eavesdrop. She said the Park Service claimed visitation was down that year, but she thought it was way up. Demand for her business had never been so great. Although the Park Service predicted visitation might reach only 3.5 million in 2005, she didn't believe it. She thought it would be closer to 5 million. The official Park Service total for 2005 was 3.3 million, but based on the crowding I observed the actual number was much higher.

Information on Yosemite Valley's visitation is even sketchier than overall Yosemite National Park visitation. A 1998 survey indicated about 80 percent of park visitors went to the Valley. This percentage is applied to the erroneous entrance station counter data to derive numbers for the Valley.

The 1980 *General Management Plan* set maximum visitation for the Valley at 10,530 and 7,711 people for day and overnight use, respectively, for a total of 18,241 per day. These numbers were based on the amount of lodging, camping, and parking present when the plan was written. The 2009 Superintendent's Compendium of regulations reiterates *General Management Plan* limits: "Visitors may enter Yosemite Valley until westbound traffic is backed-up from Lower Yosemite Fall to Curry Village Four-Way intersection, or all day use parking spaces have been filled, and/or the 18,241 person capacity has been reached."

Valley visitor surveys from 1998 showed averages of 7,624 and 17,496 people per day in April and August, respectively. The average numbers for the entire peak (summer) season were 10,950 day visitors and 6,383 overnight visitors, for a total of 17,333 per day. While these numbers fall below the 18,241 limit, they are averages, and they hide the fact that weekends, especially summer holiday weekends, are much more crowded than weekdays. Because the averages rise almost to the limits, the limits clearly are exceeded on summer weekends. By some accounts, as many as 30,000 people have visited the Valley on a single summer weekend day.

More than 50 percent of Yosemite's visitors come in July and August, and a disproportionate amount of resource damage occurs during this period, particularly on weekends and holidays. The quality of the park experience is compromised severely as well. The Valley suffers. Plants are trampled, bears get in trouble, litter abounds, and garbage cans overflow. Dirty diapers and piles of human waste flagged with toilet paper streamers are left behind trees and rocks. Coyotes are corrupted by hand feeding, and visitors face horrific traffic congestion, noise, exhaust, and lines.

Memorial Day weekend, 2003, came and went. Tom and I mistakenly left the Valley that Monday, the holiday, to do errands in Fresno. Leaving was not the mistake; returning home was. We made good time on the Wawona Road and through the long tunnel, but cars and people clogged the parking area at the tunnel's northeast end. Bumper-to-bumper traffic descended into the Valley. Our speed slowed to about five miles per hour. The line of cars was rock solid when we arrived at Southside Drive and merged east to head home. Like Los Angeles during rush hour, it was much more stop than go. An hour later we arrived at the Yellow Pine picnic area, with about three miles to go. We pulled into the picnic area, parked, and walked home, returning later that night for the truck. It was not a happy trip.

In the 1990s the Park Service occasionally limited Valley access. When all parking spaces were filled, and there were long delays at intersections (in other words, when the Valley came close to gridlock), rangers re-routed incoming day visitors to other park areas. If the entire park was too crowded, rangers turned day visitors around at entrances and told them to try again later. Between May 20 and July 2, 1995, rangers restricted access on all but one weekend day. Access was not restricted in late July or August because personnel were not available, even though traffic volumes were even higher than they'd been earlier in the season. On a few occasions while I was living in the Valley, rangers took it upon themselves to stop traffic coming into the Valley to relieve congestion.

Regardless of how or why discrepancies in visitor use data crept in, through traffic counters, calculations, or multipliers, during my tenure in Yosemite, the Park Service did not know with any precision how many people visited Yosemite National Park every year. I believe the reported estimates were too low, and that the number of people who visited Yosemite Valley also was underestimated, possibly by a substantial amount. The only thing that can be said with certainty is that too many people visit the Valley, based on resource damage and overcrowding.

On a more positive note, in 2010 and 2011, the Park Service was trying to get more accurate visitor counts, an important first step in developing a valid plan for the Merced River, and for protecting all Valley resources in perpetuity.

Resource damage increases in direct proportion to visitor numbers. Some managers deny this, saying damage is a function of visitor behavior rather than numbers, that 1 million "good" visitors who don't feed wildlife, drive too fast, or trample river banks cause less damage than one hundred, or even a dozen, "bad" visitors. This may be true, but if it's assumed a certain percentage of all visitors will be predisposed to behave badly, the actual number of such scofflaws increases in direct proportion to the total number of visitors. In addition, even so-called "good" visitors have substantial cumulative effects on resources over time.

Overcrowding in national parks also creates social problems. To illustrate, not long ago I noticed Yellowstone National Park advertising a position that seems incongruent with national parks: Supervisory Criminal Investigator. Yosemite has similar positions, and the Valley has its own courthouse, jail, and U.S. Magistrate. Several factors led to the need for serious law enforcement in Yosemite Valley, including too many visitors and too many employees, as well as a number of concession employees hired without adequate background checks. Ultimately all of these factors are a function of too many visitors for the rangers to manage. The solution for Yosemite Valley is obvious: reduce visitation and reductions in both resource impacts and crime will follow.

Yosemite Valley's crowding problems are linked to day visitors. The roughly 475 campsites and 1,260 lodging units in the Valley automatically limit overnight use. Approximately 20 percent of Yosemite National Park visitors stay overnight and 80 percent come for a day. The *Yosemite Valley Plan Supplemental Environmental Impact Statement* reported overnight use was relatively stable between 1981 and 1996, but overall visitation soared in that time frame from about 2.5 million to over 4 million. The huge increase was due to day visitors.

Surveys conducted in the early 1990s revealed Valley day visitors who drove personal vehicles, as opposed to those riding buses, stayed an average of 4.2 hours. Overnighters stayed an average of 2.7 days. Day users had time to drive in, find a place to park (maybe), go to the restroom and a gift shop, have a burger and ice cream cone or a picnic, photograph Half Dome and Yosemite Falls, and drive out again. Many day users may never set foot off of pavement. While they may be impressed with Yosemite Valley's grandeur, it's unlikely their hearts and souls are touched by the Valley's unique spirit. Most will go home with little more than a few photos, and perhaps a keychain, t-shirt, or mug.

I believe visitors who stay overnight are more likely to touch and be touched by the Valley. Most of them learn to manage trash and store food properly. They have more opportunities to attend ranger programs or spend time in the visitor center. They take longer hikes. Many of them park their vehicles and walk, bike, or use the shuttle buses. In most cases, they've made advance reservations. The energy expended in planning their trip indicates their Valley visit is special and important to them. As a result, they're more likely to become more sensitive to, and respectful of, the place, and more likely to make a life-changing connection with nature.

The Park Service knows day use is the crux of the Valley's overuse problem. To their credit, the agency planned to launch a day-use reservation system in 1997. After the flood, though, local business owners argued vehemently against the idea. The Park Service backed down and agreed to wait until 1998 to start the new program. The system was never implemented.

The topic of limiting visitation in national parks makes National Park Service managers squirm. They know establishing limits for Yosemite Valley is the right thing to do, but they don't want to do it. Instead, they opt for actions like erecting boardwalks, fences and signs, or closing sensitive habitat areas. This is fine if resource damage and crowding remain minimal. For this approach to work, though, managers must establish exceptionally high standards of quality for both resources and visitor experiences, and, as soon as conditions even begin to approach those thresholds, they must be willing to take quick, decisive action to ensure the thresholds are never crossed. Yosemite's managers have done neither.

The National Park Service's answer to crowding during my period of employment was the Visitor Experience and Resource Protection, or VERP, framework. In the words of Dr. Robert E. Manning, from *Parks and Carrying Capacity: Commons without Tragedy*, the framework "was designed to identify and protect what is important about parks and not to inherently limit visitor use." Parenthetically, Dr. Manning admitted that "...such limits are needed in some places and at some times," and later said, "Limitations on visitor use are an important part of the management arsenal, but other less draconian alternatives are possible."

With all due respect, I disagree with the idea that limits on use are "draconian." Limiting access to popular places is not a new idea. Our society readily accepts all kinds of limits. We recognize that goods, services, and spaces are finite, and we adapt accordingly. We understand theatres, stadiums, and restaurants have limited seating. We know museums can accommodate only so many people before the experience is ruined because no one can see the exhibits. So we plan ahead and make reservations when we want to do something or go somewhere with limited space. In Yosemite, visitors already reserve rooms, wilderness access, cabins, campsites, tables in restaurants, and space on tours. The number of people who can stay overnight in Yosemite's wilderness has been limited since the 1970s to protect resources and ensure a high quality visit. We accept limits and the subsequent need for advance planning and reservations because they ensure our experience will be something special, something to cherish.

In 2008 Yosemite's version of VERP, formerly called the User Capacity Management Monitoring Program (more recently re-named the Visitor Use and Impacts Monitoring program), identified eight variables, or indicators, to be monitored. Only five of the eight were really indicators: water quality, riverbank erosion, wildlife exposure to human food, extent and condition of informal trails, and number of encounters with other parties in wilderness. The remaining three "indicators" were data collection exercises to support development of future indicators related to crowding (measuring "people-at-one-time" in popular areas), impacts to archeological resources, and transportation studies. Of the five real indicators, only the first four applied to Yosemite Valley, and they were grossly inadequate. They ignored the majority of the Valley's most critical natural resource problems, including impaired hydrology, introduction and spread of non-native species, light and noise pollution, and disappearing species, all of which are linked, at least in part, to visitor use.

Yosemite managers established standards for their indicators, but the standards set the bar extremely low by only requiring maintenance of the status quo. Managers made the assumption that present resource conditions were acceptable, but, as the judge's decision made perfectly clear, they were not. Additionally, Yosemite's User Capacity Program did not state the actions to be taken if standards were exceeded.

The program implemented in 2010 was similar to the work done in 2008, and primarily involved monitoring of current conditions. One new indicator, natural soundscapes, was added to the program. At this point, it appears the park has not made much progress in establishing meaningful standards for any of the indicators. On the bright side, the program has evolved, and ultimately may become more effective. Some of the earliest, completely meaningless indicators, like the number of exposed tree roots in campgrounds, and the percentage of time a visitor can find a picnic table, have been dropped from the program. However, the Visitor Use and Impacts Monitoring program as it is currently being implemented does not further the establishment of high standards for resource quality, nor does it help managers determine how much damage is too much.

When the Park Service failed to implement the day-use reservation system in Yosemite, the agency revealed the real reason they resist use limits: such limits are bad for business. The chosen alternative, a VERP-based program, allows managers to dodge limits endlessly.

Managers also claim visitors will react badly if limits are imposed. Some visitors may be angry. They may resist limits because people don't like change, and many have difficulty letting go of their own personal desires in the interest of the greater good. I'm no exception. I would not like to have my chances of visiting Yosemite Valley reduced, but I would adapt. I would make reservations, and then I would revel in the clean, quiet splendor of an uncrowded, healthy Yosemite Valley.

If limits are poorly received, the lion's share of the criticism probably will come not from the public, but from concession operators and businesses. This point is illustrated by the public's response to the first fences and boardwalks built in the Valley to protect Stoneman and Sentinel meadows. Park managers resisted these structures, fearing the public would be angry at the visual intrusion and limitations to their freedom. I remember the visitor's responses because I heard them firsthand; people were ecstatic and wondered why the Park Service had taken so long to act. Limiting use in the Valley, including limiting the number of people that can come into the Valley, will be similarly well-received. It also has been noted that visitor numbers should have been limited *before* there was a need for fences or boardwalks; construction of these structures was a clear indication that visitation already was too high.

The National Park Service's mission has two key components: caring for resources and providing opportunities for visitors to enjoy parks. In Yosemite there is an unwritten third part to the mission: to support businesses that make money from the park. It's time for the Park Service to leave this insidious third part behind forever. It's not the purpose of the Valley, or of any national park, to make money for any person, business, or corporation. If making money dropped off Yosemite's priority list, limiting visitors would be no big deal.

In a July 2007, Los Angeles Times opinion piece the writer said determining the number of people that can be in Yosemite Valley at one time and still have an enjoyable experience is like determining how many angels can dance on the head of a pin. I agree in part, because everyone's definition of enjoyable is different. Similarly, determining the number of visitors that can visit the Valley without causing resource damage or impairment presents a considerable challenge. Neither of these tasks, however, is impossible.

Establishing the numbers of visitors compatible with optimal resource condition and visitor experience will require experimentation. The limits in the 1980 *General Management Plan* can be used as a starting point. Those numbers may be too high, though, because they were derived from infrastructure capacity present in 1980, including the number of campsites, lodging units, and parking spaces, not on resource conditions or the quality of a visit.

The Park Service could begin by modifying the limits in the *General Management Plan* to reflect present infrastructure capacity, and then adjust the numbers down from there.

Better yet, they could be bold and try the opposite approach: limit the numbers of people in Yosemite Valley significantly at the outset. The limit could be gradually raised over time if resource conditions show improvement. This way, any future changes to the limit would be welcomed instead of resisted.

I suggest the Park Service change its thinking about use limits. Instead of focusing on the extremes of a number or no number at all, focus on crafting a new vision for Yosemite Valley's future in which resources *always* come first and the desired visitor experience is, using Olmsted's word, contemplative, emphasizing connection with nature. Acknowledge the obvious correlations between visitor numbers and resource deterioration, and don't wait to act until all the science is done. Data collection can go on indefinitely, while resources continue to suffer. Raise the standards of quality to optimal levels for enhancing resource health, stop accepting the already degraded status quo. Accept the fact that the only way to do this is to limit visitor numbers and activities. Recognize Yosemite Valley has a much more important role to play in the world than that of playground, or backdrop to social activities. Understand the Valley is ready to serve as ambassador to the wild, to be the place where we demonstrate that humans can engage in respectful, symbiotic relationships with the Earth.

The Los Angeles Times opinion piece concluded by saying limiting visitors to Yosemite was a debate without end. I disagree. The debate can and must end, and it's up to the Park Service to take the steps necessary to end it, to establish visitation limits and a day use reservation system. These steps will signal an increased level of respect for Yosemite Valley, and the willingness to control humans, not Nature, in her grandest temple. We must all learn these steps, and learn them soon. They are the first steps in the angel's dance of right relationship with Yosemite Valley.

CHAPTER 29
Liberate Natural Processes

Journal

The Valley sent me a message yesterday, translated by a large glossy raven perched in a tall pine. Two of his cohorts stood nearby on lower branches of the same tree, nodding agreement at appropriate moments. With each caw, translator raven's breath sailed out into the world, puffs of white steam in the cool morning air—the breath of the wild. He didn't mince words. Here's what he said:

> "Yosemite Valley wants clean air, and clean water
> that flows unhindered from the highest peaks,
> races down steep walls and canyons, and floods freely.
> Yosemite Valley wants less pavement, fewer polluting vehicles,
> dark, starry nights, and days filled with river and wren song.
> Yosemite Valley wants robust populations of great gray owls,
> red-legged frogs, foothill yellow-legged frogs, Mariposa sideband
> snails, and all the other species driven out by humans.
> Yosemite Valley wants coyotes who don't beg for food,
> mountain lions who are not shot for being mountain lions,
> bears without ear tags or toe tags,
> and, last, but never least,
> well-fed ravens."

♦♦♦

Efforts to reverse unwanted changes in Yosemite Valley's appearance began soon after Euro-Americans arrived. The 1890 Biennial Report of the Yosemite Commissioners said: "The policy of the Commission is to preserve the floor of the valley as nearly as possible in its natural state...to restore as rapidly as consistent with well-ascertained principles of forestry, the park-like condition of the valley." The commissioners wanted to turn back the clock, to return vegetation to its 1851 state by reducing the impact of humans, clearing underbrush, and encouraging the growth of flowering plants.

Almost 100 years later, in the late 1980s, park employees and volunteers began concerted efforts to remove non-native plants, plant and protect black oaks, build fences to protect meadows and river banks, plant native species in denuded areas, and remove old trails and asphalt from meadows and other wetlands. Between 1890 and now, the motivations and objectives behind restoration efforts have changed a bit. Desires to restore ecological structure and function for the health of Valley ecosystems replaced the earlier focus on views and beauty, although vista clearing for the sake of aesthetics still has its proponents. Additionally, vegetation removal to reduce the risk of wildfire has been a perpetual goal.

The restoration efforts of the early Euro-Americans aimed largely to restore a lost scene in Yosemite Valley, to return the Valley to the way it looked when the Mariposa Battalion rode in. Despite over a century of considerable effort, though, the Yosemite Valley of today looks quite different from the Yosemite Valley of the 1850s. This raises an important question: Can the Valley really be "restored?"

If the target of restoration is a scene from the past, the answer is no. Our knowledge of past conditions is too limited. Some information exists on historic forest structure, meadow extent, and Merced River channel structure and dynamics. Old photos illustrate some aspects of earlier conditions. Researchers collect additional data every year to fill the gaps, but the details required to replicate past conditions in the Valley don't exist and are probably beyond our grasp.

Even if we knew exactly what the Valley looked like in the 1850s, the changes that have occurred since then are irreversible. For example, even if we removed every human contrivance in the Valley, and then walked away and never returned, natural systems and processes would regain their dominance, but they would never recreate precisely the conditions of the past. We've severely altered Valley hydrology; the odds of successfully replacing the recessional moraine are slim. We've moved, mixed, buried, eroded, contaminated, and otherwise upset soils; no matter what we do, they won't recover in our lifetimes, or even those of our great-great-great grandchildren. Removal of every non-native plant from the Valley may be possible, but would require funding similar to United States military budgets. Even with a great deal of money, the task might never be finished. It's highly unlikely the full complement of wildlife that once occupied the Valley will ever live there again, as much as I'd love to round a corner on the Mirror Lake Trail and spot a grizzly foraging for gooseberries.

A third major deterrent to recreating a vignette from the past involves the dynamic nature of ecosystems; they are not static or isolated. Yosemite's natural systems are always in flux, constantly changing in response to local conditions as well as to an unfathomable range of external factors. The changes can be as small and localized as a minor rockslide or a mama vole being eaten by a coyote, or as massive and universal as solar flares or volcanic eruptions. The range of things that induce change ensures humans will never be able to restore or re-create conditions of the past.

These obstacles are not cause for despair. They simply indicate the need to look forward, not backward, when we envision Yosemite Valley's wild future. Instead of trying to restore a particular scene in the Valley, let's liberate natural processes, including water movement, fire, soil development, native plant succession, and native wildlife use to support the Valley's ability to restore itself. Instead of trying to control or derail natural processes, let's shift our efforts to support and nurture the Valley's ability to self-organize, to be self-willed, to be wild. Let's remove obstructions to natural processes and get out of Nature's way.

Although efforts to date have not "restored" the Valley, the park's ongoing restoration efforts are crucial steps in the right direction. Yosemite's resource managers and volunteers are heroes. They fully understand the need to restore natural processes, and they know that form, the way the Valley looks, follows function, the way the Valley works. But restoring natural processes in Yosemite Valley requires strong management support and the commitment of significant financial resources. To date, these two essential ingredients have not been forthcoming. It's time for this situation to change.

I stepped outside and was met by a breezy, overcast late October day. A mosaic of leaves of all shades of gold and yellow covered the front lawn. The beat of steady rain had echoed in and out of my dreams throughout the night; it was the first significant storm of the season. The clouds parted as I walked toward the Village. I'd almost rounded the corner by the cemetery when I heard the low rumble of thunder running across the Valley from the east. I looked up to admire the clouds that could produce such a racket. There were no clouds. The rumble continued. A shiver raced down the back of my neck like a tiny lightning bolt. The thunder was generated by falling rocks.

Valley residents are tuned to the key of falling rock. From wall to wall and from end to end, much of the Valley floor lies within rock fall range. Towering, cone-shaped piles of splintered rock along the Valley's margins testify to unstable granite faces. Boulders the size of small houses lie scattered up and down the Valley; they weren't put there by Park Service landscape architects or their contractors.

Rock falls occur in all seasons, but often accompany intense rains, snow melt, and fluctuating temperatures that enhance the freeze-thaw cycle. A 2007 United States Geological Survey report suggests several hundred rock falls, rock slides, and debris flows of varying magnitude have dropped into Yosemite Valley over the last 150 years. Since 1857, fourteen people have been killed and at least sixty-two injured by Valley rock falls.

On the evening of July 10, 1996, rock masses estimated to weigh over 160,000 tons fell from cliffs just east of Curry Village. The rocks slid along a steep plane before free-falling roughly 1,500 feet to the talus below. The falling rock generated an air blast that knocked down or snapped about 1,000 trees. The event killed one person, seriously injured several others, damaged the Happy Isles Nature Center, and destroyed a snack bar. On December 26, 2003, a rock fall originating west of Glacier Point sent debris flying into Curry Village cabins, injuring visitors. On October 8, 2008, another rock fall injured three people at Curry Village. The Park Service evacuated over 1,000 visitors after the event.

More recently, in March 2009, a rock fall near Half Dome knocked down hundreds of trees and buried long stretches of the Mirror Lake Loop Trail. Seismographs registered the impact as a magnitude 2.4 earthquake. Early reports estimated the material weighed about 115,000 tons. No one was injured.

The Park Service permanently closed over 200 accommodations after the October 2008 rock fall at Curry Village. True to form, as soon as the closure was announced, some people bemoaned the loss and clamored for replacement facilities. The combined forces of the 1997 flood and the 2008 rock fall reduced overnight accommodations in the Valley from about 2,300 to about 1,500.

Many people are upset by this reduction; I celebrate the changes. I celebrate the fact that nature does indeed bat last—so far, at least.

The rocks I mistook for thunder that cloudy October day in 2005 fell just west of Curry Village, where contractors were building the new employee dorms. I learned later the rock fall sent workers scrambling to get out of the way. A few people were injured, but details surrounding the event were kept very quiet. New construction in an active rock fall zone was not something the Park Service wanted to advertise.

In *Yosemite: The 100 Year Flood*, writer Mark Goodin called the Merced River, "shaper, nurturer, comforter, destroyer." After telling the story of the flood, he said the river "seemed the true ruler of Yosemite during those first three days of 1997, and as the waters abated, few dissenting opinions were heard."

Since 1916, the Merced River has caused substantial property damage via eleven large floods, all occurring between November 1 and January 30. The largest floods occurred in 1937, 1950, 1955, and 1997.

Despite intensive control efforts, including armoring river banks with rocks, re-channeling flows, removing log jams, clearing channels, and blowing up glacial moraines, high water ultimately prevails, thankfully. The Valley's natural cycles of high and low water and occasional big floods play a critical role in maintaining healthy ecosystems. If humans had succeeded at fully curtailing the effects of flooding, the Valley's ecological fabric would be much more tattered than it already is.

On a warmish autumn day with little wind, a dark-haired gentleman dropped down on one denim-clad knee on pine needle littered ground not far from the banks of Tenaya Creek. His other foot stayed flat on the Earth to support his body. He leaned over and deftly spun a narrow wooden dowel between his palms. Friction produced by the lower tip of the dowel generated heat as it swirled in a slight depression on another piece of wood. Bits of dried plant material were mounded around the point of contact between dowel and wood. Rhythmic chanting from a small group of people surrounding the man helped him focus on his task. A whisper of pale smoke swirled up to bless the gathered crowd.

It was October of 2005. The fire-maker was a Native American with ancestral ties to Yosemite Valley. Members of the Southern Sierra Miwuk Nation and the Tuolumne Band of Me-Wuk had joined the National Park Service to ignite a prescribed burn in an area traditionally used for gathering plants. The piece of ground had been largely overrun by dense infestations of the non-native Himalayan blackberry, which would be knocked back by the fire, giving native species a chance to return to the site.

The Yosemite Valley that was described as a sublime piece of paradise by early Euro-American visitors was a product of lots of fire. Lightning strikes are rare within the Valley proper, but fires that ignited elsewhere probably burned up to, and over, the rim on occasion, starting fires down below. In addition, the Valley's Native American residents lit a lot of fires. Some meadow areas show evidence of annual burning. Some ponderosa pine and black oak habitats burned as often as every two years, while other areas supporting these species burned less frequently, with six to eighteen year periods of no fire. Most of these fires probably were low intensity surface fires, as opposed to raging crown fires.

Of the three major processes acting on Yosemite Valley's behalf—rock falls, floods, and fires—rock falls are the least well-suited to control by humans. As soon as geologists produced maps of probable rock fall zones for Valley planning, Nature deposited rock outside the delineated areas. Rock fall is not a process the National Park Service can manage. High water also defies control, even though past efforts to thwart hydrologic processes have been substantial and have severely impeded water flow in many areas. Together, rock fall and high water create a dilemma for the Park Service; most of the Valley floor will, sooner or later, be affected by falling rocks, rising water, or both. After the October 2008 rock fall and subsequent closure of Curry Village lodging, a Yosemite employee noted with a sideways grin, "Yosemite's managers are caught between a rock and a wet spot."

Clearly, the process of falling rock doesn't need to be restored or liberated; park managers just need to remove existing infrastructure from rock fall zones, and stop constructing new buildings.

Relative to the Valley's hydrological processes, many impediments to the natural flow of water into, through, and out of the Valley still exist and are ripe for removal. These impediments are obvious and their removal, for the most part, is straightforward. Fire, on the other hand, is the wild card when it comes to restoring nature in the Valley. Liberating fire in Yosemite Valley is not a simple enterprise.

For hundreds, maybe thousands of years, humans have strongly influenced fire regimes in Yosemite Valley. When the practice of regular burning ceased in the mid-1800s, pronounced effects emerged within a few decades. As early as 1880, the Commissioners' Report stated the upper portion of the Valley was largely overgrown with willows and young pines.

Too little fire in the Valley changes almost everything. Tree density increases. Tree species composition shifts in favor of shade-tolerant species like incense-cedar, at the expense of species requiring more sun, like black oak. Trees encroach on meadows. The risk of major crown fire increases because of excessive fuel build-up. Disease or insect outbreaks become more common as forest density and the stress produced by crowding increase. Plants that rely on fire for reproduction suffer. Wildlife populations change in response to changing habitat. The presence of more trees in the absence of fire alters hydrologic cycles as the trees take up more water and re-direct surface flow. Nutrient cycles are disrupted because nutrients remain in storage in trees, instead of being recycled by fire to other organisms. Processes of decomposition are altered when fire doesn't come through and clean house.

The fact that the health of many ecosystems depends on periodic fire was not widely understood for most of the history of most national parks. Considered destructive, fires were suppressed. Once the beneficial effects of fire penetrated their consciousness, Park Service crews began to ignite fires intentionally in some parks, including Yosemite, in 1970. In 1972, Yosemite's managers also stopped putting out some naturally-occurring fires, if humans and developments were not put at risk by doing so. Additionally, crews cut and burned piles of small trees and shrubs routinely to reduce vegetation density, mimicking some of fire's ecological effects and reducing the risk of catastrophic wildfire.

Fire is a wild card because we don't know how frequently Yosemite Valley would burn in the absence of humans, without human-caused fires or fire suppression. We also don't know what percentage of past fires in the Valley was lit by Native Americans, as opposed to lightning. We do know the Valley's ecological structure and processes evolved with a lot of fire, and, if ecosystems are to remain healthy and viable, they need a lot more fire than they've been getting for the last 150 years. Despite sincere intentions and efforts, fire crews have had limited success at reducing tree density in the Valley with thinning and prescribed fire. Crews burn Valley meadows fairly often, but other habitat types have proven more difficult. The present density of both trees and infrastructure in the Valley precludes letting natural, or even prescribed, fires, really do their jobs. And complaints about smoke and blackened landscapes make superintendents reluctant to allow more widespread prescribed burning.

Clearly, the Park Service can't allow all wildland fires with potential to ignite the Valley to burn, so the periodic fires required to keep the Valley healthy must be prescribed fires. But, should the Park Service burn the Valley as frequently as did the Native Americans? Or should the target be a more "natural" frequency, one that would occur in the absence of humans?

Approximate natural fire return intervals for the Valley can be determined by modeling the probable paths and rates of spread of lightning fires that start outside the Valley and have potential to ignite the Valley. No one knows what the Valley would look like under either of these regimes—burning as frequently as the Native Americans did or burning at "natural" intervals—because neither regime has been systematically applied since the mid-1800s. And, because conditions in the Valley today are so different than they were in the mid-1800s, even if managers did burn the Valley as frequently as did the Native Americans, the resulting landscape could look very different from the vision beheld by the Mariposa Battalion. No one knows.

Both past and current conditions of Valley ecosystems are the result of many types of human manipulation. It's been a very long time since the Valley operated under purely natural conditions. And, as I mentioned earlier, it's highly unlikely humans will voluntarily remove all their accoutrements and leave the Valley forever, allowing nature to reign totally supreme once again. I have little doubt that humans, in this case the Park Service, will continue to manipulate Yosemite Valley's natural processes to ensure visitors can come and have a reasonably safe visit. Restoring nature and natural processes under these conditions is challenging. It's up to park managers to determine how much "naturalness" to strive to retain or attain, and to decide how much manipulation of nature is acceptable and desirable. The Park Service and other land management agencies struggle with this issue constantly, and many are now working to define "desired future conditions" for areas under their care. In Yosemite's case, the question is "What do we want Yosemite Valley to look like, to be like, in the future?"

Questions about desired future conditions are very difficult to answer because of several factors. First, there are many variables to consider. The complexity of natural ecosystems tends to paralyze the human decision-making process. Second, many people are uncomfortable claiming they "know" or even have the right to suggest the best possible future for a given landscape. Playing God is a scary prospect. Third, we know, deep down, we aren't in control. Park managers could describe in great detail exactly what they want for the Valley in 5, 10, 20, or 50 years, but nature probably has other plans that will render thousands of hours and millions of dollars completely inconsequential.

We have to start somewhere, though. If park managers intend to try to "manage" nature, they need to develop targets for their management actions. With respect to Yosemite Valley, rock fall will prescribe its own future conditions, and managers should strive for maximum "naturalness" with respect to hydrologic processes.

Identifying desired future conditions for fire frequency and fire effects, such as the resulting plant species composition and distribution, is more complicated and elusive. No one seems to want to make a commitment to a target. The tools and techniques for burning in Yosemite Valley are available to do the work once desired future conditions are developed.

It would be in the best interest of Valley ecosystem health if managers would decide what they want and then fully commit to getting it done. Make the commitment to reestablish fire in the Valley regardless of smoke, charred landscapes, or inconvenience to humans. If the initial targets prove unattainable, infeasible, or undesirable, they can be changed. For the sake of Valley resources, someone must step forward and get the process started. As long as the Park Service fails to actively and consistently apply fire in Yosemite Valley, the health of Valley ecosystems will continue to decline, and ecosystem structure and function will move even farther away from the conditions present in the mid-1800s.

I don't know exactly what's best for the health of Yosemite Valley's ecosystems. There's no doubt past human use has damaged Valley ecosystems. If the status quo is maintained relative to the amount and distribution of infrastructure in the Valley and the numbers and activities of visitors, ecosystems will continue to deteriorate—they will be further impaired. Efforts to remove non-native species, plant natives, fence people out of sensitive or damaged areas, and remove old infrastructure represent small, but critical steps toward liberating Yosemite Valley's wild nature. There is, however, much more work to be done.

Although I don't have all the answers, I do know the Park Service, despite its claims, is not restoring nature in Yosemite Valley in any significant way. The Yosemite Valley Plan and the Lower Yosemite Fall facelift, despite the way they were sold to the public, were not restoration plans. I know that when the Park Service finally chooses to take the equivalent of the $30 million once allocated to Lodge renovation, the $15 million that went to the Lower Falls facelift, and the untold millions that were poured into dorm construction, utility upgrades, and scenic overlooks, and instead uses the money to further our understanding of Valley ecosystems and human impacts on those ecosystems, we will be much better able to co-exist with the Valley without causing harm. I know when we change our way of relating to the Valley, and finally put ecosystem health ahead of economics and narrow self-interests, we will be able to figure out what the Valley needs and does not need from us.

Although today's park managers don't try as hard to impede natural processes in Yosemite Valley as did managers of earlier times, the current process of gradually lessening impediments is not good enough; it amounts to little more than tinkering. It's time to do everything possible to free natural processes, put more resources into removing non-native plants and animals, take steps to reduce the number of visitors and their impacts, and let time, nature, and the prescribed fire crews take care of the rest.

CHAPTER 30
Cultivate Reverence, Not Relevance

Journal

In his Introduction to The Heart of the World *by Ian Baker, Tenzin Gyatso (His Holiness the Dalai Lama) describes ancient texts discovered centuries ago in Tibet that spoke of beyul, or hidden lands. The texts told of valleys "reminiscent of paradise that can only be reached with enormous hardship." The sacred lands were not places for people to escape from the world, but rather places where they could enter it more deeply. The qualities inherent in beyul revealed the interconnectedness of all life and deepened one's awareness of hidden regions of the mind and spirit.*

Beyul are places where physical and spiritual worlds overlap. Protective veils guard these sites, allowing only those with the karma to do so to enter their depths. The texts describing beyul are not only narrative maps of the hidden worlds, but treatises that can alter the way we see our surroundings, transforming waterfalls, cliffs, and other natural features of the landscape into doorways to exalted perception. Only those with faith and merit actually experience the beyul's spiritual qualities. A beyul is an earthly paradise, a celestial realm here on Earth.

The beyuls the Dalai Lama discussed are in his homeland of Tibet. If there are beyuls in the United States, and I have no doubt there are, Yosemite Valley is one such place, or at least it was. And it can be once again—if we make the right choices.

♦♦♦

The Soul of Yosemite

To reach Yosemite Valley in the 1860s, one took a boat from San Francisco to Stockton, rode a stagecoach for sixteen hours to Coulterville, and then joined a horse and pack mule train for a fifty-seven mile, thirty-seven hour trek. Early tourists experienced rustic conditions, usually in sharp contrast to their lives at home. The time required to get to the Valley ensured all visitors stayed over at least one night. A visit was a unique, special adventure.

On June 25, 1859, the *Tuolumne Courier* reported on Yosemite Valley's Lower Hotel, located south of the Merced River, near the base of today's Four Mile Trail: "Every accommodation possible is given to visitors, and all the appointments of a first-rate hotel are found in Yo-Semite House." According to one early visitor, though, staying at this "first-rate hotel" involved sleeping in a stall in a shed with no windows. Stars were visible through the roof. The door was fastened with hinges of cow skin with hair still attached.

The epic adventure afforded by traveling to Yosemite Valley aboard steamship, train, and horse-drawn wagon changed over time into a fast, insulated drive on smooth, paved roads and cushy seats in air-conditioned vehicles. The vast majority of today's visitors stay in the Valley less than one day. For those who stay overnight, lodges with swimming pools, fluffy pillows, TVs, and central heating have replaced the rugged comforts of the Lower Hotel. Roughing it outdoors by sleeping on narrow cots in musty canvas tents gave way to "camping" in massive motor coaches with satellite television and hot showers inside, and murals depicting regal Serengeti lions outside.

Today, with good weather and light traffic, one can drive to Yosemite Valley from San Francisco in less than four hours. The traveler with little time can take a day trip, a Sunday drive, or a picnic outing. If driving is not an option, a day trip via commercial tour bus can be arranged. For many people, the Valley is little more than a pretty place to cool off when the Central Valley's heat becomes unbearable. Today's visitors need not prepare for the trip in any way; everything a visitor might want can be purchased in the Valley. A trip to Yosemite Valley, once a true adventure, has become a generic outing.

The loss of a sense of adventure and the homogenization of experience, the fact that a visit to this unparalleled wonder differs little from a trip to a city or county park, devalues Yosemite Valley. The opportunity to go to Yosemite is no longer a special, wonderful gift, and this dulling of the edges of a wild adventure has ramifications for wild areas everywhere. As goes Yosemite, so goes the wild of the world.

The Park Service inherited Yosemite Valley in 1916. Despite having almost a century to do so, the agency has never clearly articulated a desired visitor experience for the Valley. In lieu of choreographing the Valley experience, the Park Service has followed trends and mirrored social changes occurring outside the park, changes that are based in ever-increasing levels of consumption and consumerism.

Along with the Valley, the Park Service also inherited the misguided belief held by early concession operators and park managers: that visitor numbers had to increase perpetually. Acting under this delusion, the Park Service supported efforts to cater to everyone's whim and desire. If visitors wanted cigars and haircuts, these "necessities" were provided. If a luxury hotel would entice more and wealthier visitors, the Park Service would build one. When visitors wanted to swim, ice skate, ride horses or bikes, or raft the river, those activities were made available. But efforts to meet every visitor's desire robbed the Valley of its most divine aspects—uniqueness and wildness—and led to creation of a small city instead of preservation of a natural sanctuary. The undying belief that visitation had to increase continually led to most of the Valley's problems, including overdevelopment, overcrowding, and resource damage. Unfortunately, although we should have outgrown it long ago, this archaic mindset that more is necessary continues to rear its ugly head.

Total visits to U.S. national parks declined by about 4 percent in the last decade or so. In response, a cadre of park managers and promoters, many with economic stakes in parks like the recreation travel industry and concession operators, have infused talking heads and the media with the idea that national parks have lost "relevance" with the American public. To regain relevance and reverse downward trends in visitation, some of these groups want the Park Service to behave like a chameleon, to change the parks to reflect the world outside. For example, those caught up in the "lost relevance" delusion believe the Park Service should actively encourage more people in ethnic minority groups to visit parks, and should provide more electronically-based information and opportunities to entice young people.

The Park Service is, once again, hiking down the wrong trail and being misled by economic pressures. Trying to keep up with the recreational or electronic fad *du jour* is like trying to hit moving targets in a dark forest with a broken bow. Rates of change in those arenas occur at a very rapid clip. People are in constant pursuit of something new to buy, to fill up their time or to give them a thrill. And trying to appeal to every ethnic group in America is as impossible as managing an Italian-Mexican-Thai-Mongolian-French restaurant and coffee house; none of the dishes served would be very good, and they all would taste the same because the cooks would be trying to do too much.

The Park Service can't keep up with America's ever-increasing diversity or its rates of technological change; they shouldn't even try. In fact, attempts to stay "relevant" probably contribute to declines in visitation. When national park visits are no different than experiences available elsewhere, many people will be less inclined to visit the parks. Visitors come in search of uniqueness, wildness, and a sense of adventure, not the same old stuff.

Some of the intentions behind this chameleon approach are laudable, and I support efforts to inspire ethnic minority groups and young people to visit and learn about parks. But it's critical that the Park Service not alter basic park functions to cater to any particular group or groups; that the focus stays on fostering connections with and understanding natural and cultural resources. I fear the relevance issue is one more thinly-disguised effort to boost visitation to more lavishly line pockets. As long as the Park Service believes visitation must increase perpetually, neither the integrity of park resources nor the unique opportunities parks can provide will survive.

Instead of worrying about whether or not the parks are still relevant to people, the Park Service can better serve the public by keeping it simple and focusing on the unique, special aspects of the areas they administer. Why were the parks set aside? What are their timeless values? What is their enduring legacy? What is the place of these values and this legacy in the lives of humans?

What is timeless and enduring about humans is our need to feel connected to something larger than ourselves, to find meaning in our lives, to feel at home on the planet, to understand who we are, where we came from, and where we are going, at least to the extent we can know these things. What is timeless and enduring about the national parks is their ability to fill these most basic human needs.

Answers to these questions will differ from park to park, but focusing on these basics will provide a solid foundation for long-term visions that won't be obsolete as soon as they are written into a plan. The latest and greatest electronic information gadgets and activities like geo-caching will go as quickly as they came, will morph into something different, and will leave the Park Service behind over and over again. I encourage park managers to stop buying into the "relevance" campaign. America's national parks have not and never will lose their relevance to people. The Park Service might, but the parks will not.

An interesting parallel exists in national parks with respect to managing both park resources and the experience of visitors. Most park managers struggle to define "desired future conditions" for resources, and they struggle equally with clearly defining desired visitor experiences. Even though these are the two primary missions of the National Park Service, it's hard to find consistent standards for either one. I believe these struggles stem from the fact that the Park Service has never defined impairment. If the agency identified clearly what it was supposed to protect, both resources and experiences, and to what standards, it could function more effectively. Just like defining desired future conditions for resources will be difficult, defining "visitor enjoyment" will be challenging, but the Park Service must do it. Otherwise, visitors will continue to define enjoyment in millions of different ways. In response, the Park Service will chase its tail forever, trying to adapt to ever-changing American lifestyles, preferences, and ethnic make-up, all the while wondering where it misplaced its relevance.

My dad's favorite stories usually begin with: "Do you remember the time..." One tale he tells time and again occurred the weekend he and Mom came to visit me in Cedar Grove, at the end of the road in Kings Canyon National Park, where I worked as a ranger-naturalist. They chose the perfect time of year to visit; the roaring Kings River danced and sparkled while the meadows rippled in waves of tall grass and wildflowers.

On a cloud-free, blue-sky Saturday morning, Mom and Dad joined me for my guided walk around Zumwalt Meadow. I led the group of thirty or so visitors down a trail that wound through the meadow, regaling them with stories of corn lily reproduction and black bear ingenuity. We circled around the far end of my planned loop hike and suddenly came face-to-face with a flooded trail. In its exuberance, the river had slipped over its banks and was running amok in the meadow.

I turned to the group and said, "Well, we have two options. We can turn back and return the way we came, or we can take off our shoes and socks and proceed. But, one way or the other, we all have to stay together." After a moment of considered silence, the group surprised me with a unanimous clamor to keep going. They immediately sat down in the middle of the trail to strip off footwear and roll up pant legs. My intrepid group smiled, grimaced, laughed, and gasped as the frigid River of Kings swirled around their feet, ankles, calves, and knees. After we finished the walk and returned to our initial point of departure, many of my guests told me wading across the river on such a glorious, heaven-sent day was one of the most wonderful, wildest experiences they'd ever had. My Dad was among the converted.

Park Service interpreters play an essential role in national parks. As a seasonal interpreter in Sequoia, Kings Canyon, and Death Valley, I spent most of my time outside with visitors, answering questions in Visitor Centers, or leading campfire or evening programs. In Yosemite, I was surprised to see how few interpreter-led walks, talks, and programs occurred in the Valley. Unfortunately, because budgets for Interpretation Divisions largely go toward salaries, budget cuts mean fewer employees. When push comes to shove and cuts must be made, keeping bathrooms clean and roads maintained trump teaching people about the park and helping them make life-changing connections with the land. And because Visitor Centers must be open and staffed, interpreters who survive budget cuts too often find themselves parked behind desks instead of leading people barefoot through cold mountain streams.

One sultry August afternoon in Yosemite Valley, I crossed paths with a group of twelve high school students and their leader as they walked along the paved bike path west of Sentinel Bridge. The students were so focused on the path, themselves, and each other, that they passed a large buck grazing on meadow grasses. He was a mere twenty feet off the trail, glorious in his velvet-covered rack, but no one in the group saw him. I stopped and quietly pointed him out. All eyes widened and conversation ceased as the students fumbled for cameras. Granted, these were high school students, but I witnessed this type of inattentiveness to surroundings frequently in Yosemite Valley. The Valley's paved trails, smooth roads, and hundreds of directional signs create a situation where visitors don't have to pay attention; they might as well be in a city.

Joseph Sax in *Mountains Without Handrails* spoke of how the tourist of "an earlier time" came to the parks and found himself "in a place where the sound of birds ruled rather than the sound of motors, where the urban crowds gave way to rural densities, and where planned entertainments disappeared in favor of a place with nothing to do but what the visitor discovered for himself." This idea encapsulates exactly what the national parks should foster: self-willed visitors experiencing self-willed, wild land. Places where people come and are changed by the coming, where they experience a world bigger and more wondrous than anything they'd ever imagined.

My strongest, most influential "a-ha" moments, times I have felt the greatest clarity and have solved some of the thorniest problems in my life, occurred when I was alone and immersed in nature, without human accoutrements, without distractions. This is also true of those moments when I felt most deeply connected to the Earth, when I knew with certainty I was not alone, even though no one was with me; moments when I felt totally comfortable in my skin and in the world. By my way of thinking, this is the highest calling for our national parks: places to contemplate life; to ruminate on nature, death, the world, the universe, and our place in the scheme of things; places to ponder the big questions.

Many people are uncomfortable with wild lands and being alone in nature, yet they are attracted to these experiences. The most popular paintings and photographs of the outdoors, including Yosemite Valley, are those lacking humans and human-created elements. Presently, the Park Service does little to help people feel comfortable in wild nature. Visitors would benefit if this became part of the agency's purpose.

Behavioral scientists and psychologists believe the events we remember most clearly, and those that continue to affect us our entire lives, are events infused with deep emotion—birth, death, illness, marriage, and other situations outside the realm of the everyday. The parks provide myriad opportunities for deeply memorable experiences. But they won't happen while visitors are reading a website or museum exhibit, or concentrating on sore butts unfamiliar with a horse's back, or drinking Pepsi and getting sunburned on a raft trip, or trying to find something geo-cached using GPS technology. The profound experiences will happen when visitors wade knee-deep through a frigid river in flood, or chance upon a bear ripping up a log in search of grubs, or look closely at the structure of a grass flower for the first time.

People are desperate for connection and meaning in their lives, and search in vain for these crucial elements outside of themselves through shopping, acquiring stuff, and watching other people's lives in movies, books, and television. I think people crave wildness, and attempt to retrieve their lost wildness in drugs and alcohol, in sports, and in reality TV shows like Survivor. But no one feels a true connection to wildness through these venues.

Many people expand their search for connection, meaning, and wildness in their outdoor experiences; they ski, boat, bicycle, raft, bungee jump, zipline, zoom around in off-road vehicles, hunt, and fish. None of these activities are good or bad in and of themselves (although they do have significant collective adverse impacts on nature), but the activities themselves are really the same as shopping. Instead of acquiring stuff, the extremely active person acquires experiences.

When we actually experience wildness in our world, true natural wildness, the wildness outside of us reflects back at us and echoes through the chambers of our ancestral experience. We remember—we were wild once, too.

Experiencing the wildness in nature and finding the wild nature within ourselves, and then connecting these two aspects of the wild require "being" in wild, natural places, as opposed to "doing" things outside. Re-discovering this vital link requires solitude, silence, and open-ended stretches of time in wild places. Yosemite Valley is perfect for fostering this connection, filling this vital role. The Valley is accessible and safe, and provides unlimited opportunities for inspiration. The only thing it needs is the return of its stolen wildness.

Ideally, the Yosemite Valley visitor would be exposed to a bare minimum of distractions from the natural environment. Anything of human origin steals one's attention from the natural: a fencepost, a boardwalk, a bike rack, an abandoned telephone line, a paved trail, a cigarette butt, a bench, a road, a restroom, a garbage can, headlights shattering the dark of night, a generator humming through the trees. Once again, there's nothing inherently good or bad about these things, but if the objective of a park is to foster contemplation, to take ourselves outside of ourselves and our routines, minimizing human-made distractions is critical. The visitor should hear mostly, and often exclusively, natural sounds, sometimes experiencing the landscape in total silence. No lawn mowers, leaf blowers, weed whackers, or diesel engines. Visitors should, more often than not, see nature without obvious signs of human culture. No power lines, no pavement, no litter.

Yosemite Valley is a perfect place for humans to fall in love with and learn to care for wild land, wild creatures, wild nature, and the wild part inside all of us that resonates with the wild outside of us. The Valley can serve as an ambassador to wild places everywhere. Where better to educate people? Almost everyone wants to go to Yosemite Valley, and the list of those eager to visit will grow once the opportunity to experience a wilder, more natural Valley becomes common knowledge. And once people are in the Valley, the Park Service has a captive and receptive audience.

In the fall of 2007, Tom and I walked the paved bike path from the Ahwahnee Hotel to Indian Caves. The Valley was quiet, with few visitors. I was hoping to see a bear. On our return trip, just east of Sugar Pine Bridge, I got my wish. A small female black bear with an even smaller cub emerged from behind a large boulder about fifty feet from the trail. We stopped to watch. Mama bear paid us no mind as she sniffed around a few downed logs. Her cub followed a few paces behind. As we watched, a man and a young girl about ten years old approached us from the west on bicycles. I held one hand up to ask them to slow down and put a finger to my lips. As they rolled up to us I pointed to the bears. With an in-rush of breath and wide eyes, they both whispered, "Wow."

Mama bear ambled in our direction. I quietly suggested we back up to give her space. She crossed the bike path and stopped at the base of a ponderosa pine. Her cub followed in a bouncing, short-stepped gait. Mama dropped down to the ground, rolled onto her back, and scratched herself in the rough bed of needles and cones. Her cub watched for a moment, and then climbed up onto her fat belly. They rolled and played in the fallen pine needles for several minutes, swatting gently at each other's faces. The forest embraced us with silence. We heard no car noise, generators, human voices, or airplanes. We heard only gruff, low-pitched growls as the bears wrestled. After a bit, they both stood, shook their shaggy coats to free needles and leaves, and wandered away into the woods. The man and the girl were beaming, radiant, hardly believing their great good fortune. They grinned from ear to ear and thanked Tom and me profusely, but quietly, still in awe, reverent over what we had witnessed together.

This experience of black bears can't be understood from reading a book, watching a movie, or peering through the window of a car or bus. The subtle sounds are lost—Mama Bear's breathy wheezes and small grunts as she scratches her itchy back, her cub's tiny mewl as he runs to catch up with her. The feel of the cool autumn breeze rippling through pine needles and ruffling bear hair is missing. The energy and essence of bear, and the impact of being in the same space as bear, are absent. And that makes all the difference.

National parks and other wild places help us remember. They help us remember what the land looked, smelled, felt, tasted, and sounded like before we changed it. They help us remember significant events in our nation's history. They help us remember the generations of people who lived on this land before Euro-Americans arrived. They help us remember that we share this land with many other species. And they help us remember how to share. What could possibly be more relevant in a society that has largely lost its connection to the Earth it depends on for its very existence?

Instead of chasing relevance for revenue, I suggest the Park Service do everything possible to cultivate reverence for nature and wildness. Beauty, nature, and wildness will never be irrelevant to human beings, but many have lost sight of or forgotten their connections to these most basic needs. The National Park Service is uniquely suited to help them remember.

In *Preserving Nature in the National Parks: A History*, Richard West Sellars suggests national parks heighten visitor's aesthetic sensibility, and may inspire a deeper understanding of, and concern for, the natural environment. Without a doubt this is true, or can be, if parks are managed with these objectives in mind. And, unlike revenue generated from postcard and key chain sales, the value of these gifts is beyond measure.

I believe these wild gifts will save our lives.

CHAPTER 31
Transcend Economics

Journal

In March 2009, a flurry of articles in various newspapers reported Yosemite's historic Ahwahnee Hotel could be closed for up to two years while the Park Service retrofitted the building for seismic safety. Park officials had requested $137 million in federal funding for the work, as part of the President's economic stimulus program, and were waiting to hear if the project would be selected for funding. The hotel generates a lot of money for the park concession operator, some of which trickles down to surrounding communities.

A few weeks later, another group of articles clearly stated the Ahwahnee Hotel would not be closed for two years for earthquake retrofitting. Instead, the work would likely be spread out over a several-year period, during which parts of the hotel might be closed. It turned out the park's proposal for federal funding was rejected.

The sigh of relief from the Park Service and others with economic stakes in the Valley could have knocked an unsuspecting bear right off her feet.

◆◆◆

The Ahwahnee Hotel has 123 rooms, and overnight rates average about $450 a night. If the hotel is full, which occurs often (average annual occupancy rates are over 90 percent), gross income for the park's concession operator, Delaware North, is approximately $55,000 per day. The hotel employs about 300 people. Adjacent counties also benefit significantly from the Ahwahnee. For example, Mariposa County draws tens of millions of dollars every year from hotel taxes. The economic consequences of closing the hotel for two years would have been substantial.

Delaware North Companies, an international food service and hospitality management corporation based in Buffalo, New York, secured Yosemite's concession contract in 1993. One of the largest privately held companies in the United States, Delaware North generated revenues of over $2 billion in 2009. Their ventures include: providing retail and food services to sports and entertainment venues; operating hotels, casinos, racetracks, poker rooms, and video lottery terminals; managing more than 10,000 video games; providing airport food service and retail companies; operating the Kennedy Space Center; and running concession services in national parks like Yosemite, Yellowstone, Sequoia, and Grand Canyon. The parent company's chairman, who is also the Chief Executive Officer, owns the National Hockey League's Boston Bruins.

The Yosemite concession contract is the largest in the National Park system, and includes management of 1,667 guest rooms, 25 food and beverage units, and 19 retail locations. In 2010, Delaware North employed about 1,800 people in Yosemite during the summer, and about 1,100 in winter. In contrast, the Park Service employed about 740 people year round, and about 1,100 in summer.

In 2008, Delaware North reported gross revenue of about $125 million from its Yosemite contract. Under terms of the original contract, approximately 20 percent of the total revenue goes to the park, primarily to fund concession-related improvements and services. Under this arrangement, the Park Service has a clear incentive to encourage increased visitation: more people means more money.

In Yosemite, Delaware North manages lodging, food and beverage services, retail sales, a shuttle bus system, tour buses, and open-air trams as well as activities including rafting, biking, skiing, ice skating, hiking, climbing, horseback riding, and educational programs. The company also hosts special events throughout the year designed to attract visitors in the non-peak winter months. Many of these two to three-day events are held at the Ahwahnee Hotel. The Vintner's Holidays showcase wine-makers from throughout California, who come to help visitors taste and learn about wine. At the Chefs' Holidays, participants can drink wine, and learn from "celebrated chefs" from around the country.

In March, Delaware North hosts the Yosemite Heritage Holidays, which started in 2002 in honor of the Ahwahnee's seventy-fifth anniversary. Now a "three-day tradition," this event celebrates the "glamour, style, frivolity and culture of the Roaring Twenties and beyond." Activities include Speakeasy entertainment, fashion shows, a Grand Ball complete with the twelve piece Royal Society Jazz Orchestra, and dancing and performances by a professional dance troupe.

The most extravagant of the Ahwahnee events is the Bracebridge Dinner, held in mid to late-December. Celebrated annually since 1927, the event transforms the hotel dining room into a seventeenth century English manor for a "feast of food, song and mirth." The four-hour long dinner features carols, Renaissance rituals, entertainment of the Middle Ages, and a seven-course meal. Ticket prices for 2011 started at $1718 for two people, including two nights lodging. None of these events have anything at all to do with Yosemite Valley.

Many people feel the presence of Delaware North fosters the trend toward more development in Yosemite Valley, and has strongly influenced the Park Service to encourage as many people as possible to visit the park despite the adverse impacts of visitation on resources. But Delaware North is not to blame; the company does business in Yosemite to make money. The only way to eliminate the pressure exerted by a for-profit concession operator is to grant the concession contract to a not-for-profit entity. The National Park Service will have a golden opportunity to do so when the concession contract comes up for renewal.

Since 1988, the Yosemite Conservancy (known as the Yosemite Fund until January 2010), a tax-exempt corporation, has given Yosemite National Park more than $55 million. The money comes from individual and corporate donors, including ChevronTexaco, Delaware North, Granite Construction, Inc., PG&E, URS, and Wells Fargo (the Conservancy's principal bank). Donors are rewarded by being associated with Yosemite. Those contributing the most money get their names included on the "Honor Wall at the Yosemite Valley Visitor Center," receive recognition in publications like the organization's annual report, get listed on their webpage, and are invited to Yosemite events and holiday parties.

The Yosemite Conservancy's mission statement indicates the group provides private funding for specific projects that further "preserve, protect, or enhance Yosemite National Park." Projects range from trail repair and wildlife research to museum exhibit production and the monumental Lower Yosemite Fall project. ChevronTexaco alone contributed at least $1 million to the Lower Fall project.

An analysis of projects funded from 2004 through 2007 reveals a distinct bias. By far, the most heavily funded endeavors are large infrastructure projects and trail repair. In 2004, 71 percent of funding went to the Lower Yosemite Fall Project, the most expensive project to date at more than $12.5 million over several years. Trail repair received more than 40 percent ($1.1 million) of allocations in 2005, and one visitor services and education project—the showy restoration of the Olmsted Point viewing area on the Tioga Road—received over 27 percent ($744,000). In 2006, visitor services and education received the lion's share at 35 percent ($1.3 million); the Olmsted Point restoration being the big winner again in that category. The second runner-up was trail repair, with 34 percent ($1.28 million). In 2007, trail repair projects received 38 percent ($1.9 million), and a new category of expenses known as Project Administration consumed 13 percent ($680,000).

Projects to study or manage park resources received funding in each of those years, but at consistently lower levels. The pattern is clear; the emphasis of The Yosemite Conservancy's efforts is on high-profile visitor use projects, not on resource management, protection, or research.

On one hand, this emphasis is understandable. Many donors want their contributions to result in a physical, tangible product. But they need to get over that. The most basic and pressing needs in Yosemite are resource inventory, monitoring, research, protection, and restoration; and the Park Service knows this. The Yosemite Conservancy's wealth, however, has given the organization tremendous power. Instead of handing the donations to the Park Service to allocate to the park's most pressing needs, managers of The Yosemite Conservancy hand-pick projects they want to fund. This approach is backwards.

In 2006, the Conservancy launched a new Campaign for Yosemite Trails to raise another $13.5 million to focus on "Yosemite's most critically compromised, high profile trails." This project made my blood run cold; the wonderful, rustic, still semi-wild Valley Loop Trail was on the list of targets for "improvement."

A third group with significant economic stakes in Yosemite is composed of tourism-oriented business owners operating in "gateway communities" near the park. The *Yosemite Valley Plan Supplemental Environmental Impact Statement* said, based on a 1998 survey, Yosemite visitors spent an estimated $238.8 million in businesses within and outside of the park that year.

A report titled "*National Treasures as Economic Engines*," prepared by the National Parks Conservation Association, indicated Yosemite tourists spent about $320 million in 2001, and this money generated 8,864 jobs. Yosemite's more than 4 million visitors pumped about $355 million into local economies in 2010. Yosemite ranked third among parks in its economic impact, after Great Smoky Mountains and Grand Canyon. It's difficult to identify precisely how much money Yosemite's presence generates for gateway community businesses, but, if the magnitude of business owners' opposition to any proposal to control or reduce visitor numbers in the park is any indication, the totals must be substantial. Unfortunately for all concerned, many local businesses rely on park-generated revenue for their existence.

A friend of mine in Boise formerly served as Executive Director for a non-profit program that provides opportunities for children with various kinds of disabilities to ride horses. The program has evolved for several years, and has experienced growing pains. Over lunch one afternoon, she explained to me how many of the people involved with the program at various levels seemed to want to be in charge of things, to take control. I made the observation that the program is such a "feel good" enterprise that everyone wants a stake in it. And each person's interest is rooted in something slightly different, something unique to their personalities. Some want to be involved because it makes them feel good about themselves, others want to spend time with the horses, and many simply want to help people. With a program like this, there is a tendency for everyone, including coordinators, board members, and even volunteers, to want to seize a large piece of the pie, because the pie is so tasty.

I believe a similar situation occurs with Yosemite Valley. Everyone, or almost everyone, who sees the Valley and experiences its magic wants to grab a piece of it, wants to remain connected to it. For some, it's a matter of ego gratification; they are somehow better, more respectable people for their association with the Valley. For others, it's purely a matter of making money. And, for most of us, it's simply a desire to remember, to experience and re-experience the wonder, because it satisfies so many of our deepest needs.

Perhaps it's time for all of us to stop holding on so tightly to Yosemite Valley, to relax our death grip of personal needs and desires, and to give the Valley back to itself; free the river, the rocks, the meadows, the mallards, and all the other sentient and non-sentient beings of the place to fulfill their own destinies. Perhaps it's time to let go. Not completely, I realize that's not possible or desirable. I still want to visit the Valley, too. But maybe we could all collectively loosen our grip to ensure a healthy, vibrant future for the Valley.

In Yosemite, the tail really does wag the dog. And the dog is big, and has many tails. One could say the corporation wags the bureaucracy, the fund-raiser wags the recipient, and the neighbors wag the primary occupant. To further complicate matters, these tail-waggers all have considerable influence with political representatives—and the politicians always wag hardest of all.

If the last remnants of wildness in the Valley are to survive, the National Park Service must regain control of its tail, and make decisions based on what is best for Yosemite itself. And people outside the Park Service who care about the Valley will have to make their voices heard over those who want to exploit its beauty. The Organic Act does not direct the National Park Service to preserve parks as opportunities for economic gain. This benefit is ancillary to the purposes of parks.

Those who make money off the park can have a voice in, but should never drive, the Park Service's decision-making processes.

CHAPTER 32
Imagine

Journal

Imagine standing in a deep, grassy valley edged with sheer granite walls laced with white-ribbon waterfalls; a valley lined with lush green meadows shivering under a thin veil of frigid snowmelt, compliments of up-canyon snow—a precious gift to grass and sedge as they begin their seasonal reach for the sky. Imagine sun-dappled trunks of ponderosa pine rising straight up from a forest floor strewn with old needles and spiky brown cones chewed to a ragged pulp, unmistakable calling cards of the Douglas squirrel.

Imagine sitting by a wild river with an ever-changing visage. In spring, a froth of urgent frenzy crashing headlong through a maze of boulders the size of elephants; in summer, a leisurely flow of smooth, long, reaches, relaxed under a beating sun; in autumn, curling slowly around rocks and bushes, pausing to idle in oxbow or pool, finally turning deep green-brown, enriched by past lives and decay; and, in winter, dark, with sharp-edged shards of ice lining shaded banks, crystalline, cold, waiting, biding time until spring when the cycle repeats and flushes all clean once more.

Imagine breathing clear, clean air that rings with children's voices divining the secrets of the wild, the world of the natural. A warm glow rises from rapt faces as adults and children of all ages, backgrounds and life stories awaken to the wonder of the place. Deep, contented sighs emanate from deeply wrinkled, weathered faces as the tranquil scene, the sweet mountain air, and the sparkling water song loosen the grip of stress and strain, wash away pain, sadness, grief, and fear. All who come find escape, transformation, re-creation.

Imagine walking through nights filled to the rim with quiet, marked by the passing hush of a great horned owl returning to nest in a one hundred year old oak, the high-pitched yip and chatter of the coyote clan dancing under the full moon to celebrate a kill, the steadfast murmur of the Merced River on its way to forever. The air carries the snap of a campfire. A park ranger regales all comers with stories of the woods and the creatures of the night as rows of faces reflect the glow of burning wood back to the flames of creation.

Imagine lying on a blanket, watching a bold, star-spangled sky emerge from hiding not long after dusk. Moon glow shimmers off smooth granite mirrors, and a trillion million stars light the way. Watch the moon turn to new, experience night without light, true darkness, until Ursa Major, Orion, and Draco leap out from the black, engaged in their endless circle dance with Polaris and the Seven Sisters. The creatures of the evening and the night: bats eating mosquitoes on the fly, mountain lions foraging for raccoons foraging for berries or insects or frogs; all living unhindered, undisturbed by humans.

Imagine being part of a valley abuzz with the activity of government workers and volunteers removing the overdone trappings of 140 plus years of misguided intentions. Their work plan reads: Remove asphalt and concrete of unnecessary roads, bridges, trails; remove lodges, homes, dormitories, swimming pools, tennis courts, restrooms, and offices; remove tons of cement used for bridge footings in the river and creeks; remove miles and miles of underground pipes carrying waste, water, power, and phone calls; remove forever all that is extraneous to the experience of the wild.

Imagine seeing disturbed soils carefully re-contoured, native plants tenderly planted, and critters—bacteria and fungi, earthworms and sowbugs, ground squirrels and Steller's jays, and all the other more-than-humans—living, procreating, and dying largely outside the influence of humans.

Imagine experiencing a deep, grassy Valley, Yosemite Valley, unimpaired by humans.

♦♦♦

Yosemite Valley needs a new vision for its future: a vision based in wildness that always protects and preserves natural and cultural elements first; a vision that allows people to come and rejoice in the Valley's grace and splendor; a vision with opportunities for visitors to connect deeply with the natural world; a vision not corrupted or coerced by economics or politics.

Identifying problems is easy. Visualizing and manifesting changes to resolve those problems is more difficult. Imagining a new vision for Yosemite Valley requires letting go of attachments to what is, in order to allow what could be to appear.

I have a vision—a new, old vision—for Yosemite Valley. It's new in that it is a product of the twenty-first century, and is unlike any plan that has guided park managers to date. It's old because similar visions have been developed and proposed, have waxed and waned, since 1864, when the Valley became a park. It's new because unlike other similar visions that for one reason or another never gained traction, implementation of this vision, or one similar to it, is absolutely necessary for the long-term ecological health and well-being of Yosemite Valley. I present this vision as a starting point.

The best way to describe my vision is to travel through the Valley to see it made manifest. Let's walk the Valley from end to end, and I'll describe the changes I envision. Keep your eyes peeled for mergansers and great blue herons as we come in view of the river.

We'll start at the eastern end of the Valley, just above Happy Isles, and walk to the Pohono Bridge, which marks the Valley's western end. It's a long walk, about seven miles, and we'll meander back and forth to see all the changes, but we'll take plenty of water and lunch and go slow. For those of you who can't walk with us, a van will depart soon for Glacier Point, where you can follow our progress with binoculars and headphones keyed to my microphone. I welcome all of you, and can't wait to share with you my dream for Yosemite Valley.

Let's imagine ourselves in 2016, the year the National Park Service celebrates its 100th anniversary. Before we begin our walk, I want to share a press release that came from the Service's Washington D.C. office just this morning: "In response to an unprecedented amount of public support in favor of re-wilding Yosemite Valley, the National Park Service wishes to formally recognize Yosemite Valley as a sacred place to be revered instead of abused, exploited, and commercialized. The Service recognizes that the primary purpose of Yosemite Valley is to sustain itself by sustaining all of its living and non-living natural elements and processes. The Valley's secondary, but also critical function is to help people re-connect with nature and with themselves. Further, it is not the purpose of Yosemite National Park to make money for individuals or corporations, or to feed undernourished or insecure egos, or to provide everything every visitor or every potential visitor could ever need or want."

I can't tell you how overjoyed I was to read this press release. After nearly one hunderd years of service, the agency responsible for the well-being of America's beloved national parks, the U. S. National Park Service, understands its mission. The agency has experienced an epiphany. Imagine that, the paradigm shift is underway. Hallelujah!

For the past several years, the Park Service has worked steadily to implement the new vision for Yosemite Valley. As Valley visitors within the vision, we had to make advance reservations before we left home, regardless of whether we planned to stay overnight or just for the day. When we arrived, we used our Valley entrance pass to gain access at the check station. All visitors, park and concession employees, delivery services, and anyone else coming into Yosemite Valley now must have a pass for admittance. For visitors, it's crucial to get advance reservations in the summer months. From October through April, you often can get a Valley pass on a first-come first-serve basis, but it's always best to make a reservation. Everyone who reserves lodging or camping space in the Valley automatically gets a Valley entrance pass with their reservation, good for the duration of their stay. Visitors staying outside the park must secure a day pass.

The park now allows a maximum of six tour buses and six school group buses into the Valley each day. This is in marked contrast to the approximately seventy-six buses per day that came into the Valley on busy days before the new vision took effect. Diesel buses are no longer allowed in the Valley. All tour and school groups spend at least two hours with a Park Service interpretive ranger, and all bus riders spend at least one night in the Valley.

Reserved Valley passes are checked, and first-come, first-serve day passes issued, at park entrance stations when fees are paid. Availability of first-come, first-serve day passes is broadcast on the park's information radio station, as well as on electronic bulletin boards in gateway communities.

The Valley's road system has changed a bit. In the past, as you entered the Valley from the south on the Wawona Road, you passed Bridalveil Falls and then turned right, or east, on Southside Drive, to enter the Valley. Now, drivers must turn left, or west, on Southside Drive, continue for a few minutes, then cross Pohono Bridge and turn right, or east, on Northside Drive to access the Valley.

Southside Drive is no longer used as a regular access road. From the Wawona Road Junction east all the way to the 4-way stop near the former Curry Village site, Southside Drive is maintained as a paved biking and hiking route. Throughout the Valley, bicycles are allowed only on paved roads and bike paths. And the Park Service has gotten serious about enforcing regulations designed to protect resources; heavy fines are levied for riding bikes off pavement. This regulation applied to the Valley before the transformation, but it wasn't enforced because there were too many visitors and not enough rangers. Believe me, all that has changed.

The Park Service still maintains Southside Drive for vehicle use in case of emergencies, including situations like fires, floods, earthquakes, or rockslides that could block Northside Drive, which now serves as the main access road into and out of the Valley.

The entrance station for the Valley is located between Pohono Bridge and El Capitan Meadow. Cars coming up the El Portal Road stay north of the river all the way into the Valley. El Capitan Bridge and crossover road, north of El Capitan Meadow, is still here, but is used only by pedestrians, bicycles, and emergency vehicles.

The history of cars in Yosemite Valley is worth mentioning. Cars have marred the beauty of the Valley ever since 1890, when the first one rolled in. By 1892, humans had built over twenty miles of roads, six bridges, twelve culverts, and twenty-four miles of equestrian trails in the Valley. In 1907, the superintendent banned private cars; they were destroying Valley vegetation and road surfaces, and posed a safety hazard when combined with the many horses used for transportation. In 1913, cars were allowed again, but only north of the river. In 1915, private cars could only be used to enter or leave the Valley, and only before 7:00PM.

In 1916, the restrictions were lifted, but all roads were designated one-way most of that year. In 1920, to alleviate traffic problems, a jitney service operated between visitor accommodations and popular hiking spots. In the 1920s, cars could only enter the Valley on even hours, and could only exit on odd hours. Twelve miles per hour was the maximum speed and cars were not allowed to travel at night. By 1929, twenty-nine miles of paved roads, fifteen miles of oiled roads, a large paved parking lot at Happy Isles, thirteen miles of bridle paths and fifteen miles of paved walkways crisscrossed the Valley. Damage to meadows from cars was extensive.

The impacts of cars, including air, water, and light pollution; noise; wildlife mortality; and impairment of visitor enjoyment, continued unabated into the twenty-first century, despite *General Management Plan* directives to eliminate them from the Valley.

The Soul of Yosemite

My old new vision for Yosemite Valley includes cars, but as the number of visitors at any one time is relatively low, and use of cars is severely restricted, they have significantly less impact. Similar to times past, private cars largely are restricted to the north side of the river, can only be driven to enter or leave the Valley, and are not to be driven after dark. No vehicles operate between dusk and dawn, except in emergencies; no headlight glare mars the dark night skies. The speed limit is twenty miles per hour, so wildlife gets to live. Once visitors arrive, they walk, ride their own or rented bicycles or the free shuttle bus. If they are unable to do any of the above, visitors can rent a small electric golf cart-sized vehicle.

Okay, are we ready to begin our visionary tour? We'll start at the site of an old water tank that sat on a flat clearing upriver and south of Happy Isles. The tank is gone, as is its service road. A little-known horse trail that winds up the south side of the river to the Vernal Falls Bridge is now maintained as a hiking trail. It was rarely used by visitors in the past because the Park Service reserved it for horses and mules coming and going from Yosemite's backcountry. But, there are no horses or mules in the Valley now; their impacts on the environment are too severe.

At Happy Isles, the Nature Center and all pavement and asphalt are gone. Trails in the area are retained as dirt trails. Pedestrian bridges remain to facilitate access among the isles.

As we progress down-Valley, you'll begin to notice almost all development south of the Merced River is gone. There are numerous reasons for this major change. The area north of the river is warmer and sunnier, and has had fewer recent rockslides than areas south of the river. Most of the existing infrastructure already was on the north side, and removal of facilities south of the river eliminated the need for any river utility crossings. Keeping the zone south of the river undeveloped allows for better natural visitor experiences, opens a wider corridor for wildlife travel, and removes the safety risks of bicycles, pedestrians, and cars using the same road.

Only two buildings remain south of the river: the LeConte Memorial and the Yosemite Chapel. They've been removed from the utility grid, and are serviced by waterless vault toilets. To access these facilities, visitors and residents walk, bicycle, or ride a Sunday church shuttle. In the future, these buildings may be relocated north of the river or removed completely.

Upper and Lower Pines Campgrounds underwent quite a transformation. There are fewer, much less densely-packed sites, and the campgrounds are no longer served by utilities. Things are much quieter and cleaner here now, and vegetation, once completely eliminated by overuse, has begun to recover. The two campgrounds now accommodate a total of fifty tent and fifty small recreational vehicle sites. Generators are not allowed. North Pines Campground, the concession stables, and all associated infrastructure are gone. And if we detour a bit toward the south Valley wall, we'll notice all of Curry Village is gone. Parking lots, cabins, tents, store, cafeteria, registration building, and all employee housing—every part of Curry Village has been removed because of its location south of the river and its propensity for rock falls.

At this point, I imagine many of you are bemoaning the loss of something, or dressing me down for having the gall to suggest such changes. Bear with me, hear me out, and hold the tomatoes. If the ecological integrity of Yosemite Valley is to recover and survive, we all must make sacrifices. Your favorite cabin or campsite may be removed, but you will have opportunities for an unprecedented Yosemite Valley experience; a much more private, quiet, and nurturing experience. If we are all willing to sacrifice, to give up something, we will all receive much more than we ever expected in return. There will be overnight accommodations at Yosemite Lodge; we'll get to that in a minute. For those of you who are angered by my proposal because it will hurt your economic bottom line, I have no words of solace. I sincerely believe Yosemite Valley has a more important role. Onward!

Let's head west across the river on the historic span known as Stoneman Bridge. The bridge has been reconstructed to substantially reduce its impact on dynamic river flows, while retaining its historic character. Experts in historic architecture re-used the original materials as much as they could. Several other historic bridges in the Valley, including Ahwahnee, Sugar Pine, and Clark's, also have been rebuilt, but may be removed in the future.

A new road lies between the Curry 4-way and the Pines Campgrounds. The old road that cut across meadow habitat is gone; the new road follows existing routes that once served Curry Village, traversing upland areas less likely to flood or support meadow vegetation. The paved bike and shuttle bus roads to Happy Isles and Mirror Lake have been retained, but were narrowed to a single lane. The pavement on the lower portion of the trail to the Vernal Fall Bridge has been removed. Remnant scraps of pavement along the entire Valley Loop Trail also have been removed.

Once we cross Stoneman Bridge, you'll see that both Upper and Lower River Campgrounds, which were literally demolished by the 1997 flood, are functional campgrounds once again. Each one supports fifty sites located away from the river, on the highest ground available. The natural drainages in the area that re-established after the flood have been avoided to the greatest extent possible, and site improvements are minimal. The Park Service understands and accepts the fact that these campgrounds will be periodically damaged by flooding. Amphitheatres are maintained at Lower Pines and Lower River Campgrounds. National Park Service ranger-led campfire programs occur every evening at these two amphitheatres and at Yosemite Lodge.

As we continue west, take a look across the river to the south and you will see nothing but trees and shrubs and rocks. Housekeeping Camp and all associated developments are gone. Additionally, the road that connects the Rivers Campgrounds to Yosemite Village is an elevated causeway that runs over, instead of on top of, the Ahwahnee Meadow, which facilitates water flow through the meadow.

The parking lot south of Yosemite Village used by day visitors, formerly the site of Camp 6, is still a parking lot, but it is a dirt lot once again, and it has been reduced in size. It can accommodate a maximum of 500 cars at one time, and no longer is used as a staging area for Valley construction. The limit on Valley day passes is 1,000 cars. Some day parking also is available at Yosemite Lodge.

Moving west and south, the old Sentinel Road and Sentinel Bridge are gone; both were down-sized to accommodate bicycles and pedestrians. All paved bike paths have been removed from Valley meadows; bicycles no longer have access across meadow habitat, with the exception of an elevated causeway that runs between Yosemite Lodge and Swinging Bridge.

The road that runs east of Yosemite Village, behind the old General Store and out to the Ahwahnee Hotel is still there. This route has been re-constructed as an elevated causeway where it crosses the north edge of Ahwahnee Meadow to allow water to flow unimpeded between and among Valley walls, woodlands, meadows, forests, and the river. The Valley's lifeblood is starting to flow freely once again.

The medical clinic, dentist office, and Superintendent's house are gone. In fact, all employee housing between Yosemite Village and the Ahwahnee Hotel is gone, with the exception of a small complex immediately west of the hotel. Very few employees reside in the Valley now; most travel to and from work every morning on small electric buses. The concession operator and the National Park Service collectively funded a large, new apartment complex in Mariposa that houses many employees. Once the infrastructure in the Valley was reduced, the number of concession employees decreased in tandem. Both the concession operator and the Park Service then identified employees who absolutely had to reside in the Valley, a limited number of people involved in hotel and food service, and emergency responders. Several employee housing units are maintained for overnight stays for personnel, like interpretive naturalists, who must be in the park after dark on occasion.

The Ahwahnee Hotel still operates, but the tennis courts are gone and most of the area previously covered by lawn is no longer maintained. The rip rap along the river near the Ahwahnee Hotel was removed to restore river processes. As a result, the river will eventually erode its banks and undermine the hotel. The Park Service may remove the hotel or relocate the structure to a less flood-prone site before this occurs.

As we head into Yosemite Village, you'll see more notable changes. All development south and east of the Degnan's Deli building, including the garage, employee housing, concessionaire's offices, art center building, and the building housing the Village Store, hamburger stand, sport shop, hair salon, and restrooms is gone. All pavement in this area is gone, with the exception of a bike path. Shuttle bus routes that once ran through the Village now bypass the Village to the south.

The building housing Degnan's deli has been remodeled. Upstairs, a restaurant serves breakfast, lunch, and dinner. A general store with delicatessen, coffee bar, and ice cream shop occupies the downstairs. All buildings between Degnan's and the Yosemite Museum, including the Post Office and the Ansel Adams Gallery have been retained and rehabilitated. The existing Visitor Center has been converted to a Nature Center. The auditorium and Indian Village are retained. The main National Park Service administrative office building has been transformed into the main Valley Visitor Center, all administrative functions now operate out of El Portal. The historic Rangers' Club was retained for employee housing.

Farther north, the building complex known as "The Fort," as well as the jail, government stables, maintenance yard, trailers, and courthouse are gone. All employee housing between the Village and Ahwahnee Meadow, and north of the Village is gone. Emergency services are now staged from the Yosemite Lodge area.

The Valley cemetery next to Yosemite Village remains. The number of houses in the residential area along Oak Lane and east of Yosemite Creek has been reduced by 50 percent. All structures and grounds have been cleaned up, and all non-native plants, including the lawns, are gone. Fences at these houses also are gone, and there is a no-pet policy in place for residents. The Yosemite School is gone. Chain saws, snow blowers, leaf blowers, and other noise-making machinery no longer operate in the Valley; natural sounds are re-claiming their rightful places. Visitors frequently send letters and emails to the Park Service applauding the changes implemented in the Valley, and almost every single person mentions hearing sounds they'd never heard before, including cottonwood leaves rustling, ravens warbling, a deer's exhalation, and a gray squirrel scratching for acorns in a dry leaf bed.

At Yosemite Falls, the paved western trail has been retained, but all rock walls, pavement mosaics and other unnecessary decorative distractions are gone. The east side trails have been restored to lovely dirt paths that once again meander through a quiet, contemplative environment. The massive bridges built during the Lower Yosemite Fall Project debacle are gone, replaced once again with simple stone and wood structures. The restroom near the Falls has been reduced in size; it can no longer service elephants or giraffes.

The Park Service finally implemented the Yosemite Lodge Reconstruction Project, and overhauled the entire area. The Lodge complex, still located south of Northside Drive, includes five single-story motel-style buildings, each with fourteen rooms; twenty-five duplex cabins; twenty-five single room wood cabins; and a one hundred site campground. None of the lodging facilities in the Valley have televisions. The central part of the Lodge has been redesigned, and includes a full service restaurant, a coffee shop, a cafeteria, a small general store and a gift shop. All temporary and substandard employee housing has been removed from the Lodge area. Across the street from the Lodge, Camp 4, or Sunnyside Campground, is still open, and has fifty campsites, an increase over the former thirty-seven sites.

All the phenomenal work that went into seeing the Yosemite Valley Re-Vision 2016 come to fruition was funded by the park's base operating budget, entrance fees, and the Yosemite Conservancy, which heroically rose to the occasion and raised an unprecedented amount of money to support the changes.

There's been one other major transformation since the adoption of the old new vision, and this change isn't limited to the Valley, it's happening throughout Yosemite National Park. In addition to nurturing Yosemite's more-than-human elements, park managers took numerous aggressive steps to improve employee relationships and morale. Employees now are strongly encouraged to think creatively and critically, and to challenge the status quo. They've been empowered to offer suggestions and ideas, and to speak their minds about what works, what doesn't work, and how to fix what is broken. Employees are much less stressed and much less over-worked as managers have clarified park priorities. The park's cadre of exceptionally talented employees with centuries of collective experience and deep love for Yosemite are finally working together to protect this precious tract of land.

The "Yosemite Way" is changing.

The new old vision rests on a solid foundation of wildness. All remaining, relatively undisturbed wild areas in the Valley are protected, and wildness is being restored to the land. The natural processes—fires, floods, rockfall, birth, life, growth, death, decomposition—are operating with the barest minimum of interference or interruption from humans. The natural structure produced by these processes, the aggregations of soils, rocks, plants, wildlife, and water courses, are left alone to the greatest extent possible. Healthy and robust populations of native species have free rein; they are living largely outside of human influence.

The new old vision transformed the Yosemite Valley experience. A visit to the Valley is special, spiritual, uplifting, connecting, energizing, relaxing; it is an unparalleled opportunity to experience joy and connection to the land. Visitors can appreciate and experience the gifts of wild nature without disrupting them.

We are no longer desecrating the temple. It took some time for the initial shock from all the major changes to wear off; but over time, those with purely economic interests in Yosemite Valley turned their focus elsewhere. And the visitors are raving about the changes.

Imagine a deep grassy valley where the safety, health, and well-being of mountain lions, bears, gray squirrels, beetles, and all the

Barbara J. Moritsch

more-than-human beings are as important as human safety, health, and well-being. Imagine the Park Service taking the lead in creating relationships with a place like this, a place where human needs don't always come first, don't always overshadow the needs of all other life forms. Imagine working together to demonstrate that this kind of relationship is desirable and possible, and can be expanded to many other places across the globe.

Just imagine...

CHAPTER 33
In Wildness

Journal

"UNLESS someone like you
cares a whole awful lot,
nothing is going to get better.
It's not."
    -*From* The Lorax *by Dr. Seuss*

♦♦♦

In 1998, I wrote the following in my journal: For how much longer will we stifle our rage? For how much longer will we fail to speak out against injustice inflicted on human beings and the land? For how much longer will we allow the path of our lives to be determined by a profit-motivated few? For how much longer will we fail to do the right thing?

I don't remember the specific environmental crisis *du jour* that prompted this outpouring, but, after my moonlit epiphany of light and water in Yosemite in the spring of 2005, I realized I no longer could or would stifle my rage. I had to describe what I was seeing and hearing, had to explain why Yosemite was being "managed" headlong down a path leading to destruction of what I, and many others, value most about the place: its natural beauty and its wildness. I gave my heart to Yosemite Valley over thirty years ago, and it's given me more precious gifts than I could ever list in return. For the Valley's sake I had to bear witness, had to call attention to the problems. It took me a long time to find my voice. I had to return to the land I loved first to find it.

I've spent a lot of time these last few years pondering the source of my deep connection to Yosemite Valley, wondering why I am so drawn to this small patch of land in the Sierra Nevada. The connection developed as I came of age and experienced rites of passage in the Valley. It deepened because, despite being uprooted numerous times as a child, I always returned to Yosemite. I relied on the consistency of Half Dome; its solid presence became a landmark that would always be there no matter how lost or confused I felt.

My connection to Yosemite Valley came about because I, like every human being, have a deep-seated need to bond to a place, to forge a solid, forever relationship with somewhere. The magic of Yosemite Valley makes it easy to forge such a bond. And it is this very magic that epitomizes why I feel the Valley is so significant, why it is so important to restore and protect the Valley's wildness. I didn't bond with Upper Pines campground, Degnan's Deli, or the Curry Village store. I bonded with rocks and river, Steller's jays and black oaks. I bonded with the warmth of the sun, and with the springtime chorus of Pacific tree frogs. I bonded with Yosemite's wild nature. Today that wild nature is at risk of extinction.

Regardless of what we do or don't do to the Valley, it will survive and outlast us. Millions of people will continue to visit every year, regardless of the intensity of crowding or the condition of natural and cultural resources. They will come to see waterfalls, rock walls, Half Dome, and El Capitan. Thus far, humans have been largely unable to damage or destroy these vertical features. Visitors will come to cool off in or near the Merced River and the creeks, regardless of degraded river banks, monocultures of non-native plants, the absence of meadows or great gray owls, or the presence of noise, pollution and litter. Most visitors won't know that they're not seeing a wild, natural park. Many won't care, as long as there are trees to picnic under, rocks to climb on, and a river to swim and raft in.

Yes, millions will still come, and they will spend millions. But, if the Park Service continues on its current path of pursuing more development, urbanization, and visitation, some native plants and wildlife will disappear; in the worst cases this will involve entire species. The behavior and health of native plants and wildlife that remain will, in many cases, continue to get worse. The air will get dirtier, the water more polluted. The sky won't be dark at night, and natural sounds will be drowned out much of the time. In addition, opportunities for visitors to bond deeply with the Valley will disappear. The Valley's identity as an unrivalled natural inspiration, its ability to profoundly affect and transform visitors, and its unique potential role as an emissary for wild places everywhere will be lost. Yosemite Valley will be just another pretty place to drive to, have lunch, take a photo, and leave behind. We can't let this happen. The magnitude of the losses to humans and to all the more-than-human lives dependent on the Valley would be far too great.

If the Park Service does not reverse its management direction in Yosemite Valley soon, the agency will have failed in its duty to the American public. It will have failed to meet the most important half of its stated mission: to conserve the scenery and the natural and historic objects and wildlife in Yosemite, to keep them unimpaired forever. The National Park Service will have failed to protect the integrity of America's beloved Yosemite Valley, the nation's very first park.

Yosemite Valley speaks in the language of floods, fires, and rock fall; a vocabulary that doesn't lend itself to the controlled verse the Park Service wants to script for it. The Valley's "advocates" speak several different languages, some accented by love for its scenic beauty, its timelessness, and its ability to nourish the human soul, and some smoky with lust for the economic benefits its rarified qualities can provide. It's time for those who love Yosemite Valley to prevail over those who lust. It's time to grow up, to mature into responsible partners in our relationship with Yosemite Valley. The Park Service must stop deferring to the stakeholders with the loudest voices, those in pursuit of economic gain. Yosemite's managers must shift to a higher level of responsibility, take the reins and guide Yosemite Valley into a future where the health and well-being of Valley resources are protected and cherished. Using Dave Foreman's term, it's time to "rewild" Yosemite Valley. The managers who dig deep and find the courage to take the initiative and truly re-establish, renew, and revitalize the natural and spiritual integrity of Yosemite Valley will be honored and celebrated far into the future. Let's get to work. Let's make it happen.

The first step is really up to those who love Yosemite. If the Valley's ecological web is to remain intact, each and every one of us must let go of our favorite things; by "things" I mean human-made things. We all have our favorites, whether it's Degnan's Deli turkey sandwiches or pepperoni pizza at the Loft, campsite #286 in Upper Pines Campground, or tent cabin number whatever at Curry Village. For the Valley's sake, we have to let go of these attachments and focus collectively on what we truly love about the Valley: the river, the rocks, the way the sun plays on the meadow grasses at dawn, the imposing face of El Capitan, the magenta hue of Half Dome at sunset, the stars, the coyotes, the deer, and the bears—the entities that make Yosemite sacred and unique. We can get pizza and have favorite campsites anywhere, but none of us will ever find the collection of sheer magnificence embraced within Yosemite Valley anywhere else on Earth. We need to come together to protect the wonder, the sacredness, the remnants of wildness, the heart and soul reasons we love Yosemite so deeply and so fiercely. This will require sacrifice.

I invite those of you who have never been to Yosemite Valley to visit, stay a few days, get away from the pavement, touch and be touched by its wildness. Then join with all of the rest of us who've already felt that touch to defend wildness in Yosemite and everywhere else it still exists in the world with all of your heart and soul.

If any part of the natural, wild world is to survive, we must all learn to be comfortable with that world and recognize we are one with it. We must acknowledge and cherish our relationships with the more-than-human entities with whom we share the Earth. At the Fishtrap Workshop, Jack Turner told his audience that once we come into relationship with the wild and all of its elements, we will feel obligated to care for and protect them, like we care for and protect our children, our parents, our pets.

In *The Abstract Wild*, Turner said: "We only value what we know and love, and we no longer know or love the wild...Most people don't miss it and won't miss it in the future." Turner went on to say: "To reverse this situation we must become so intimate with wild animals, with plants and places that we answer to their destruction from the gut. Like when we discover the landlady strangling our cat."

Envision Yosemite Valley as a place of wildness. Envision it as a proving ground, a place to demonstrate that we can restore wildness to overly humanized, damaged land. We can put nature before economics. We can worship the sacredness of land and nature instead of money and stuff. We can. We must.

When Tom and I walked out of the Yosemite Chapel after our wedding ceremony, the lone coyote sitting on his haunches in the snowy meadow across the road howled his congratulations. I howled back.

I howl now for that coyote and all his kin: Please don't let Yosemite's wild soul die.

EPILOGUE

The floodwaters that bathed Yosemite Valley early in 1997 gave the Park Service a great opportunity. The natural house cleaning set the stage for the agency to finally pursue the 1980 *General Management Plan*'s intent to restore the Valley to a state of *"nature uncluttered by piecemeal stumbling blocks of commercialism, machines, and fragments of suburbia"* and to carry out infrastructure removal called for in the Yosemite Valley Plan.

The Park Service took advantage of the flood, but not to restore nature. Instead, they asked for enormous amounts of money for flood "recovery," which translated to upgrading infrastructure. To add insult to injury, the Park Service claimed it was restoring nature in the Valley because not every campsite, lodging unit, and parking space damaged by the flood was replaced in kind. Fifteen years later, Yosemite Valley is still far from uncluttered; it is still a small city.

If history is any indicator, the National Park Service will not, or cannot, put resources first in Yosemite Valley. It doesn't matter if this is due to pressures from politicians, gateway businesses, and concessionaires, inadequate funding, internal issues, or some combination of these factors. What matters is the Valley is in trouble from an ecological perspective, and restoration and protection must become the park's highest priority. Because the agency can't seem to put nature and wildness first in Yosemite, it is up to citizens of the United States to watchdog the agency and demand this shift in priorities. In a footnote to the Introduction of *Mountains Without Handrails*, Joseph L. Sax defined his use of the term preservationist: "Those whose inclinations are to retain parklands largely (though not absolutely) as natural areas, without industrialization, commercialized recreation, or urban influences." Then he said, "Among the organizations that speak most consistently for such views are the National Parks and Conservation Association, the Wilderness Society, the Sierra Club, and Friends of the Earth."

Relative to the environmental debacles I witnessed in Yosemite Valley, three of these four organizations largely were silent. The Sierra Club was the only one that actively argued for retention or restoration of some semblance of wildness in the Valley, and those efforts were weakened by a lack of internal consistency. The two groups that did change the course of planning and development in Yosemite—Friends of Yosemite Valley and Mariposans for the Environment and Responsible Government (formerly Mariposans for Environmentally Responsible Growth)—were small, dedicated, and hard-working grassroots organizations. We can't rely on large environmental groups to ensure protection of parks or wild lands; each and every one of us who cares about such places must step forward, individually and collectively.

What can we do? Some people question the value of standard methods such as writing letters to the editor, or writing, calling, or emailing Congressional representatives, but I believe these efforts are worthwhile. If enough people support nature and wildness, if a critical mass, or tipping point, is reached, politicians might take notice, and protection of parks, wild lands, and biodiversity may become higher priorities. The problem is we are running out of time.

The need to protect national parks and all remaining wild land from human manipulation and degradation, and to restore as much damaged land as we can, has never been greater. The threats to Earth's ecological web posed by global climate change, regardless of how much of the change is due to humans, appear staggering. Recent wildlife inventories conducted by the University of California, Berkeley, indicate some species already are on the move in Yosemite, in search of higher ground and cooler temperatures, looking for habitat that meets their needs and will allow them to live.

The Park Service has convened meetings and workshops, and formed committees to figure out what to "do" about climate change. The best thing the agency can do within parks is restore natural processes that have been altered or impeded by humans, which will increase the resilience of ecosystems, their ability to withstand or adapt to change. Additionally, ecosystem stressors such as air and water pollution, and non-native species, must be reduced both inside and outside of parks. Restoring natural processes and reducing other stressors will, in some cases, require limiting visitor numbers or activities.

The Park Service also can work hard now to expand their land base. Park and protected area boundaries can be extended north, south, east, and west, as well as up and down in elevation, to create buffer zones that will allow species to move, to find new places to live, if at all possible, as conditions in their old homes change.

The problems we face in Yosemite Valley are not unique. The entire Earth is in trouble. We read and hear these words daily in one form or another. We know it's true, we feel it deep inside our bones. It's time to stop dancing around one another's sensitivities and mincing words. It's time to speak our truth as best we can about what is wrong and how it may be righted.

Although the focus of my vision for a new, healthy relationship between humans and land is Yosemite Valley, the Valley is only the beginning, the perfect place to start. Once we implement the vision in Yosemite Valley, I see similar paradigm shifts radiating out to the rest of Yosemite National Park, other national parks, and, ultimately, beyond all boundaries.

If the old adage is true and wisdom comes with age, after almost one hundred years the National Park Service should be getting pretty smart. As the agency approaches its second century of existence, I hope all Park Service employees can be empowered to find the courage and the spirit to speak their truths and stand up for the parks, to hold their agency accountable to the National Park Service Organic Act and ensure park resources remain unimpaired (or repaired, when needed) forever.

The Park Service may have missed its chance to restore Yosemite Valley after the 1997 flood, but another golden opportunity waits just over the horizon. On August 25, 2016, the National Park Service will celebrate its 100th birthday. This is a perfect time for the agency to dream big, to re-vision, to rise to a higher level, to find ways to achieve the greatest good and fulfill its highest potential in Yosemite Valley. If we start now, we can make great progress toward implementing the new old vision in Yosemite Valley by 2016. I can't imagine a better way to celebrate the National Park Service's 100th birthday.

Yosemite Valley is only seven miles long and about a mile wide. If we can't prevent deterioration of this small, dearly beloved piece of land, if we can't find a way to preserve the Valley's remaining wildness and restore areas we've damaged, it's extremely unlikely we'll be able to preserve any natural area, any wildness, anywhere in the world.

We need to get busy; there is work to be done.

Journal

November 15, 2016

As the gray light of dawn chased night from the Valley, ravens from all directions left their night roosts to gather in a low swale north of the river, just east of Leidig Meadow. The birds convened over breakfast: the carcass of a large doe taken down two days earlier by a mountain lion. The ravens behaved with a high degree of decorum. One or two descended to pull at large pieces of meat while the others waited their turn, perched on an adjacent log or incense-

cedar branch. The birds called back and forth, discussing the cool of the morning, the first snow lacing the ridges above the Valley, and the blessed lack of noise from cars, generators and other noisy human accoutrements.

A young boy watched the show from his seat at the base of a tall ponderosa pine about fifty feet away. The rising sun crested the Valley rim and illuminated the red-gold tree bark, the ebony tips of raven feathers, and the pale blond crown of the boy's head. The boy noted the deer's remains had moved since the previous morning; a coyote or a bear, or perhaps the lion herself, had hauled the body about thirty feet south under cover of night. As he watched, the high-pitched call of a red-shouldered hawk pierced the quiet, and a coyote approached the scene from the west. The feeding ravens took flight at the coyote's approach, and then returned quickly after the heavy-coated dog tore off a piece of bright red meat the size of a small duck and trotted off to eat it in peace.

The boy rose from his seat and bowed his thanks to the sun for its welcoming warmth, to the ravens for their good company, and to the tree for its solid, reassuring presence. He walked slowly across the swale to the north, away from the ravens, picking his way carefully over small branches, flattened grass clumps, and brambles of wild rose. Stepping up onto the porch of a small cabin, he passed the twin cots he and his mom had slept on the night before. He opened the cabin door, stepped in, and was greeted by the aroma of fried eggs and potatoes, and the warm, welcoming voices of his family

FOR FURTHER READING

Anderson, M. Kat. *Tending the Wild: Native American Knowledge and the Management of California's Natural Resources.* University of California Press. Berkeley, Los Angeles, London.

Brower, David R. with Steve Chapple. 1995. *Let the Mountains Talk, Let the Rivers Run: A Call to Those Who Would Save the Earth.* Harper Collins West, New York, NY.

Bunnell, Lafayette Houghton, M.D. 1990. *Discovery of the Yosemite and the Indian War of 1851 Which Led to that Event.* Yosemite Association, Yosemite National Park, CA; Copy of the 4th reprint of 1911 by G. W. Gerlicher, Los Angeles, CA.

Clark, Galen. 1907. *Indians of the Yosemite Valley and Vicinity.* Published 1992 by Kings River Press, Lemoore, CA.

Ernst, Emil. 1949. Vanishing Meadows in Yosemite Valley in Yosemite Nature Notes 28(5). Available on line at www.yosemite.ca.us/library/yosemite_nature_notes/28/

Farabee, Charles R. "Butch" Jr. 2003. *National Park Ranger: An American Icon.* Roberts Rinehart, Lanham, MD.

Gibbens, Robert F. and Harold F. Heady. 1964. *The Influence of Modern Man on the Vegetation of Yosemite Valley.* University of California, Division of Agricultural Sciences, California Agricultural Experiment Station Extension Service. Manual 36.

Goodin, Mark. 1997. *Yosemite: The 100 Year Flood.* Sierra Press, Mariposa, CA.

Griffiths, Jay. 2006. *Wild: An Elemental Journey.* Penguin Group, London, England.

Heady, H. F. and P. J. Zinke. 1978. *Vegetational Changes in Yosemite Valley*, National Park Service Occasional Paper Number Five, U.S. Department of the Interior.

Hutchings, James M. 1886. *In the Heart of the Sierras: Yo Semite and the Big Tree Groves* (1990 edition, Peter Browning, editor), Great West Books, Lafeyette, CA.

Maclean, Norman. 1976. *A River Runs Through It and Other Stories.* The University of Chicago Press, Chicago and London.

Milestone, J. F. 1978. *The Influence of Modern Man on the Stream System of Yosemite Valley.* Master's Thesis, San Francisco State University. May 1978.

Muir, John. 1912. *The Yosemite.* The Century Company (referenced 1962 Natural History Library Edition, Anchor Books, Doubleday & Company, Inc., Garden City, NY).

Nash, Roderick Frazier. 2001. *Wilderness and the American Mind*, 4th Edition. Yale University Press, New Haven and London, *Nota Bene.*

National Park Service. 1994. *Yosemite Valley Cultural Landscape Report*, Volumes One and Two, Yosemite National Park, CA. Prepared by Land and Community Associates, Charlottesville, VA and Eugene, OR in association with Jones and Jones Architects, Seattle, WA.

Olmsted, Frederick Law. 1865. *Yosemite and the Mariposa Grove: A Preliminary Report* (Reprinted August 1995 and 2009) by The Yosemite Association, Yosemite National Park, CA.

Roper, Laura Wood. 1973. *FLO: A Biography of Frederick Law Olmsted*. The Johns Hopkins University Press, Baltimore and London.

Runte, Alfred. 1990. *Yosemite: The Embattled Wilderness*, University of Nebraska Press, Lincoln and London.

Russell, Carl Parcher. 1959. *One Hundred Years in Yosemite*, Omnibus Edition (Referenced 1992 High Sierra Classics Series by the Yosemite Association).

Sax, Joseph L. 1980. *Mountains Without Handrails: Reflections on the National Parks*. The University of Michigan Press, Ann Arbor.

Sellars, Richard West. 1997. *Preserving Nature in the National Parks: A History*. Yale University Press, New Haven and London.

Snyder, Gary. 1990. *The Practice of the Wild*. North Point Press, New York.

Solnit, Rebecca. 1994. *Savage Dreams: A Journey into the Hidden Wars of the American West*. Sierra Club Books. San Francisco, CA.

Turner, Jack. 1996. *The Abstract Wild*. The University of Arizona Press, Tucson, AZ.

ABOUT THE AUTHOR

Barbara J. Moritsch worked for the National Park Service as an ecologist and interpretive naturalist in the western United States. She holds Bachelor's and Master's degrees in natural resource planning and interpretation, and environmental science. She currently lives in Eagle, Idaho with her husband Tom, two cats, a dog, and three horses.

www.ingramcontent.com/pod-product-compliance
Lightning Source LLC
Chambersburg PA
CBHW071954290426
44109CB00018B/2021